EUROPE'S NIGHTMARE

EUROPE'S NIGHTMARE

THE STRUGGLE FOR KOSOVO

MIRON REZUN

PRAEGER

Westport, Connecticut
London

Library of Congress Cataloging-in-Publication Data

Rezun, Miron.
    Europe's nightmare : the struggle for Kosovo / Miron Rezun.
      p. cm.
    Includes bibliographical references and index.
    ISBN 0–275–97072–8 (alk. paper)
    1. Kosovo (Serbia)—History—Civil War, 1998– 2. Europe—Politics and
government—1989– I. Title.
DR2087.R49 2001
949.71—dc21   00–032378

British Library Cataloguing in Publication Data is available.

Library of Congress Catalog Card Number: 00–032378
ISBN: 0–275–97072–8

First published in 2001

Praeger Publishers, 88 Post Road West, Westport, CT 06881
An imprint of Greenwood Publishing Group, Inc.
www.praeger.com

Printed in the United States of America

The paper used in this book complies with the
Permanent Paper Standard issued by the National
Information Standards Organization (Z39.48–1984).

10 9 8 7 6 5 4 3 2

FOR VERONICA, WHO WAS THERE FOR ME

CONTENTS

A photo essay follows chapter 4

PREFACE: A LOSS OF FACE

The Balkans are comfortably warm in the spring. The place I ended up in, though, was more a grim reminder of somber winter.

I came to Macedonia to conduct research. I was teaching International Humanitarian Law and Eastern Europe in Canada. War crimes were also on my agenda. There were several unhygienic refugee camps on the Macedonian border, where local Macedonian police and camp guards were quite unwelcoming. Sometimes they even abused the Kosovars who came there. The camp I visited was an utterly distressing and morbid sight. The predominantly Muslim Kosovars were surrounded by heavy rolls of barbed wire. But they were safe; they had adequate food and shelter, and legions of international relief workers were ministering to their needs. To the northeast a vista of breathtaking mountain scenery offset the dreariness. The very afternoon that I arrived I could see the pale light of a gray sky. The wind was up, and billowing clouds rose above the mountaintops in distant Kosovo. When dusk settled over the encampment, small fires were stoked all around; the air had a dank taste, full of the eerie sounds of night. The whole place felt clammy like a grave.

A straggle of women with bundles came around the bend on a route leading into the camp. The sight of them made my heart sink. There were thousands of weary people, and more and more pouring in—so many that the place looked thoroughly cluttered as well as dreadfully muddy. Behind them, at an army checkpoint, rolled a line of rickety tractors and beat-up cars, twisting forward like a serpent, groaning under their human cargoes. The wounded, the sick, and the hungry appeared bewildered. Chaos reigned everywhere. A rancid and sour smell of sweat, decay, and suppuration seemed pervasive. A more woeful scene than this I could not possibly call to mind. It was as if I had stumbled into Hades—it was a netherworld of mourning and obsequies. On my second day at the camp, the wind suddenly ceased. A heavy cloud hung over the sprawling tent city like a giant sponge ready to be squeezed. A dazzling flash cut the horizon as lightning forked across the mountain range. It was almost a torrential rain that came, making the mud walks even thicker than before. I stopped beneath an awning to await a pause in the downpour. Half-seen in the shadows, desperate figures scampered here and there for shelter. A deafening sound all but tore the heavens. I couldn't make out whether it was a clap of thunder or a booming jet overhead.

I made my way straight to a makeshift hospital that was set up near a grassy hollow. I had been welcomed to interview the medical team and some of the patients. The hospital constituted several small reception tents and a fairly large metal barracks that doubled as sleeping quarters and an infirmary. I could see many women there, waiting; they were stamping their feet and drawing their collars close against the pelting rain. A team of Israeli doctors and nurses had set up the obstetrics compound to help in the delivery of babies. They were also performing abortions for women with unwanted pregnancies. The plight of these women was particularly acute. I found it ironic that Jewish volunteers were ministering to the traumas and shocks of Muslim women, all innocent victims of violence. I had been under the impression that Jews were more in sympathy with the Serbs than with the Albanian Muslims. Surely enough, Jews were apt to support an indivisible Yugoslavia, not an independent Kosovo. Most Israeli Jews were saying that the Muslim Kosovars would turn on them with as much hatred as the Kosovars felt for the Serbs and Gypsies in their homeland.

At least this Israeli field hospital made me realize that human kindness was not dead. I was told the Israeli doctors were tending to rape survivors. The women were seeking to obliterate the consequences of their defilement.

A woman in her thirties, Safete (not her real name), told me she had been "dishonored by a sexual act." The other girls standing by refused to say anything about sexual assaults by Serbian men. They denied it had happened. Most of them looked frail and delicate. A pretty adolescent with auburn hair stammered in a low voice, "We were manhandled, ordered about and threatened, beaten up by Serb soldiers, driven out of our homes." She looked at Safete with sharp reproof. Her gaze seemed to ask, "Why are you revealing all this to strangers?" Another woman, somewhat older, cried in a voice laced with sarcasm, "No one was raped!" Her hollow eyes blazed from sunken sockets.

"So why the abortions?" I asked.

Safete looked very sullen. She shivered.

"A stigma of dishonor goes with it," offered the physician from Haifa. He introduced himself as Dr. Amnon. With a shock of thick white hair, he looked every bit the part of an army doctor. He spoke in a deep voice, his eyes revealing no emotion: "The older women are more apt to talk about it, the girls keep silent, and we don't ask any questions."

"The Kosovars, I suppose, are similar to other Third World cultures," a woman medic from Tel-Aviv said with a humorless smile, as she joined our conversation. "They have a strong kinship culture, strong patriarchy, ties of blood, patrilineal descent; the wife's a husband's possession, his property."

William, a Dutch relief worker who was standing by, added: "Rape is a weapon of war, worse than marital infidelity—it is treated practically the same; considered a shameful act!" He continued gravely, "Remember that most of these people are rural; they would seldom even see a large town, especially the womenfolk."

"I had read about this and experienced this in Arab Bedouin culture," I said. "So a husband's honor is tarnished by a violent rapist. It is as if the rapist were his wife's seducer, which isn't really the same thing. What happens then," I asked, "when a husband or the male members of his family find out about the rape? What if, for instance, the wife gets pregnant—is she punished?"

"No," the European relief worker answered. "He simply dismisses her. She's got to leave—she either goes back to her father's house or moves in with relatives, a brother or sister perhaps."

A young Kosovar woman who answered to the name of Xheraldina (not her real name) was just then being led to the hospital by UN aides. Her face and body drooped as she approached. She looked nervous, her hands were trembling.

Amnon leaned back in his chair and let out a deep sigh. The deluge had stopped.

"I am not in the least surprised," I told him. I explained that I used to teach International Human Rights Law and was now doing research on this war and its refugees.

He nodded. "This is not so strange," he said. "These people and their leaders are still the prisoners of their own cultural values."

It was easy to concur. "Many in the West are oblivious to the cultural differences of the Balkans. We are not dealing with sexual indiscretions here. In the Western view a person can neither legally nor morally be held responsible for the acts of another. Consequently rape is no more a case of sexual misconduct than a wife who runs away with the delivery man, nor does it constitute some kind of dishonor to both husband and kin."

"Their family and kin never come to the hospital to see them," said the doctor from Tel-Aviv. Speaking more philosophically, she proceeded to describe how Muslim women are changing. "But" she paused, with a slight hint of resignation, "given the traditional Albanian Muslim's value of 'face,' which really means 'honor,' it is impossible for any of these women to act differently."

"I know that in both Western and Balkan-Muslim culture 'saving face' and 'losing face' is the outward manifestation of honor," I argued. "A woman will try to preserve this front; it's very essential to her, to her identity, whether she has committed a dishonorable act or not."

Amnon added, "Rape, which some of these women experienced a month or so ago, and the risk of being impregnated—all this may not be so dishonorable to a Western woman. A criminal act it certainly is, and absolutely repugnant, but never to the same degree that it might be to a Kosovar mother and daughter." He looked pensive for a moment and then added, "I do not wish to diminish the trauma that a European or American woman may experience." He looked at the relief envoy, who was nodding his head.

"Islam and this general Balkan culture have much to do with the stigma of shame that a woman feels," the Dutchman said.

What I was able to conclude from these exchanges was that as long as such an action of disgrace remains unknown, a woman's face is saved in her culture. If the dishonorable act becomes known (known, that is, by both kith and kin), she loses face. It is like saying that a woman's self-respect depends entirely on the respect she gets from others, only from others around her and close to her. The Kosovars' system of virtue is primarily oriented outwardly—it is highly patriarchal by European standards.

I must have had an incredulous look on my face, for the medical team told me I looked puzzled. I kept shaking my head. It was baffling to see how on the one hand the Kosovars were fighting for democratic rights and freedoms, while on the other hand these men were unprepared to accept their womenfolk on equal terms.

Rape, the dehumanization of women, is at long last a crime of war, even more than war itself, I repeated to myself. These refugees of Kosovo, I thought, are truly a knot of contradictions . . . and though the media portray this conflict in very graphic terms, it often becomes a daunting task to explain it objectively.

ACKNOWLEDGMENTS

The book I published in 1995, *Europe and War in the Balkans: Toward a New Yugoslav Identity*, was a general introduction to the breakup of Yugoslavia. Kosovo was given only a brief mention. Slobodan Milosevic had not yet come to a showdown with the West for control of that province. With each successive conflict, it seems, the situation in the Balkans becomes more and more complicated. This is evident in *Europe's Nightmare: The Struggle for Kosovo*, which indicates how the number of players has increased exponentially. Institutions, relief agencies, and foreign governments are so involved, so immersed in this conflict that I have had to adopt a policy approach to explicating the Kosovo quagmire. A simple narration of events would not do this tragedy the justice it deserves. This book is about the pathos of war, about very lifelike—but not always sane and rational—things. It is thus intended for lay readers and experts alike. It is my hope that international policymakers, members of lobbying groups, and general readers will benefit from my findings and observations. I hope the book will promote critical reflection and enable us to peacefully move toward rational conflict resolution.

The sources for this book are voluminous. For want of space, they do not all appear in the bibliography. However, I have consulted Serbo-Croatian–language newspapers; translations from Albanian; Russian newspapers and magazines; and documentation in German. Sources from the Internet proved invaluable, giving all the perspectives that are relevant to the unfolding drama in Kosovo. A good example is the U.S. Department of State's presentation of countless relevant briefings, debates, congressional resolutions, and views and notes from the Pentagon and the Oval Office in an online format via an International Information

Program in four languages (English, Russian, Serbo-Croatian, and Albanian) in order to attain the widest possible readership. The International Criminal Tribunal at the Hague, which is part of the UN, offers a web site filled with bulletins of the Court's activities; it lists all the cases and gives all important legal publications. But notions of justice and bringing a perpetrator of a crime to account are themselves mooted. At the other end of the spectrum is the Znet Kosovo/NATO web site, drawn from Z magazine's very vocal left. Nothing seems to be impartial, neither the books nor the articles that now appear at booksellers, not even the seemingly unbiased documents and statistics of the United Nations. A quick perusal of the foolish way the Rambouillet Accord was crafted will no doubt bear this out. And the utterances of the lunatic fringe are scarcely worth discussion. Clearly, much depends on an author's point of view or on personal bias. Otherwise, disinterested objectivity would result in yet another tedious account of what has occurred in Kosovo. For the Balkans are, to be sure, full of surprises and irremediably charged with high drama.

Presenting that story in an understandable way requires a process of accumulation and sorting, demanding much more than scholars and journalists are doing at present. Rigorous reasoning is also needed, because the story involves foreign cultures and ways. Instinctively uninhibited, when writing this book I felt a compelling need to point out the irony and the antithesis of mainstream views; seldom does this subject make it easy for anyone to exercise restraint.

Individuals and governments are not the only actors in this story. NATO, EU, OSCE, UN, UNHCR, UNMIK, and KFOR are just some of the actors and institutions that have become enmeshed in helping Kosovo. I did what I could to keep the abbreviations to a bare minimum, so as not to confound the reader with unneeded acronyms. Place names and proper names have been stripped of their accents and diacritical marks, with due apologies to experts in the field.

In the spring and summer of 1999, I travelled to Macedonia to meet and speak with many refugees and relief workers. I interviewed other refugees when they arrived at a Canadian Armed Forces base located at Gagetown in the province of New Brunswick, not too far from where I live. These meetings helped me to weigh some of the recorded testimony. Personal observation and the evidence of refugees were frequently much more telling than NATO's dubious information campaign. Privately, of course, I talked to soldiers. I met with diplomats and economists. I argued with lawyers and jurists. I heard stories from Muslims and Jews, from Greek, Russian, and Serbian Orthodox Christians, and from Gypsies. When observing the sufferings of innocent people, witnessing their profound loss, seeing the sorrow of broken dreams, and catching, through this pain, a flicker of hope for a brighter tomorrow, one struggles, almost as much as they do, to make sense of it all. Long after this episode in the Balkans is laid to rest, we will continue to puzzle over questions of virtue and justice in the human predicament.

The book you are about to read is a grim reminder of war and the folly of humankind. Many works will no doubt follow that will set down a clearer historical record and will reinterpret what I and others have said. There does not seem to be an absolute truth about anything anyone will say these days about the Balkans. Most writers, whether they are near or far from that corner of Europe, are either too prejudiced, too influenced, or just too far removed to be able to juggle truth, myth, and fact.

My sincere gratitude goes to Heather Staines of Praeger. She offered enthusiasm and patience when the project first germinated and the Kosovo war, or bombing, was drawing to a close. She and I seemed to be of one mind when it came to discussing distinct civic cultures and political communities. She really thought this book should get the widest readership possible. The organization Médecins Sans Frontières (Doctors Without Borders) helped with information and some valuable photography. The work of Doctors Without Borders in Kosovo and in other areas of the world earned them the well-deserved Nobel Peace Prize in 1999. My heartfelt thanks go to the renowned experts on the subject who read earlier drafts of the book and offered valuable suggestions—Sabrina Ramet, Aurel Braun, Fuat Borovali, and Eric Gordy. Many thanks to Marybeth Mackenzie. I should also like to thank Canada's Department of National Defence for both photographic and financial support. Special thanks here must go to Lieutenant-Commander Jacques Fauteux, in Ottawa.

Last but not least, I am deeply indebted to Veronica Price Brown. When she learned that I hadn't written anything in years, she kept on pushing me to finish the project. It was Veronica who saw to it that the manuscript got to Heather on time.

While writing this small tome, I followed no theoretical or semiotic signposts. I embraced no political ideologies. Nor am I to be regarded as an official spokesperson for any governmental or nongovernmental organization. However, with a subject such as this, neither I nor anyone else could possibly be dispassionate when it comes to drawing conclusions. Indeed, readers might find discrepancies in my research, in my tone; I must plead then—the fault lies entirely with me.

PROLOGUE

I was making the finishing touches to my manuscript when, in early October 2000, Slobodan Milosevic was ousted from power after a democratically held election. Not two weeks earlier, the strongman of Yugoslavia was suspected of trying to rig the electoral vote: he had done it before. He tried to get the Constitutional Court to keep him in power until June 2001. He stalled and wavered, before finally stepping down. So at long last, thirteen years of his rule ended ignominiously.

Now the opposition, unified if not completely unanimous, buffeted by years of in-fighting, finally got its act together under Vojislav Kostunica. Milosevic did indeed have a strong showing, but the people had had enough. His henchmen were powerless to help this time. It was practically a bloodless, non-violent revolution of civil disobedience that paralyzed an entire nation. Transit workers had left their jobs and miners protested against the regime. Students, intellectuals, and urbanites from Belgrade, Nis, Novi Sad, and even masses from the countryside, rallied in support of Kostunica. Russia's pragmatic president, Vladimir Putin, no longer had any use for Milosevic. As the federal parliament was stormed and the main grids of power were seized by the people in the streets of Belgrade, Milosevic's army and police preferred to stay out of the general fracas.

It reminded one of the day the shah of Iran, Mohammad Reza Pahlavi, had lost his throne. Nor does one forget the non-violent overthrow of the Marcos' regime that crumbled to dust in the Philippines; or the "Velvet Revolution" that toppled Communism in Czechoslovakia—led by a mere playwright. We are alternately surprised and not surprised that it should happen this way. Demonstrations against Milosevic have occurred in the past. He was roundly condemned (if not despised) by many of his people. A case in point would be members of Serbia's orthodox church who criticized him, for instance. Labour leaders and workers grew to hate him. The middle class was never with him.

Simply put, Milosevic had lost his grip on everyday reality, not just his political power because in modern society, political power is never "absolute" anyway. For one thing, he had lost the war in Kosovo against the West—an ordeal that came with bombings, sanctions, and isolation. Everywhere, there were too many refugees; too many soup kitchens; too much unemployment; gangsters running amok; thugs masquerading as soldiers; a half-censored media that lies. What democracy; what justice? We are reminded of the man in the tragic play whose handful of ever diminishing loyal informers were prompt to convey only good news to him, the things he wanted to hear, even if it was false; and the increasingly isolated leader of the nation is oblivious to whether or not his meddlesome wife is despised by the people, or that his corrupt son has flown the coop.

All dictators fall, it is true . . . sooner or later. I must admit that during the months I was writing this book, I could not have predicted the ruler's downfall so readily, even though that possibility stared me in the face. In fact, it was hard to believe the overthrow would have come from within. Few would have expected it that way. Many are those who claim now that NATO and American policies have been justified and that Milosevic and his henchmen were the sole wrongdoers. Presumptuous. Naive. But, enough said—let us examine Milosevic's downfall and the story of Kosovo from beginning to end.

EUROPE'S NIGHTMARE

1

INTRODUCTION

---

66 is the path of a people in flight, refugees from dust and shrinking
land, from the thunder of tractors and shrinking ownership, from the
twisting winds that howl . . . the people are in flight, and they come
into 66 from the wagon tracks, the rutted country roads. 66 is the
road of flight . . . and 66 goes on over the terrible desert, where the
distance shimmers and the black center mountains hang unbearably
in the distance . . . until at last the mountains rise up again, the good
mountains, and 66 winds through them. Then suddenly a pass, and
below the beautiful valley.

—*Grapes of Wrath*, by John Steinbeck

Halfway down a windswept hillside in central Kosovo stands a remote
cemetery. The place is desolate. When spring comes, it is often chilly. A
tall, bearded young man sits by a burial mound, weeping. His eight-
year-old daughter kneels beside him and gazes long and longingly at
the fresh earth. She too is inconsolable. No gravestone, no markings
adorn the site. Father and daughter must leave soon; by nightfall the
Serbs will be coming, looking for them.

"None of this is God's will," the man says haltingly. "Here . . . here
lies your mama . . . remember, remember this place, my little one," he
stammers in a rasping voice, pointing at the mound.

The girl turns and looks at his hard face. She then runs off frantically.
But in a few moments she runs back to the gravesite, into her father's
comforting arms, and the tall bearded man gently wipes away her tears.

In a village near Pristina, a woman bundles up her children. Fear and
anguish burn in her tired eyes. Gutted houses, potholes, and hollowed

earth are all she sees. The bodies of another family lie rotting in a ditch, their eyes glazed and sightless. Charred carcasses of cattle litter the nearby fields. The stench of death is everywhere. The mother gathers up some of her personal effects and heads for the open road. Her husband and oldest son have stayed behind to fight the Serbs. For all she knows, both could be dead. And she worries about her parents now—too old and too sick to make the long trek south.

The mother joins a group of younger women in agony over the loss of loved ones. Hordes of children look up at her with tear-filled eyes. Most of the procession is horror-stricken; with mouths agape, the children cling to their mothers as they trudge down a winding dirt road. Safety is in numbers, they say. The mother soon discovers that her parents were murdered in their beds and her husband may have perished in an ambush. Her son survived and will surely join with the Albanian nationalists in their revenge killings. Thus, the cycle of hatred continues.

The year could be 1913, or 1945, or 1999, an example of the many instances of Albanians being driven from their homes.

But on March 24, 1999, NATO jets started dropping lethal charges on Serbia. The air war would be a short one. Its gruesome image would be brought home to television viewers across the world. Hundreds of thousands of Kosovars—1.8 million ethnic Albanians, in fact—had to flee their native Kosovo from the onslaught of the Yugoslav army and police. This traumatizing odyssey is now told and retold in the general accounts of the refugees.

Prince Otto Eduard Leopold von Bismarck, Germany's nineteenth-century so-called Iron Chancellor, once remarked that the Balkans weren't worth the bones of a single Pomeranian soldier. Kosovo and the surrounding area have long been the breeding ground of ethnic hatreds. It is also an area cursed by an especially virulent nationalism, one that has pitted nations of different faiths and cultures against one another. For those foolhardy enough to intervene in this quagmire, it would take years and effort to cope with the enormity of the tragedy.

The breakup of the former Yugoslavia is only the latest instance of the struggle for national identity that has taken place countless times in this corner of Europe throughout the last one thousand years. Since 1991, the events in Yugoslavia have been a relentless war of histories. The Balkan powder keg once led to a world war. History has a way of repeating itself in the same places. That repetition was narrowly averted in the 1999 bombing of Serbia, to be sure, but it was only in view of fortuitous timing and world political reality that NATO and the United States were able to succeed in the endeavor. The United States and the European Union were lucky to pursue policies at a time when Russia was incomparably weak. Had the once mighty Soviet Union existed, the Western alliance against Serbia would have come to naught. For the Serbs have not been without friends and allies, including the Greeks, who are members of NATO. Explaining the ambiguities of the division and alliances in this region is no simple matter; Russians and Greeks are drawn to the Serbs in ways that others are not. And Chinese opposition to NATO is based more on self-interest than on cultural loyalties. In the end, however, only self-interest prevails, even in the case of Yugoslavia's Greek and Russian Orthodox supporters.

It is easier to divide than to bring the peoples of this region together. This part of Europe we call the Balkans is bounded in the north by the Danube and Sava Rivers, in the east by the Black Sea, in the southeast by the Aegean Sea, in the south by the Mediterranean, and in the southwest by the Ionian and Adriatic Seas. As a peninsula, the region is cut off from the neighbouring lands to the east, west, and south. The Balkan countries include Greece, Albania, the former Yugoslavia, Macedonia, Bulgaria, Romania, parts of Croatia, Bosnia-Herzegovina, and the European part of Turkey. The rivers are short and can't carry much water traffic. Even the Danube is hard to get through. The mountains have divided the region into habitable areas and have effectively prevented regional cooperation by insulating the people in their own enclaves. Throughout the centuries the term *balkanization* has become synonymous with fragmentation and division.

The dissolution of Yugoslavia has created a number of separate countries. Where there was once one Yugoslavia, there are now Croatia, Slovenia, Bosnia-Herzegovina, Macedonia, and what's left of Yugoslavia (Serbia, Montenegro, and the Serbian provinces of Vojvodina and Kosovo). Is there room for more, perhaps? Montenegro is experiencing nationalist stirrings. So too is Kosovo (whether the Kosovar Muslims choose independence or opt to join Albania), with far more immediacy. Sections of Vojvodina could possibly decide to join with their Hungarian brethren to the north.

Some Western analysts have argued that with the example of Yugoslavia growing more and more fragmented, there is little to stop any nationalist group from claiming sovereignty elsewhere in the world. The Basques of Spain, for example, have been fighting for years for an autonomous country of their own. The French Canadians in Quebec never give up in one referendum after another. Consider also the Tibetans in China, the American Indians, the Armenians, the Kurds. The list goes on and on. Aren't they all equally deserving of a nation-state? Before the advent of the "modern" state, the world was divided into hundreds of principalities. Are we slowly returning to that world order again? In this century the breakup of empires has led to the creation of dozens of countries. Why not dozens more? Are we to say, then, that federalist entities are doomed?

The globalization of government was once the watchword for the twenty-first century. The idea of a world government is just that: an idea. More and more, it is becoming obvious that the legacy of the last few decades of the twentieth century is fragmentation, not globalization. Before 1990, the East and West were effectively split among the Soviet bloc, the American-led allies, and the Third World. With the fall of the Soviet bloc, it seems that these power blocs are no longer needed; dissolution was the byword of the 1990s. True, the creation of the European Union has drawn together much of Europe, but there's still much to be done before that union is complete. The United Nations is also seen as the chief agent for globalization; it has done much to pursue that cause. However, it has very little actual power of implementation without the approval of the United States, Russia, and China—in that order, it seems. If it can be said that American political, military, economic, and cultural domination of the world fosters rapid globalization, one must ask what manner of globalization, and in whose image? There now appears evidence of a silent and not-so-silent backlash. Increasingly, violent anti-American groups are springing up all over the world, even in America's own backyard.

At first glance, it may appear presumptuous for NATO and the United States to be dictating policies and behaviour to any country at all. It may seem unfair that the United States can virtually dominate UN policies while Washington's membership and operational dues to this world body are in arrears. What of the other industrialized countries that make up and contribute heavily to UN operations? These so-called Western allies of the United States have some heavy baggage; none are without skeletons in their closets. All have dark pasts. The colonial empires of England, France, Spain, Portugal, Germany, the Netherlands, and Russia, not to mention American empire-builders in the South Pacific, exploited colonial native peoples for their own benefit, often reducing the colonized population to a second-class status. They slaughtered indigenous peoples to quell discontent. The British in Australia, the Spanish in Central and South America, and white men who subdued American Indian tribes—all have engaged in the destruction of cultures, all have practised wholesale genocide.

Britain, for instance, is the NATO country most eager to bomb the Serbs. England, it is often argued, would certainly not appreciate NATO telling London it must settle the problem of Northern Ireland or risk getting bombed. Certainly, the British might counter by saying that they are not evicting and expelling the Irish Catholics from their homes, not anymore, not today anyway. But during the Boer War,[1] the British did herd thousands of women and children into concentration camps, where as many as 26,000 died of disease and malnutrition. This fact is shrouded in much mystery. Clearly, then, NATO countries cannot justify their actions any more than the Serbs can (reprehensible as Serbian actions in Kosovo have been), given their own histories of conquest and encroachment.

No NATO country is immune from racism and hatred. England has hate groups that seek to restrict immigration from non-white countries. The same is true of France, especially the *Front National* under Jean-Marie Le Pen. White Aryan militias cause turmoil in the United States; the French want Arabs out of France; the Germans want Turks out of Germany. Ultra right-wing nationalism is rife, everywhere in Europe. In Russia, an ultranationalist like Vladimir Zhirinovsky, leader of the ironically named Liberal Democratic Party, garners considerable support. Russia and other mainstream majority groups (e.g., the Russians in Russia, the Poles in Poland, the Hungarians in Hungary) seem to perceive themselves as victims, taking out their frustrations on minorities. How difficult it must be today (is it not?) to be a Gypsy anywhere in Eastern Europe!

However, the greatest self-righteousness is often ascribed to the policies of the American government. Indeed, American history is hardly the yardstick by which human rights can be measured. African Americans are still treated as second-class citizens. In many cases, their ancestors were brought to America in the holds of slave ships and treated as chattel by their "owners." Tortured, beaten, sold like cattle, families separated— surely these moral wrongs violated basic freedom. And when at long last that freedom was won, discrimination began to rear its ugly head. The treatment of the Native Americans was far worse. Whole tribes were slaughtered, their lands stolen, their way of life shattered. The American Indian still faces discrimination today, living in poverty and struggling in a substandard existence. The treatment of Hispanics, Asians, and many other minorities is equally reprehensible. During World War II, for example, most Japanese Americans were interned in detention camps and had their property taken away just for being of the wrong race. Ironically, many of the hate groups currently operating in the United States today—be they anti-black, anti-Semitic, anti-Hispanic, misogynistic, or anti-gay—are members of fundamentalist religious groups—religions that, for the most part, preach tolerance. To be sure, the U.S. government has dealt harshly with some of these groups (e.g., Waco, Ruby Ridge), but others hide behind a respectable facade of established religion.

The Yugoslav wars brought a new term into the international political lexicon. *Ethnic cleansing* is a term of horror used to describe the wholesale removal of a people from their homeland by another ethnic or dominant group. Certainly the scale of this phenomenon in Kosovo and in Bosnia is shocking and unbelievable, but it is by no means a new phenomenon nor is it limited to the former Yugoslavia.

The first examples of ethnic cleansing date back to the eighth century B.C. Jews suffered ethnic cleansing in Christian Europe for centuries. Between 1290 and 1492, they were forced out of England, France, Hungary, Austria, Lithuania, Poland, Portugal, and Spain (which also expelled Muslims in 1502). In more recent times, Americans were involved in an ethnic cleansing of their own in the wild, wild West of the American frontier by either killing off or forcing Native Americans onto reservations. England expelled many Irish from northern Ireland in 1688. Examples in the twentieth century include the Turkish ethnic cleansing of Greeks (in Cyprus) and Armenians (leading to the Armenian genocide of 1915). Perhaps in this sense the Holocaust is the most extreme form of ethnic cleansing. Six million Jews were murdered between 1933 and 1945 (almost one and a half million were children) and many others were deported; 1.2 million Poles were also cast out from their own country. After World War II, 12 million Germans were removed from Eastern Europe, especially from Poland, Czechoslovakia, Hungary, Romania, and Yugoslavia (during these expulsions, 2.1 million Germans also died of war, hunger, cold, and disease). The Soviet Union cleansed 600,000 from "unreliable" regions during Stalin's reign of terror. In retaliation, the Crimean Tatars killed between 70,000 and 120,000 Russians. The advent of Communism allowed, for the first time, the cleansing of an economic class (the bourgeoisie), and in China the intellectuals bore the brunt of this effort during the Maoist Cultural Revolution. In Yugoslavia during World War II, the Croatian Ustasha Party, Hungarians, and Bulgarians slaughtered Serbs.[2] One is loath to excuse the actions of ethnic cleansers and murderers in the former Yugoslavia, yet history shows that such activity is not a new phenomenon—moreover, many who have been condemning the Serbs are themselves guilty of atrocities.

After World War II, America regarded itself as the leader of the free world. Since the fall of the Soviet Union and the end of the Cold War, the United States has become the only superpower. With this status of leadership in the world come the trappings of an American way of life. Self-interest is important to a nation that must preserve that status and that ideal. America's commercial, political, and military preeminence must be maintained at all costs. This attitude reflects an ethic born of political pragmatism, a *Realpolitik* that follows the dictates of reason in a given space and at a particular time.[3] This pragmatism has led to questions about why the United States has intervened in some areas and not in others. It raised the question of consistency in the policies pursued and implemented. Why in Europe but not in Africa? Why in the Middle East for some people (e.g., the Kuwaitis) but not others (e.g., the Kurds)? Is the answer only economic? Is it racial? As mentioned, the Turks have been repressing the Kurds since 1984, and they ethnically cleansed Cyprus of the Greeks in 1974 and brought in thousands of Turkish settlers.

But then again, Turkey is a member of NATO and is thus an American ally.[4]

Some critics believe that U.S. intervention in other countries is undesirable and futile. In a paper published in *Policy Analysis*, Barbara Conry outlines the basic tenets of this view. She states that American intervention often exacerbates the situation, leading to further violence. It can also lead to anti-American sentiment and diminish American credibility if the mission fails. Conry believes that global instability is normal and poses no threat to America. Instead, she states, only when national security is at stake should the United States intervene and encourage regional initiatives. Conry believes that even though democracy, human rights, national self-determination, and humanitarian assistance are lofty ideals, they do not provide sufficient reason to intervene inasmuch as the opportunity to intervene begs the question of inconsistency. Results are often a form of duplicity in American foreign policy when choosing areas to get involved in.[5] The same can be said of NATO, the European Union, and of course, the UN. The media all too often explained the intervention in Kosovo in purely humanitarian terms.

Madeleine Albright, the U.S. secretary of state, sees American foreign policy in a different light. She believes that although there is no longer a Soviet Union to worry about, the United States still has a vital role to play on the international scene. She believes that the United States must help other governments to achieve full participation in the world system and assist the poorer countries in helping themselves. To do this, she argues, Americans must promote the principles of democracy, open markets, law, and a commitment to peace.[6] Max Frankel, writing in the *New York Times* of May 13, 1999, echoes this messianic role of the United States in no unambiguous terms:

> Someday in the next century we will acknowledge that there can be no global human rights without global laws and no way to write and enforce the laws without a global congress, courts and cops . . . as the lion in the jungle of nations, the United States is obviously not ready to yield to a higher authority. . . . The time will come when Americans recognize that anarchy among nations constitutes a threat to our interest and welfare. We would then take the lead in creating a canopy of law across the globe.

Albright's former mentor, Peter F. Krogh, wrote a scathing article in the *Wall Street Journal* that condemned a foreign policy that has significantly marginalized the Russians diplomatically and called the shots on virtually every issue of importance to them.[7] "They (Americans) instruct the Russians and the Japanese on their economics, the Chinese on their politics, the Iraqis on their military, the Serbs on their provinces, the

Latin Americans on drugs and the UN on reform. . . . It is a foreign policy of sermons and sanctimony accompanied by the brandishing of Tomahawks."[8]

The independent Russian press screams every day about American arrogance in the Balkans; every day Russians call for a return to Communism, a return to red/brown coalitions, a return to a monarchy with an authoritative tsar. "This is a clash of civilizations," stated Alexei Podberezkin, deputy chairman of the foreign affairs committee of the Russian parliament's lower house. "Theirs is an aggressive, Protestant model of democracy—no, they impose it on us. What is happening in Yugoslavia and what happened in Bosnia and Croatia is an attempt to impose the Western understanding of values."[9] For this reason, Russian public opinion has been wholeheartedly on the side of Serbia.

The cases of Iraq and Yugoslavia leave a message that cannot be ignored. America has twice bombed Iraq, and still Saddam Hussein remains in power. The same is true of Slobodan Milosevic in Yugoslavia. Increasingly, this policy of duplicitous inconsistency leads other sovereign nations toward anti-Americanism. Iranians have thought of the United States as "the Great Satan" for years. Middle Eastern and Asian countries feel the same way. Throughout the twentieth century, the United States removed from power many leaders it didn't feel promoted the best interests of America (e.g., Salvador Allende in Chile, Manuel Noriega in Panama, Muhammad Mossadeq in Iran . . . and the list goes on).

A sidebar to this argument is America's use of foreign policy to distract the American public from domestic issues. There is nothing new in this, certainly—and it is not limited to the United States. Serbia's Slobodan Milosevic is a virtual master of the strategy. He started two wars in order to keep himself in power. But the release in 1998 of the American film *Wag the Dog*, produced by Barry Levinson, goes to the heart of a lively discussion. In the film, the U.S. president is caught having sex with a visiting "Firefly" girl in the White House a few weeks before the presidential election (this film was, ironically, released weeks before "Monicagate" hit Washington). In order to defuse the situation, Conrad Brean (played by Robert De Niro), the president's spin doctor, hires Hollywood producer Stanley Motss (Dustin Hoffman) to "produce" a war that will distract the nation. They use modern movie-making magic to stage a war between the United States and Albania. They concoct terrorist attacks, bomb villages, and even divert *Air Force One* to Boca Raton in the rain so the president can appear to give his coat to an old Albanian woman and have her thank him on national television. There's even a bogus hostage who writes a song about the event and passes it off as a 1939 ballad. That man turns out to be a psychopath who is killed by a farmer while trying to rape the farmer's wife. This allows a full-scale military funeral, which is televised throughout the country. Everything works perfectly until Motss decides he wants full credit for the production and ends up being killed by government agents. Is truth stranger than fiction? Not long after the Monica Lewinsky scandal hit Washington, the United States bombed Iraq. It wasn't too long before the Pentagon and president got involved in Kosovo. Strange coincidence? What about the fact that America invaded Grenada a few days after 241 marines were killed in a bombing of their barracks in Beirut in 1983? What about the reelection of Britain's Margaret Thatcher soon after the Falkland Islands invasion? It certainly makes one wonder how much of a nation's political life is manipulated.

The foreign policy of the Clinton administration, indeed of the entire presidency, seems to be hobbled by the polls. The American public did indeed support the war in the former Yugoslavia, especially after a settlement was proposed. The Republican-controlled Congress, anxious at first to rein in the popularity of the president's initiatives in what can only have been intra-party rivalry, voted the president more money when it looked like they could ride the coattails of his renewed popularity. Instead, the Republicans appeared foolish. They had distanced themselves from the war from the very beginning, claiming it was Clinton's fault. Now that peace has arrived, Clinton can take full credit and leave the Republicans holding the bag. The main reason for this popularity, it seems, is that no American lives were lost in Kosovo until after the peacekeepers went in, and then only in accidents that could just as easily have happened on home soil. This precedent could have dire consequences on the future of American involvement in international conflicts. Americans cannot expect that the United States will only become involved in conflicts where there will be no Americans killed. But policymakers in the United States do hope to manipulate actions from behind the scenes—much like the "Great and Powerful Oz"—and expect the British, the French, the Germans, NATO, or the United Nations to suffer the brunt of the casualties.

This war has also proven to be a sad commentary on the state of the United Nations. When the Americans couldn't get help from the UN before going into Kosovo, mainly over the objections of Russia and China in the Security Council, Washington opted for the next best thing: NATO. Although the UN Charter forbids violating a state's sovereignty with force, the Universal Declaration of Human Rights guarantees the rights of individuals against oppressive states. This unclear distinction requires a case-by-case examination and a vote on where to intervene and how. In the case of Kosovo, the Russians had a stake in keeping the United States out of the area, so the UN was hobbled by internal Security Council problems.

Many say that the plight of the Albanian refugees was one of the major causes of Western intervention in the area. However, there are millions of refugees throughout the world: to wit, Armenians, Hindus, Palestinians, Cubans, Bengalis, Vietnamese, Chileans, Somalis, Rwandans, and Afghans. Neither NATO nor the UN significantly intervened in helping these groups to return home. In fact, world aid organizations must literally beg Western countries and sponsors for more money to address the refugee crisis in Africa. The United Nations High Commissioner for Refugees has raised 90 percent of the money it needs for the Kosovo refugees but only 60 percent for the 6 million refugees in Africa.[10] Why are the Kosovars seen as being more worthy than the Africans? This is an area with only 10 percent of the world's population, but 50 percent of the world's wars and conflicts take place here. Certainly, the fact that Kosovo is closer to the West than Africa is has something to do with it. The fact that very little media coverage is given to the crises in Africa is another reason. The signatories of the 1951 UN Refugee Convention are today taking in fewer and fewer refugees. Many are sent home to face torture and death or end up in detention areas, with no home and no future. The main problem regarding refugees is how to handle them. Should they be given a safe haven within the country they flee to, be moved to camps outside the region, be resettled in other countries, or be allowed to return home? The last option is the ultimate goal. And now, for the first time, some states are seriously talking about UN reform, without which there can be no lasting solutions in world crises.

This has been a war of firsts: the first time that NATO forces attacked a sovereign country; the first time the Internet was a source of news and propaganda in a major world conflict; the first time a leader who was still in office was indicted for war crimes; the first time a war was ostensibly fought for human rights.

Is this the beginning of a new morality for international relations? The ostensibly "human rights" war seems to show that it's possible. But what about other countries whose governments mistreat and massacre their own civilians? Consider Chechnya or Rwanda. Why is Kosovo regarded as the first humanitarian war? NATO has no vital interest in the area. Kosovo produces nothing that is an essential trade item; it has no strategic commodity. It isn't situated along any major trade route. Serbia didn't attack any NATO country. Kosovo is a province of Serbia and has been since the founding of Yugoslavia (except for a brief time during World War II when it was united with Albania under Italian and then German occupation). Thus, it seems there is more to the invasion than has been revealed. There must surely be policies, or ulterior motives, in the minds of NATO planners that are long term.

Who is the real culprit here? What is the real cause of the fighting? Certainly a leader like Milosevic. But like Saddam Hussein, he must have a following—in the armed forces, among his generals, among the police, in the population at large. Milosevic could not act alone. His support may be summed up in the term *nationalism*. Nationalism can be defined as the belief that the good of the nation into which a person is born is the most important political value. A person's nation is not necessarily the same as a person's country. A nation implies a common language or history or religion. But it is not the only loyalty. A person living in Paris, for example, may consider himself a Parisian, a native of France, a Roman Catholic, a Christian, a member of the European Community, and a Westerner. National identity is thus a state of mind. The people of France may be regarded as the French people because of the commonality of their language, their culture, their religion, their history. However, there are natives of France in other lands who are no less members of the French nation as a whole, just as in France there are members of other nationalities who don't consider themselves as belonging to the French nation. In today's world, only 10 percent of countries are formed of a single ethnic community. However, in some countries, nationalism subordinates the individual cultures that comprise it. A good example of this is the United States—a country, not really a nation, made up of people from many different ethnic groups. Yet the idea of the melting pot makes them all Americans, and therefore a nation.

Nationalism has been the strongest political force in the last two hundred years. All attempts at globalization seem to have failed. There is no doubt that there are international organizations and groupings (e.g., the European Union [EU], the former Warsaw Pact). These were (the EU is still) supranational, but a truly universal government is not likely in the near future. The great political theorist Alexis de Toqueville once said: "Few will burn with ardent love for the entire human species. The interests of the human race are better served by giving every man a particular fatherland than by trying to inflame his passions for the whole of humanity."[11] Indeed, the only way that the current world, given all its divisions, could truly come together is to face an immediate global catastrophe. For the moment, that appears to be the stuff of Hollywood fiction (e.g., *Armageddon, Deep Impact*).

Nationalism, like most ideologies, has positive and negative aspects. It's positive if it involves pride in one's country and fosters patriotism. It can become negative, however, if it means oppressing another people. An example is the ancient Greeks, who saw themselves as the epitome of civilization and the rest of the world as barbarian; or the Chinese ideologues which celebrated *Zhongguo*, their Middle Kingdom, and believed their center of civilization was surrounded by offal. Another example involves the members of a particular religion who see themselves as believers and members of other religions as infidels. Samuel Huntington claims that the major source of conflict in the twenty-first century will be cultural. Before the French Revolution, conflict was between rulers eager to expand their territories and create nation-states. Following the Revolution, conflict was between nations. After World War I, conflict generally arose over ideology (i.e., communism, liberal democracy, fascism). During the Cold War the world was divided into First, Second, and Third Worlds. Since the end of the Cold War, conflict may very well escalate to become wars between cultures.[12]

Nationalism can be a destructive and violent force that, when spurred by hatred toward the "other," becomes devastatingly warlike in character. Already the wars between the Serbs and Croats and the Serbs over Bosnia show that cultural and religious nationalism is dangerous. Here ethnic hatred has reached such new levels that the cruelties and barbarism of these wars will long be remembered. No one can forget the images of concentration camps, torture, executions, and rape as a weapon of war—all part and parcel of ethnic cleansing.

At the heart of this type of nationalism is prejudice. Prejudice can be defined as hostility toward an individual or group or race on the basis of their supposed characteristics. It is human nature to want to place the blame for one's problems at the foot of someone else. What child has not blamed a broken dish on the nearest animate object in the vicinity? But this propensity for blame-giving has not been outgrown as the last few generations have matured. Perhaps it is because post-Kennedy and post-Vietnam America lost its idealism and its conviction that it was the moral compass by which the rest of the world could steer. With the loss of innocence came the problem of facing reality—a reality in which the government did not always have the individual's best interests at heart and the bad guy didn't always wear a black hat. This has led to the phenomenon of people taking the easy option of blaming their problems on their parents, their teachers, their friends, their lovers, their children, even people who pass them on the street just this very minute or looked at them in a funny way fifteen years ago.

Members of such a society put the blame for personal, economic, and political problems squarely at the feet of whomever they think can legitimately, or illegitimately, be blamed. It is always easier to blame those who are different, no matter their innocence. This has led to racism, ethnic and religious intolerance, and hatred. Guilt and frustration can also cause people to blame someone else. For example, the economic and political frustration and the guilt forced on the Germans by the Allies after World War I led the Germans to transfer these feelings to naked aggression against a traditional scapegoat, the Jews, with cataclysmic results.

Granted, during times when the economy was tough and when people were hungry and homeless, hatred against the "other" has always prevailed. At such times, racism becomes useful as a way to distract people from their troubles. A scapegoat is especially useful. The notion of the scapegoat dates to the Book of Leviticus, where it was explained that on the Day of Atonement the high priest would place the sins of Israel on the head of a goat and send the animal out into the desert, thereby transferring the sins from the people to something that could be physically as well as spiritually banished. The scapegoat reduces our responsibility for our actions.

In Serbia, it seems that Albanians are an easy scapegoat. Rather than face a declining economy and a potential loss of power, Milosevic attributed all of the problems to the Albanians as people not belonging in Serbia. He set about dehumanizing them, taking advantage of Christian prejudices against Muslims.

Nationalism became a true force in the world following the end of the imperial age after World War I. Before this, much of the world was divided into colonizers and colonized. The great empires of Europe, Japan, and the United States began to disappear after World War I as nationalist sentiments arose. Asian, African, South American, and the South Pacific nations began to throw off the yoke of colonialism and asserted themselves as international entities. The beginnings of the Cold War following World War II led to the creation of three separate blocs into which nearly every nation fit: the East, the West, and the non-aligned. With the fall of the Soviet Union in 1991 and the independence of its former empire (Eastern Europe and the fourteen republics that went on to form nations), nationalism has again become a potent force for change. The revival of nationalism was inevitable. The Soviets and the Yugoslav government sought to replace nationalism under a socialist society. Thus, in the Soviet Union they tried to form—instead of a Ukrainian or Russian or an Uzbek—the composite Soviet citizen. The same was true in Yugoslavia. But it couldn't be done. Once the party and the security apparatus fell, there was nothing to keep nationalism in check. In addition, other countries such as the Czech Republic, Slovakia, Eritrea (from Ethiopia), and Somaliland (from Somalia) have been created by these forces. These breakups can be peaceful, such as the Velvet Divorce of Czechoslovakia in 1993, or extremely violent, as the breakup of Yugoslavia shows.

The situation in the former Yugoslavia is unique. A large area made up of twenty-four ethnic groups, three main languages, three main religions, two alphabets, and six republics each having a majority ethnic group, Yugoslavia seemed a ticking time bomb that portended war and destruction. Serbia was the largest republic, along with the autonomous regions of Kosovo and Vojvodina. Vojvodina has a Serbian majority but at least ten different ethnic groups and five languages, making it the most ethnically diverse area in all of the former Yugoslavia. The largest ethnic minority are the Hungarians, who are considered an alien people by the Serbs. Kosovo was settled by Albanians and came under the control of an Italian- and then German-controlled Albania between 1941 and 1945 before it was taken back by Yugoslavia. Slovenia is the home of the Slovene people, who are Catholic, highly Westernized, and formerly part of the Austro-Hungarian empire. They split from Yugoslavia in 1991 with very little problem. Croatia is home to the Croatians, a people who have long been the traditional enemy of the Serbs despite the fact that they are ethnically the same, separated only by religion (i.e., culture)— the Croats are Catholic, and the Serbs are Orthodox. When the Croats declared their independence, the Serbs were very reluctant to let them leave (mainly because of a large Serb minority within Croatia) and attacked. Croatia is now independent. Bosnia-Herzegovina is the centrally located republic. Although the majority is Muslim, there are large populations of Croats and Serbs within its borders. This very division caused the years-long war over possession of Bosnia and eventually resulted in international intervention and the partition of Bosnia among the three main ethnic groups. Macedonia has long been under contention among Serbia, Bulgaria, and Greece. It was divided many times throughout its history. Today's Macedonia contains a large population of Albanians. It declared independence in 1991 and avoided the major problems of other provinces trying to separate. Montenegro is today a province, along with Serbia, of the former Republic of Yugoslavia. A mountainous region, it would like to be independent as well. It also has a small population of Albanians.

War in Yugoslavia is especially dangerous because the borders touch many other countries that have the potential to be drawn in. Italy, Hungary, Romania, Bulgaria, Greece, and Albania all have ethnics living within the former Yugoslavia's borders, and all may decide to come to the rescue of these minorities if they are threatened by Serbia.

Miroslav Hroch, in an article appearing in the journal *Nations and Nationalism*, outlined six favourable conditions for the growth of nationalism:

1. vacuum at the top not filled and fighting for political power is a nationally relevant conflict of interests

2. decline of economy, so one can blame "others"

3. differences based on religion

4. political culture forgotten or absent or difficult to improve

5. members of former ruling nation are degraded to the level of ethnic minority under the rule of a formerly oppressed nation

6. national traditions and myth include a tradition of fighting and dying for "nation" as an extremely positive and morally bonding value[13]

All these conditions were at play in the former Yugoslavia.

Politically, the death in 1980 of Marshal Tito, the strongman who'd led Yugoslavia since World War II, left the country in a vacuum. The "father" of modern Yugoslavia, Tito was a shrewd politician who was able to keep the distrustful minorities at bay from the time of the creation of Yugoslavia until his death by a call for national unity. There were laws forbidding racial, national, or religious hatred. Tito's ideology, which can be described as Marxist-Leninist-Stalinist-Titoist, claimed to be stronger than nationalism. But with the fall of communism came nationalism. After all, nationalism and communism had much in common. They were both a struggle against the "other": in communism, against the capitalists; and in nationalism, against all who weren't members of the nation. In both cases, the highest allegiance was to the state. Although Tito succeeded in defusing ethnic tensions, he never created a Yugoslav identity that was stronger than the nationalisms of each state. Thus, when he died and his overwhelming authority was absent, the nations were free to exert their long-suppressed political muscles. Tito didn't want another leader to take his place in the minds and hearts of his people, so he left behind a collective leadership with power changing hands at the top echelons every year. The Serbian frustration at not being in control was an opportunity for Slobodan Milosevic to seize power.

The decline of the Yugoslav economy in the 1980s and early 1990s was obvious as they tried to forge a new economy following communism. Several methods were tried before capitalism was attempted. The new leaders decided to democratize, but by then it was too late. The northern republics tended to be more highly developed. Vojvodina was rich in mineral wealth, whereas the other republics exported raw materials and agricultural products. The north grew weary of supporting the south, and this led to independence talks. By then, the Serbians found an easy scapegoat for the economic failure in the Kosovar Albanians because they had kept the area poor. When many Serbs moved out of the region because of the poor economy, Serbia blamed Albanian terrorism, thereby stirring up hatred against them.

Religious differences also have played a role. The Serbs tend to be Orthodox Christians. Converted when they were part of the Byzantine Empire, in 1219 they created their own Serbian Orthodox Church. It has long been a political entity as well as a religious one, and it has sought to protect the Serbian culture. The Croats and Slovenes are Roman Catholic. Many of the people of Bosnia-Herzegovina and the vast majority of Kosovo adopted the Islamic faith of their Ottoman conquerors. Thus, the Serbians see the Albanians as religious traitors.

The political culture of the Serbians was nearly absent after many years within the Yugoslav federation. Yet the Serbs remembered the glory days of having their own state and were unwilling to remain just one of many nationalities. They wanted to control the Yugoslav government. Serbia's growing nationalism also played a part in the disintegration of Yugoslavia. Many of the other republics were concerned that Serbia would try to force its culture on them. The army, government, and bureaucracy were overwhelmingly Serbian in character. In fact, Serbian nationalism tends to frame the Serbs as history's victims. They feel that everyone is out to get them. They have been conquered or attacked by Muslims, Germans, Croats, and now the NATO allies. They are xenophobic and feel isolated in the world system. As Steve Crawshaw, writing for the *New Statesman*, put it: "According to a view held widely in Serbia today, anybody who accuses the Serbs of anything (yes, anything) either has been duped by or is part of an international conspiracy—an à la carte mixture of Bill Clinton (trying to distract from cigars and moral decay in the Oval Office), Germany (with its well-known ambitions for a Fourth Reich) and international Islam (seeking a fundamentalist takeover)."[14] The Serbs felt that they were the only ones who loved Yugoslavia and had done the majority of the work to make it succeed, only to be economically exploited by Croatia and Slovenia. They are sure all the other nations hated them. They felt discriminated against because they had to share their state power with Vojvodina and Kosovo while no other state had to share its power at all. The principal problem became one in which non-Serbs didn't want to be ruled by a Serbia in the guise of Yugoslavia, and the Serbs didn't want to be a junior partner in areas where they were minorities.[15]

Their culture also was a factor as they remembered that they had fought the Turks and the Nazis and didn't feel that they'd been given their proper due for those efforts. They felt underappreciated for the Battle of Kosovo in 1389, for trying to save Europe from the Ottomans, and for defeating the Nazis during World War II. With all these conditions at play, it's hardly surprising that the Serbs chose to go their own way. Kosovo was an easy target, especially following the debacle in Bosnia. Because Kosovo was a Serbian province, they believed that the international community would not involve itself. Because they considered Kosovo an important part of their history, comparing it to the Jews' Jerusalem, they thought they could expel the Albanians with little or no consequences.

As Massimo Calabresi noted, "Diplomats can negotiate peace, and foreign soldiers can enforce it. Well-intentioned civilian supervisors can even provide day-to-day public services. But no one has ever figured out how to make former combatants bury their hatreds along with their casualties."[16] Herein lies the difficulty of Balkan politics. For when one member of a family is killed by the hated enemy, his or her children swear revenge and the cycle of violence continues through another generation. This is a region where the concept of blood vengeance, or *krvna osveta*, was prevalent until a mere generation ago and, no doubt, continues to form a part of the cultural history of these people.

Parties in conflict identify the position of the adversary as the exact opposite of their own experience of reality. Thus, we must be careful in our capacity as critics and analysts and observers, and above all, as peacekeepers—we must not push too far the norms of the mainstream culture of diplomacy. We must remember that all the nations of the former Yugoslavia (including Albania) underwent nearly fifty years of Communist repression; in such a post-Communist environment one cannot suddenly embark on Western notions of liberal democracy. One can hardly expect the rapid transition to a multi-party electoral system to come spontaneously with a free press, the protection of minorities, guarantees of human rights, tolerance of opposing political views, responsive legislative bodies, and nonviolent transfers of power. Peacekeeping by mediators bodes ill in these conditions if it is not accompanied by peacemaking. The impartiality of the international brokers will always be called into question.

History is the problem. Yes, it is; there has positively been too much history here. Too many of the atrocities committed in the past are told to the next generation, who are admonished never to forget. "Those who cannot remember the past will be condemned to repeat it." Santayana's maxim is now a truism. The problem in the former Yugoslavia is not that the people don't remember the past; they remember it too clearly and look upon it as a personal affront to themselves and their people—affronts that must be avenged. In a speech to U.S. troops in Bosnia on December 22, 1997, U.S. president Bill Clinton said: "The real differences around the world today are not between Jews and Arabs; Protestants and Catholics; Muslims, Croats, and Serbs. The real differences are between those who embrace peace and those who would destroy it; between those who look to the future and those who cling to the past; between those who open their arms and those who are determined to clench their fists." The only way lasting peace can occur in the Balkans is if a policy of *Vergangenheitsbewältigung* (a German word meaning "overcoming history") is implemented. This war was perhaps inevitable, no matter the solutions suggested. It took place along the dividing line of southern Europe—between the Ottoman and Austro-Hungarian empires; between Orthodox and Roman Catholic Christianity; between Greater Serbian and Greater Albanian nationalism. Tensions have been seething here for centuries. The war in Kosovo was only the latest manifestation of these divisions.

This tome will try to point out the signposts, the alternative policies that were accepted, rejected, and missed. What does the future have in store? A new panacea? A reform of the UN? Hindsight always comes with 20–20 vision. If mistakes were made, much can be learned from them.

The following chapters present a history of what has exacerbated nationalist aspirations and led to the rise of a leader like Milosevic. The text examines Serbia's and Kosovo's cultural antecedents and the ambiguities of the Western position, both prior to and after Russia's slow decline in Europe. Before NATO's intervention, before the peacekeepers actually moved in, were there any signs of reconciliation? How peaceful can the Balkans become? What will be NATO's role in Europe? And what opportunities were missed—deliberately or accidentally—that might have prevented bloodshed and ethnic cleansing in the first place?

Whatever happens in this Balkan corner of Europe never happens in a void, oddly enough, no matter what Bismarck said about the inconsequence of the Balkans.

NOTES

1. The Boer War (1899–1902) involved Great Britain and the Transvaal and Orange Free State of what was to become South Africa. Britain increased its territory at the expense of the Boer (Dutch) people already living there, especially after gold was found. The two sides eventually went to war and the British prevailed, making South Africa another colony in its empire.

2. Andrew Bell-Fialkoff, "A Brief History of Ethnic Cleansing" in *Foreign Affairs*, vol. 72, no. 3, Summer 1993, pp. 111–17.

3. Samuel P. Huntington, "The Lonely Superpower: The New Dimension of Power" in *Foreign Affairs*, vol. 78, no. 2, p. 3 (reprinted from EBSCO).

4. Ignacio Ramonet, "A Fine Mess" in *Le Monde Diplomatique*, May 1999, p. 4 (www.monde-diplomatique.fr/en/1999/05/?c=01leader).

5. Barbara Conry, "The Futility of U.S. Intervention in Regional Conflicts" in *Policy Analysis*, no. 209, May 19, 1994, pp. 1–10 (taken from http://www.cato.org/pubs/pas/pa-109.html).

6. Madeleine K. Albright, "The Testing of American Foreign Policy: Present, Again, at the Creation" in *Foreign Affairs*, vol. 77, no. 6, Nov./Dec. 1998, p. 51.

7. Peter F. Krogh, "Scold and Bomb: Clinton's Failed Foreign Policy" in *Wall Street Journal*, April 28, 1999, p. A18.

8. Ibid.

9. *Pravda*, June 10, 1999.

10. Karl Vick, "Africa Has Refugees, Kosovo Gets Money: Needs of War Exiles Deplete Donations" in *Washington Post*, October 8, 1999, p. A24.

11. Quoted in Michael Lind, "In Defense of Liberal Nationalism" in *Foreign Affairs*, vol. 73, no. 3, May/June 1994, pp. 94–95.

12. Samuel P. Huntington, "The Clash of Civilizations?" in *Foreign Affairs*, vol. 72, no. 3, Summer 1993, p. 23.

13. Miroslav Hroch, "Nationalism and National Movements: Comparing the Past and the Present of Central and Eastern Europe" in *Nations and Nationalism*, vol. 2, no. 1, 1996, p. 42.

14. Steve Crawshaw, "A Whole Nation Goes Mad" in *New Statesman*, vol. 128, no. 4438, May 31, 1999.

15. Where they were minorities, the Serbs invariably considered the majority to be "Serbophobic." Ivo Banac, "The Origins and Development of the Concept of Yugoslavia (to 1945)" in *Yearbook of European Studies #5: The Disintegration of Yugoslavia*, eds. Martin van den Heuvel and Jan G. Siccama (Atlanta: Rodopi, 1992), p. 22.

16. Massimo Calabresi, "No to Reconciliation" in *Time*, September 28, 1998, p. 44.

2

THE BACKGROUND:
A PANDORA'S BOX
OF HATRED AND CONFLICT
THROUGH THE AGES

Yes, there is too much history here ... but how else will you understand these people?

—overheard at a conference on the Balkans

Kosovo did not appear from the ether. It has a history. It has relevance and must not be seen as expendable.

"Yugoslavia" was composed of six major national groups: Slovenes, Croats, Serbs, Montenegrins, Macedonians, and Muslims (the first five had their own republics, and the Muslims were within a multiethnic Bosnia-Herzegovina). It was also the home of twelve minority nationalities: Albanians, Hungarians, Turks, Slovaks, Gypsies (or Roma), Bulgarians, Romanians, Ruthenians (a Slavic people from western Ukraine), Greeks, Italians, Vlachs (descendants of the Romans from Wallachia), and Ukrainians.

The history of these peoples has largely been penned in blood and tears. It is more complicated, perhaps, than any paperback mystery.

THE SERBS: THE BOOGEYMEN OF THE LATE 1990s

Since the Soviet Union's last gasp and the discovery that the Russians can be America's trading partners and intimate friends, the world realized it needed a new villain to despise. Sure, with his dark mustache, his sinister look and stare, Saddam Hussein cut quite a figure for a while. Alas! After two efforts to unseat him from power failed miserably, Americans grew weary of him. Besides, he was just one man. And it was painfully obvious that the people of Iraq, not Hussein himself, had been suffering from our efforts to unseat him. With Serbia, however, there was a villain we could all hate and condemn. Television brought the reality of wars in Bosnia right into our living rooms. While eating dinner, glued to the television, we could shake our heads at the images of mass graves, of concentration camps, of the homeless and the wretched. We would never allow anything like this in the West! Why were the Yugoslavs (read: Serbs) permitting such atrocities? They must have known. And so we felt justified in condemning the Serbs as the world's latest blackguard.

But who are the Serbs? And how did they develop into the people they are today?

The Serbs are Slavs, Europe's largest ethnic and linguistic group. The Slavs are split between the west (Poles, Czechs, and Slovaks), the east (Russians, Ukrainians, and Belarussians), and the south (Serbs, Croats, Slovenes, Macedonians, and Bulgars). In terms of religion, these peoples are divided between the Eastern Orthodox and the Roman Catholic churches. The Slav peoples most likely originated in Galicia (southeastern Poland and western Ukraine). Those that settled in what became Yugoslavia emigrated from the north between A.D. 500 and 700, probably fleeing the advancing Hun invasions. They were organized under warlords and eventually developed a nobility. As they settled the land, the tribes became divided by the physical landscape and were never united again. The early kings adopted Christianity in order to gain legitimacy for their rule. During the late fourth century a major division between the Roman Catholic and Byzantine empires took place, causing the land to be divided between the Catholic and Orthodox churches.[1] Thus, the Russians, Greeks, Serbs, Bulgarians, Romanians, Georgians, Cypriots, and Ukrainians became Orthodox (for a discussion of the Orthodox faith and the reasons for the split, see note 1).

The first Serbian king was crowned in 1077. At the time he converted the Serbs to Catholicism. It wasn't until 1159 that Stephen Nemanja founded the dynasty that would rule Serbia for two centuries, during which time the Serbs were converted to Orthodoxy. Although they ruled as members of the Byzantine Empire, the Serb kingdom known as Raska did not gain full independence until 1217, and then for only a little over a century. The greatest of the Serbian kings, Tsar Stephen Dushan, conquered many of the surrounding states—Bulgaria, Macedonia, Greece, and Albania—and united them under Serb rule. After his death, his empire fell apart.

The year 1389 is probably the most well-known date in Serb history. On June 28 at the Field of Black Birds, or Kosovo Polje, the forces of Prince Lazar Hrebeljanovic were defeated in battle by the Ottoman Turks. This historical defeat has been transformed into the myth of Kosovo; it still explains why the Serbs want control of Kosovo, which was the heartland of the Serbian medieval kingdom. It is said that the prince died in battle rather than live with the shame of becoming a Turkish vassal. Over the centuries since the event, a range of poems, plays, and paintings have depicted the events in ways that have little to do with the actual battle and its results. Part of the legend has it that a gray falcon flew from Jerusalem to Kosovo carrying a book from the Mother of God to Lazar and dropped it in his lap. It instructed him that if he embraced the Kingdom of Heaven and built a church, he and his men would all die. But if he embraced the Kingdom of Earth he would kill all the Turkish invaders. Lazar chose the Heavenly Kingdom because it would last forever. As a result his son-in-law, Vuk Brankovic, betrayed him and all the defenders perished.[2] Lazar was thus transformed into God's servant who sacrificed himself for the common Serbian good. Kosovo became likened to a Serbian Jerusalem under the control of Muslims. Although Muslim Albanians, Christian Bosnians, and Catholic Croats probably fought on his side too, and Serbs probably fought on the Ottoman side, the Battle of Kosovo is seen by the Serbs as a Serb-only achievement. Those who fled to the mountains or to Austria and the Orthodox Church kept the story of the battle and an independent Serbia alive, transforming the defeat into a moral victory that could sustain the Serbs under foreign rule. The oppressed Serbians turned to the church as a source of self-identity to keep their embattled culture alive.

Lazar's son Stefan was allowed to rule over a diminished and divided Serbia. Although it had been reduced in size, the Serb kingdom did manage to survive almost 100 years after the events at Kosovo. By 1456, arguments over the succession to the last Serbian king led to a complete annexation by the Ottoman Empire.[3] The Turkish rule grew increasingly oppressive as time went on. Those who weren't Muslims were forced to grow food and supply horses and oxen for the Ottomans. The Christians became an underprivileged class. It was not surprising that many non-Muslims, including many Albanians, converted to Islam[4] in order to avoid becoming serfs. The Serbs were spread around the provinces so as not to cause problems, their sons were taken as tribute to be converted and trained as soldiers for the empire, the nobles were exterminated, and the Serbs were deprived of contact with the west. In 1690 after the Austro-Hungarian Empire[5] abandoned its war with the Ottomans, the Serbs, who had backed Austria-Hungary, were forced to flee from Kosovo to Hungary under the Archbishop of Pec. The Austro-Hungarians promised them religious freedom and settled them in a buffer zone between the two empires. Between 1718 and 1791, the Austro-Hungarian frontier and northern Serbia changed hands several times between the empires. In 1737, after Austria again abandoned a war it had started (along with Russia) against Turkey, the Serbs were forced to emigrate north again. By 1774, however, through the Treaty of Kutchuck Kainardji, the Russians were given the right to protect the Orthodox subjects of the sultan.

In the early 1800s the Serbs were reunited under Djordje Petrovic, a peasant and sergeant in the Austrian army who became known as Karadjordje, or Black George. They began a revolt, after renegade Turks murdered Serbian leaders, which took nine years for the Ottomans to contain. Karadjordje's resistance led to a reawakening of the Kosovo tradition and the idea of a united nationalist Serbia. The revolt eventually failed, and Karadjordje was forced to flee abroad.

The revolt also reawakened the idea of pan-Slavism, a theory that espoused the unification of all Slavs. In the seventeenth century Juraj Krizanic called for the unification of Russians and South Slavs. The Serb group Omladina, operating in the 1870s, foresaw the creation of a state of Serbia, Montenegro, Bosnia-Herzegovina, and Bulgaria. By the late 1800s Petar Preradovic expanded on the idea of Yugoslavism (or union of the Southern "Yugo" Slavs) and pan-Slavism. At the same time, the Croatian Catholic bishop of Djakovo, Josip Strossmeyer, was calling for a union between the Catholic and Orthodox churches and a South Slav union.

In 1815 there was another revolt, this time led by Karadjordje's lieutenant, Milos Obrenovic, who seized control of the Serb nationalists. Within months most of Serbia was free, and two years later Obrenovic was made prince after the assassination of Karadjordje by an Obrenovic supporter, thereby setting off a dynastic feud. Although Obrenovic denied complicity, he did send the head of Karadjordje to the sultan, winning limited self-government. Russia, which had supported Karadjordje, became an opponent of the Obrenovic dynasty. The Russo-Turkish war of 1828–1829 gave the Serbs further autonomy. By 1839 Obrenovic was forced to abdicate in favor of his son Michael. In 1842 the Russians helped Aleksandar Karadjordje become king, but he was deposed by the Obrenovic dynasty in 1858.

The idea of the creation of a Greater Serbia dates to this time. In 1844 Ilija Garasanin, the minister of internal affairs of Serbia and later foreign minister and prime minister, wrote a book entitled *Nacertanije* (Outline). In it he stated that Serbia must take its place among the other European powers. To do this, all Serbian people must be united by the absorption of Bosnia, Herzegovina, Montenegro, northern Albania, Slavonia, Croatia, and Dalmatia.

The Serbs believed that they should play the leading role in the emancipation of the Southern Slavs and that all Slavs should be united under them. During the 1860s one of Mikhail Obrenovic's policies was to unite the Turk-held Balkans, and he signed treaties to that effect with Montenegro, Romania, Bulgaria, and Greece. The long-term goal of this plan was the creation of a Yugoslav state that would include Serbia, Bosnia, Herzegovina, Montenegro, Albania, Macedonia, Bulgaria, Thrace, Croatia, Sirmia, Dalmatia, Istria, Carniola, Stryria, and Karst. Obrenovic negotiated an Ottoman withdrawal by 1867 but was assassinated and replaced by his cousin Milos the next year.

In 1878 the Congress of Berlin declared Serbia a state after a war between Russia and Turkey during the previous year. Soon thereafter, 30,000 Albanians were expelled to Kosovo. However, the new state was subservient to Austro-Hungary. In 1885, King (until then, the leaders were known as princes) Milan Obrenovic declared war to subjugate Bulgaria and was saved from complete defeat only by the intervention of the Austro-Hungarians. The king was soon forced to resign in favor of his son. Aleksandar I Obrenovic made his father the commander in chief of the army. He was a known agnostic, which drove a wedge between him and his Orthodox subjects. His reign was very unpopular and corrupt, and he and his wife were brutally assassinated in 1903.

The new king, Peter Karadjordjevic, liberalized Serbia. Like the rest of his family, he maintained close connections with Russia by marrying into the Russian royal family. The Russians further supported him because he was seen as a pan-Slav advocate. The year 1905 saw the creation of a Croat-Serb coalition that fought for the freedom of Southern Slavs in Austro-Hungary and sought to join Serbia. Between 1905 and 1907 the Serbs were involved in the Pig War, a trade dispute over livestock duties that worsened Serbia's relationship with the Austro-Hungarians. Certain high officials in the empire called for the elimination of Serbia. In 1908 the empire seized Bosnia and Herzegovina.

During this time the Ottomans were having problems of their own. The late nineteenth century massacres of Armenians had alienated the rest of the world from Turkey. In 1909 the Young Turk movement, a reformist and strongly nationalistic group, forced the restoration of a constitution and deposed the sultan. The movement, which promised many social changes, soon degenerated into a dictatorship and Islamization. This led to the Balkan Wars of 1912 and 1913. The first war, against the Turks, ended with the Treaty of London giving Serbia almost all the remaining Ottoman lands in Europe, including Kosovo. This led to massacres of Albanians and Turks in Kosovo, Montenegro, Bosnia, and southern Serbia. Bulgaria attacked its allies in 1913, setting off the second Balkan War. The results of this war lead to Serbia doubling in size. Serbia wanted to create Greater Serbia, just as Albania now sought to create a Greater Albania, but both were hampered by the boundaries thrust on them. Each wanted to recover the lands it felt belonged to it outside its own territories.

This period saw the creation of a number of expansionist, nationalist secret societies in the Serbian army. The most significant was the Black

Hand, or Unification or Death, created by Colonel Dragutin Dimitrijevic. This group played an important role in the beginning of World War I. ○ On June 28, 1914, the anniversary of the Kosovo defeat, Austro-Hungarian archduke Francis Ferdinand and his wife, Sophia, visited Sarajevo. They were warned not to come because of the way the date was memorialized by the majority of Serbs, and the Serbs would not want dignitaries from a foreign occupier there on that day of all days. Still, the archduke and his wife came, only to be assassinated by Serb nationalist Gavrilo Princip, who was trained by the Black Hand. In retaliation Austro-Hungary demanded and received a large number of concessions such as the elimination of propaganda against Austro-Hungary, suppression of subversive movements, and the arrest of the murderer. Serbia accepted all the terms but did not allow Austro-Hungarians to investigate on its soil. However, the Germans joined the Austro-Hungarians and war was declared on July 28. In August, Serbia was invaded. Within two weeks Russia, Germany, France, Belgium, Montenegro, and Britain, as well as Turkey, were drawn into the conflict. In October, Bulgaria invaded Serbia. By December, Serbia was occupied and the king and government had fled to Corfu. In 1915 emigrés from Croatia and Slovenia formed the Yugoslav Committee of London. By the end of the war, U.S. president Woodrow Wilson in his famous Fourteen Points speech agreed to let the states of the former empires form their own unions. On April 8, 1915, Italy convened the Congress of Oppressed Nationalities of Austro-Hungary, which declared that each people could establish a separate state. The English and Americans took an extra step and recognized the anniversary of Kosovo as a special day for Serbia and other oppressed peoples in Europe.

The end of World War I saw the creation of the Kingdom of the Serbs, Croats, and Slovenes. But before discussing the creations of two very different Yugoslavias, we should first try and understand the Kosovar Albanians.

THE KOSOVAR ALBANIANS: HISTORY'S VICTIMS?

As Kosovo is considered the home of Serbia, so too do the Albanians consider it the cradle of their national culture. The Kosovar Albanians traditionally are made up of many members of a *fis*, or clan, with the leader being the *vojvoda*, or oldest patriarch. They had a history of common property, with the tribe being fully behind the individual as long as the individual maintained the tribe's rules. There was, and to some extent still is, the notion of blood feud in Albanian society. The Serbs also have a history of blood feuds and equated the use of physical force with right. Such feuds are common in societies where there is no formal state to impose order. They are also prevalent in states where the government is feared and distrusted so much that only private justice is seen as reasonable. In today's Kosovo the latter is closest to the truth, explaining why there are so many revenge killings of Serbs.

The Albanians in Kosovo are not the only Albanians in the former Yugoslavia. There are large populations in Macedonia and Montenegro as well. In fact, Albania is one of the only countries whose internal population is almost equalled by the population outside its borders. The Albanians in Kosovo have one of the highest birthrates in the world. Although they are regarded as being only Muslim, there are also Orthodox and Catholic minorities. The Albanians are descended from the Illyrian tribe, which settled the area around 1200 B.C. They were a powerful tribe whose members were finally conquered after nearly two hundred and forty years by the Romans. The Albanian mountain tribes were never fully conquered.

By the end of the twelfth century the Albanians were conquered by the Serbian leader Stephen Nemanja. Life under the Serbs was hard. They were subjected to heavy taxes, and their leaders and priests were badly treated. In the thirteenth century Charles I of Naples formed the Kingdom of Arberie and proclaimed himself the king of Albania. During this period some tribes and, at times, all of Albania came under the rule of the Bulgarians, Serbs, Normans, and Venetians.

In 1389 the Ottoman army and the Serbs met at Kosovo Polje. Before the Ottoman invasion, the Albanians were Orthodox or Catholic. Some converted soon after the invasion in order to get the land vacated by the Serbs. By and large, the Albanians were well integrated with the Turkish population and administration.[6] The mid-fifteenth century saw a rebellion by the Albanians under Gjergj Kastrioti. Kastrioti was the son of a prince of northern Albania who had been taken as tribute and raised in an Ottoman military school. He was made a general but left the army and captured his father's principality in Kruja. He united the Albanian princes in the League of Lezha in 1444. For twenty-five years he fought the Turks under the name Skenderbeg and was supplied by the Papal State, Venice and Naples. He died in 1468, and his troops resisted the Turks for another twelve years. In 1480 Albania was conquered and thereafter remained a quiet province of the Ottoman Empire for almost four hundred years.

After the Turkish war with the Serbs in 1876–1878, the Serbs expelled the Albanians, even though they promised not to if the Albanians didn't choose sides. On July 1, 1878, the League of Prizren was formed by the Albanians to resist Ottoman rule. The chieftains from the area also founded the League for the Defence of the Albanian Nation. Both groups sought to create a Greater Albania to include Kosovo, parts of Serbia, much of Macedonia, and parts of Greece and Montenegro. Turkey moved against them, and the two sides clashed in Kosovo. Many Albanians were killed and their leaders exiled.

In 1881 a provisional government was formed. A second league, called the League of Petch, was created in 1896. Between 1909 and 1911, after the Young Turks took over the empire, there were a series of Albanian revolts. The last, in 1911, drew in Kosovo, southern Albania, and western Macedonia. In June, leaders met and adopted a twelve-point memorandum demanding such concessions as recognition of their nation, self-government, elections, schools, the use of their language, employment, and a general amnesty.[7] Turkey allowed all the demands except for autonomy.

In 1912 the end of the first Balkan war saw the expulsion of the Ottomans from Kosovo, with the aid of the Serbs. After 1912, Serbia placed Kosovo under military rule and annexed more than 40 percent of Albania. Greece, in turn, annexed Albania's southern region of Cameria. By July, rebels freed all the towns of Kosovo as well as Skopje in Macedonia. In November, a number of Albanian societies met and proclaimed an independent Albania.

In 1913, after the second Balkan War, the Great Powers (Austria-Hungary, France, Germany, Great Britain, Italy, and Russia) forced Albania to give Kosovo to Serbia in the London Conference. The resulting Albanian rebellion was dealt with severely. Serbs looted and massacred the Kosovar Albanians. Thousands fled to Turkey. Albania itself was made independent. During World War I, Albania was occupied by Serbs, Montenegrins, Greeks, the French, and Italians. After World War I, the Serbs helped Esad Pasha take the leadership of Albania over the Western choice of the German prince Wilchelm von Vled. In return, Pasha gave overlordship of Albania to Serbia.

THE FIRST YUGOSLAVIA

The end of World War I saw the dissolution of both the Austro-Hungarian and Ottoman empires and the creation of nation-states in the Balkans. Pushed together by international powers, the leaders of Serbia, Croatia, and Montenegro announced the creation of the Kingdom of the Serbs, Croats, and Slovenes. Kosovo was also made part of Yugoslavia as confirmed in the Versailles Conference of 1919. The resulting rebellions were again put down harshly. Serbs were brought in to restore a Serb balance in the area set up by a Colonization Commission which also expelled the Albanians. Because the Serbs did not believe that the Macedonians, Bosnian Muslims, or Montenegrins were separate from them ethnically, they used the Commission as an excuse to expand.

Meanwhile, South Slav soldiers were returning from the Russian front with socialist ideas. Socialism came late to the Balkans, mainly because of their relative economic backwardness and lack of an industrialized working class. Trade union movements did not arise in this part of Europe until the 1890s. Even though Marx called the South Slavs "the trash of nations," "it has been said that the socialists saw the history of the Southern Slavs as tragic and therefore regarded the unification of the Southern Slavs as an act of revolutionary justice and liberation."[8] In 1919 the Socialist Party was founded, but it was outlawed in 1921 after the minister of the interior was murdered by a Muslim communist. The international communist movement wanted to split Yugoslavia into separate republics, but the Yugoslav party did not follow the party line.

From the beginning of the Kingdom, the Croatians wanted concessions. They saw the Kingdom as another version of the Austro-Hungarian Empire with the Serbs as the oppressors. They wanted a federation under one king but with several states. The Serbs wanted one king, one state, and one people. Matters came to a head in 1928 when a pro-Serb Montenegrin murdered a Croat leader and was not severely punished. A royal dictatorship under King Aleksandar was soon pronounced to end the fighting and to stomp out nationalism. The dictatorship lasted until the king was assassinated in 1934 (while on a state visit to France) by members of a terrorist organization sponsored by the Italian government. In 1929 the country was renamed the Kingdom of Yugoslavia and divided into nine provinces. A democratic system was set up in 1931.

During the late 1920s fully 60,000 Serbs were settled in Kosovo. Many left because Serbia kept it a poor area. Many Albanians were cleared out of Serbia and expatriated to Turkey.

After the king was assassinated in 1934, his son Peter came to the throne under the regency of his cousin, Prince Paul, who in effect ran the country even though he had little political experience. In 1937 Vaso Cubrilovic, one of the assassins of Francis Ferdinand who had gone on to become a historian, presented a memorandum to the Serbian Cultural Club called *The Expulsion of the Albanians*. He wrote that the Albanians should be completely expelled from the Kingdom through the use of propaganda; taking away their rights, land, and jobs; and destroying their culture. If none of this worked, armed terror tactics, riots, and the burning of villages would force the rest out. Cubrilovic warned that if the Albanian problem was not dealt with speedily, Serbia would pay a weighty price in the future.

To this end, in 1938 the government worked on an agreement with Turkey to expel all Muslim Albanians to Turkey and confiscate their land. The agreement was never ratified, however, due to the situation in Europe prior to World War II.

In 1941, Stevan Molevic wrote *The Homogenous Serbia*. This work was a call to create a Greater Serbia including Albania, Macedonia, parts of

Romania and Bulgaria, Montenegro, Herzegovina and Dubrovnik, and parts of Croatia. Molevic insisted that the Croats be sent to Croatia and the Muslims to Turkey and Albania.

As World War II loomed on the horizon, Paul, realizing that Yugoslavia couldn't be prepared to go to war in time, declared the country's neutrality. He recognized the USSR but remained uncommitted. Meanwhile, the British sought to create a united Balkan front based on a Yugoslav, Greek, and Turkish military alliance and wanted to be rid of the noncommittal Paul. Hitler agreed to anything Paul asked, even to respect Yugoslavia's independence, in order to get him into the pact. When Paul was finally forced to sign, he was overthrown by a Serb military junta that put his young nephew, Peter, on the throne. Hitler vowed to destroy Yugoslavia and invaded on April 6, 1941.

By April 19, Serbia had fallen. The Germans set up an independent State of Croatia under Ante Pavelic. Slovenia was occupied by troops from Germany and Italy. Vojvodina was taken by Germany and Hungary. Macedonia was given to Bulgaria. Montenegro was taken by Italy. Serbia was taken over by the pro-Fascist puppet Milan Nedic. Kosovo was given to Italian-led Albania. The Italians forced the Serb colonists to leave, and the Albanians took revenge on the departing Serbs for all they had been through.

At this point an important individual joins our narrative: Josif Broz Tito, who ruled Yugoslavia until his death in 1980. To talk about Yugoslavia without discussing Tito is like talking about China without Mao or the Soviet Union without Lenin. Tito was so influential on the Yugoslav people's lives that one cannot discuss one without the other. Tito was born in 1892 to a Croatian father and Slovene mother. As a young man, he joined the army and was taken prisoner by the Russians during World War I. After he was released he took part in Bolshevik demonstrations and joined the Bolshevik Red Guards. Following the war he returned to Croatia. He joined the Communist Party in 1920 and was arrested for revolutionary sedition in 1928. In prison he met Moshe Pijade, who taught him about Marx, Engels, Lenin, and Stalin. After his release he went underground and became a top party leader, eventually winning promotion to the Balkan secretariat of the Comintern (Communist International) in Moscow. Tito created a small multinational clique to help him run the party, including Milovan Djilas (a Montenegrin), Edvard Kardelj (a Slovene), Moshe Pijade (a Serbian Jew), Rade Koncar (a Croat), Ivo-Lola Ribar (a Croat from Serbia), and Aleksandar Rankovic (a Serb). To Tito, communism seemed the only hope for his country, which was rife with poverty, social injustice, corruption, and Serbian hegemony. After the Soviets signed a non-aggression pact with the Germans, Tito stopped all preparations for war. But when the Germans broke that pact and invaded the Soviet Union and Yugoslavia, he called on the people to rise up and defeat the German aggressors.

There were a number of groups operating in Yugoslavia at the time. In Croatia, the Ustasha (or Ustasha Croatian Revolutionary Organization; *Ustasha* means "Insurgent") were in power. They regarded Serbs as racially inferior and wanted Croatia cleansed of them. One-third of the Serbs were deported (over 300,000), one-third were to be converted (although they eventually created a Croatian Orthodox church instead), and the rest were to be liquidated. The Croatian concentration camps were horrifying and the barbarism unmatched. Serbs were forced to wear blue armbands with the letter P for *Pravolslavac* (Orthodox) on them.

In Serbia, one of the main opposition groups was the Chetniks (guerrilla fighters). Founded in 1804 as a way for Serbs to resist the Ottomans, the various groups of Chetniks were eventually united under Staff Colonel Dragoljub-Draza Mihailovic, who was sanctioned by the Yugoslav government-in-exile (led by King Peter and under increasing British control). His goals were the creation of a Greater Serbia and the restoration of the monarchy. He tried to reconcile with Tito's Partisans (the Communist resistance) but was unsuccessful. Eventually the Chetniks sought German aid to fight the Partisans. The British turned against the Chetniks and discredited them before finally abandoning them in 1944. They forced King Peter to tell the Yugoslavs to join Tito. Mihailovic was executed by Tito's government in 1946.

Tito established the Partisans, the revolutionary arm of Yugoslavia's Communist Party. He was ruthless in his tactics, not caring if the Germans burned villages and killed people because it would drive the people to the Partisan cause out of revenge and despair. In 1942, Tito set up his own administration called the Antifascist Council for National Liberation of Yugoslavia; it supported democracy, ethnic rights, private property, freedom, and economic initiative. He created his own cult of personality and was made marshal of Yugoslavia, prime minister, and minister of defence. He gained the support of Britain, the United States, and the USSR.

In 1943 the Germans occupied Albania, encouraged the Kosovars to join against the Serbs, and created an SS division of Kosovar Muslims. In early 1944 the Antifascist National Liberation Council of Kosovo-Metohija adopted the Bunjan Resolution, which declared that Kosovo wanted to unite with Albania. In late 1944, under a Yugoslav army campaign in Albania, thousands were arrested and killed. After the war, hundreds of thousands of "collaborators" were returned to Tito by the British to be executed. Bands of free Chetniks and Ustasha continued to assassinate Communist officials for years.

When Yugoslavia was liberated, Tito held a quick election and was voted leader of the country. Peter was deposed and exiled. He married Princess Alexandra of Greece and lived in England for the rest of his life. Their only child, Alexander, is now the crown prince of Yugoslavia. The royal family is still active and has spoken out against both the NATO bombing and the activities of Slobodan Milosevic.

○ TITO'S YUGOSLAVIA: IMPOSED ETHNIC HARMONY

This time the new Yugoslav state was not a kingdom. Instead it was communist. But it experienced a different sort of communism brought to the country through guerrilla warfare, not by imposition or force. Indeed, in Eastern Europe only Yugoslavia and Albania had that distinction. Tito wanted to create a Yugoslavia where there was no ethnic tension, where all were equal, where all were "Yugoslavs." He wanted to make people forget their national and ethnic history. In Kosovo, for example, he did not return the expelled Serb colonists but resettled them in Vojvodina and created an autonomous province of Kosovo. Still, after this declaration, thousands of Kosovars declared themselves Turks and emigrated to Turkey.

Tito set up a political and economic system based on the Soviet model. But soon problems arose between Tito and Stalin. Stalin demanded that Yugoslavia take over Albania, join with Bulgaria, and let the USSR handle its foreign policy. Tito refused, thereby leading to Yugoslavia's expulsion from the Communist Information Bureau (Cominform). This drove a serious wedge between Yugoslavia and Albania, whose leader, Enver Hoxha, was a staunch Stalinist (although he eventually split from Stalin and became closer to China). A brutal de-Stalinization campaign was carried out within the party ranks. Many were expelled, thousands imprisoned, and thousands more killed.[9] Still, no other East European leader was able to get his country away from the domination of the USSR as successfully as Tito. By the mid-1950s Tito became a leader, along with India's Pandit Nehru and Egypt's Gamal Nasser, of the Non-Aligned Movement.

Tito wanted one nation of Yugoslavs, and as such he did discriminate against the Serbs to stave off their hegemony. Indeed, the Serbs saw Tito as a type of devil in their history. After all, he dethroned the Serb dynasty; he defeated the Serbian-dominated royalist army; he executed Mihailovic; he humiliated the Orthodox Church; he made Serbia equal with the other republics although it had been a separate kingdom before; and he was a Slovene-Croat.[10] In the mid-1950s, fully 100,000 Turks and Albanians declared to be Turks were deported to Turkey. In the 1960s Tito allowed Albanians to settle in Kosovo. In 1963 he created the autonomous province of Kosovo-Metohija but dropped the last part of the name after anti-Serb demonstrations took place. In 1966 there was more freedom in Kosovo after the fall of Aleksandar Rankovic, the head of the state secret police who had been using repressive policies of Serbianization against the ethnic Albanians. Large demonstrations in Kosovo demanding republican status in 1968 led to the right to display their own flag (based on the Albanian flag), the creation of their own universities, and the right to use their language in 1969. The year 1971 saw the normalization of relations between Yugoslavia and Albania. Despite calls by Kosovars to unite with Albania, its leader, Enver Hoxha, was unlikely to want to rule a country with two types of government (Stalinist and anti-Stalinist). This would create something like the two Germanies and the two Koreas, and he said just that. Indeed, Hoxha only wanted the Kosovar Albanians to make trouble for Yugoslavia.[11]

The Croatian Spring, which lasted from 1967 until it was crushed in 1971, was a strong revival of nationalism (not only in Croatia but throughout the country) to demand economic changes. In 1970, Tito created a collective presidency to succeed him when he died. Through it, Yugoslavia was to have a different president every year. In this way, Tito could preserve his unique place in Yugoslav history. In 1974 he made Kosovo a republic in all but name, giving it the closest to republican status it would ever have. Despite this, the number of Kosovo liberation movements continued to grow, demanding full independence or union with Albania. Tito recognized that the problems between the republics were not going to go away. When he died on May 4, 1980, the problems had only gotten worse.

POST-TITO YUGOSLAVIA: THE STORM GATHERS

Before Tito's death, three things had kept the ethnic groups from fighting: Tito, communism, and fear of the Soviet Union. Any major conflict in the area could draw in Hungary, Romania, Czechoslovakia, Bulgaria, Albania, Italy, and Greece. Each of these countries had differing populations of natives within the former Yugoslavia, and each had its own populations of Serbs, Slovenes, Croats, and Albanians. Yugoslavia needed another Tito to pull the groups together, but there was no one. The economy was plagued by mismanagement, heavy foreign debt, and inflation. All the ethnic groups agreed to reject communism because the system wasn't working. They only gradually changed to a market economy and democracy. Communism had also failed to create any political institutions to contain nationalist aspirations. That failure was an important cause of Yugoslavia's demise. Soon there would be no Soviet Union. The three blockades to nationalism had fallen. The stage was set for insurrection.

Soon after Tito's death, Albanian students began to agitate, demanding better living conditions at Kosovo University. Soon workers and citizens joined in demanding that Kosovo be made a republic. The demonstrations were put down and harsh repression followed. The Kosovo republican leadership was purged, leading to a nearly two-month-long series of demonstrations. These fuelled a major Serb backlash. Between 1981 and 1986, thousands were arrested. By 1984, the Movement for an Albanian Republic in Yugoslavia was formed by the unification of several parties (most of whose leaders had been assassinated while in exile). Repression was also going on in Macedonia, where officials were dismissed and Albanian names and religious teaching were banned. In June 1986, Representative Joseph J. Dioguardi and Senator Bob Dole of the United States presented two resolutions to the U.S. government about violations of Kosovar human rights.

In 1986, 206 Belgrade writers, economists, historians, philosophers, and linguists drafted the Serbian Academy of Arts and Sciences Memorandum as a critique of the Yugoslav system. They felt that Serbia had been weakened by the 1974 constitution (the one that had given Kosovo near-republican status) and that the Serbs were victims of physical, political, legal, and cultural genocide in Kosovo. They felt that the hundreds of thousands of Serbs who had left Kosovo had done so because of this genocide (although the weak economy and high unemployment rates constituted the most likely reason). At first this document was labelled nationalist and was condemned. Later, when Slobodan Milosevic, the new leader, purged many of the Communists who'd condemned the document, he appropriated many of the ideas for himself. Many Serbs and Montenegrins returned to Kosovo after this and were given priority in housing and employment.

In July 1988 in Novi Sad, Vojvodina, two thousand Kosovo Serbs protested Albanian repression and were joined by tens of thousands of Vojvodina Serbs. In August, Yugoslavia's presidency gave special powers to federal police in Kosovo. In November, the ethnic Albanian Azem Vllasi from Kosovo was forced to resign from the government, sparking demonstrations and a general strike. In response, a peaceful 400,000-strong, 50-mile protest march was led by Trepca miners in Kosovo. This was the last pro-Yugoslav demonstration ever held in Yugoslavia.

Slovenia and Croatia, noting the way that the Kosovar Albanians were being treated, began to agitate for their own independence. In February 1989, Serbs living in Croatia said that they would work to secede from Croatia. Slovenia was forced to prevent a mass rally by Serb nationalists trying to topple the Slovenian leadership. Macedonia took its own incendiary step by passing a constitutional amendment deleting "Albanian and Turkish minorities" from its definition of the republic.

In February 1989, miners in Kosovo protested the firing of two Kosovar leaders from the Politburo. They ended the protests only when three provincial Communist Party leaders resigned after 100,000 Slovenes and Albanians signed the protest petition. Fully 500,000 Serbs marched on the Yugoslav government demanding that Serbia reinstate the politicians.

Rising protests among the Serbs about Kosovo led Milosevic into power. On April 24, 1987, at a Serbian rally in Kosovo Polje, Milosevic had listened to tales of murder, rape, layoffs, and burning of crops by Albanians against Serbs. Milosevic gave a speech when Kosovo police had to force Serbs back who were trying to rush the building. In the speech Milosevic said: "No one will beat the Serbs again." This became a rallying call for his election. Further on in his speech, he said:

> This is your country, these are your houses, your fields and gardens, your memories. You are not going to abandon your lands because life is hard, because you are oppressed by injustice and humiliation. It has never been a characteristic of the Serbian and Montenegrin people to retreat in the face of obstacles, to demobilize when they should fight, to become demoralized when things are difficult. You should stay here, both for your ancestors and your descendants. . . . Yugoslavia does not exist without Kosovo! Yugoslavia would disintegrate without Kosovo! Yugoslavia and Serbia are not going to give up Kosovo![12]

It is little wonder that he promptly won the hearts and souls of his Serb compatriots.

Who is Slobodan Milosevic? What made him the leader of the Serbs, who felt that they were being discriminated against? Milosevic was born in 1941, the son of parents who both eventually committed suicide (his father, Svetozar, was a teacher who killed himself upon learning that a student had killed himself for getting a bad grade; his mother, Stanislava, a devout Communist, killed herself after an altercation with Milosevic's wife).[13] He has a law degree and entered politics in 1984. He married Mirjana Markovic, the daughter of two Partisan fighters (her mother was killed by the Gestapo; her father, who rose to become very powerful in the party, did not recognize her as his daughter until she was a teenager), and they used her connections to rise through the power structure. She is a committed Socialist (in fact, she is head of her own party, the Yugoslav United Left), but Milosevic has emphasized his ties to Communism only when it is useful. He is described as opportunistic and combative, although he tends to work in secret and avoid direct confrontation. Milosevic rose through the ranks of the party with the help of his mentor, Ivan Stambolic. However, when the time was right, he betrayed his friend and grabbed power. He was the first leading Communist to support the mass movement of the Kosovo Serbs. To do this, he abandoned Communism and embraced nationalism wholeheartedly, donning the mantle of Prince Lazar himself. He has created his own cult of personality. Most important to Milosevic is his own personal power, and he will do anything to keep it. He and his wife both have portrayed Serbia as the victim of American aggression and the only nation strong enough to fight it.

After his election on May 8, 1989, Milosevic forced the Vojvodina leadership to resign and be replaced by loyal Serbs in order to isolate Kosovo. He then abolished Kosovo's autonomy and purged the leaders. Kosovo was placed under military occupation, its media was suppressed, and language education was suspended. Instead of protests and armed confrontation, the Albanians, by and large, went the route of Mahatma Gandhi: civil disobedience. As a result many Albanians were fired, evicted, or faced other forms of discrimination. Thousands fled. Why did Serbia, flexing its newly formed muscles, do this? Janusz Bugajski has written that "The persecution of minorities by newly independent nations may also be a form of aggressive compensation for their own prior oppression. It can also be an indication of political immaturity or over sensitivity, sometimes based on exaggerated fears of domination, absorption, or extinction."[14] Like Germany between the two world wars, Serbia was full of extremism and saddled with high inflation and unemployment. Milosevic was holding mass rallies at which Albanians were portrayed as the main enemies of the Serbs. They were seen as "chauvinist beasts, murderers, arsonists, poisonous, defilers of Serb women, desecrators of Serb graves and holy places, a primitive and violent people who deliberately used a high birth rate to Albanize and take holy Serb lands away."[15] The Serbian leader claimed that the Albanians rejected all Serb calls for an open dialogue. They wouldn't serve in the army or vote or pay taxes, and they established their own sub-par schools; but they wanted all the benefits that Serbia had to offer, such as health insurance and employment.

When Milosevic tried the same tactic on the other republics, he got a far different response. Slovenia and Croatia led the resistance and were followed by Macedonia and Bosnia-Herzegovina. In January 1990, multiparty democracy was allowed. However, divisions over reforms led to 170 Slovenes walking out of parliament, effectively ending the Communist Party's rule. Three months later, Slovene separatists won the republic's elections. In January, Albanians demonstrated for an end to the state of emergency the province had been under. Milosevic sent in troops and claimed the demonstrators were terrorists incited by Slovenia and Croatia.

Enver Hoxha's death in 1985 led to an opening of Albania after forty-one years of reclusiveness. His successor, Ramiz Alia, began to take the

Kosovo issue more seriously. In February 1990, Alia's foreign minister appealed to the United Nations over the situation in Kosovo.

In May 1990, all the Albanian members of the Kosovo government resigned to protest Serbian interference. On June 20, Albanian delegates from the Kosovo Assembly tried to block the new Serb constitution, which would take away all the province's autonomy, and proposed making Kosovo independent. The Assembly president, a Serb, responded by locking the delegates out of the Assembly. On July 2, they met and voted for self-determination. In response, the Kosovo parliament was abolished on July 5 and its leaders fled to Macedonia, where they declared Kosovo's independence. The Serb Assembly took power in Kosovo. On September 7, two-thirds of the Kosovo deputies met in secret and declared Kosovo a republic (although only Albania recognized the independence declaration). The president of Yugoslavia feared that the Kosovo crisis would lead to the end of the federation and tried to reason with the Serbs to no avail.

By the end of the year, Franjo Tudjman had won the Croatian elections and wanted independence. The Croatian Serbs declared their autonomy in a referendum (although it seemed that 200,000 more Serbs voted than the known population in the area would account for). Tudjman stripped them of their status as a nation and adopted a constitution that allowed Croatia to secede. Both Slovenia and Croatia tried to find solutions, proposing a confederal system allowing free elections, free enterprise, property rights, common services, and independent armed forces. They both saw Milosevic as the real problem.

On January 10, 1991, Milosevic warned that if Yugoslavia became a confederation, Serbia would demand the return of territory from other republics to draw in all Serbs. He aroused fears that the Croats were planning a Serbian genocide with the help of such disparate organizations as the Vatican, Comintern, Islamic fundamentalists, Nazis, Freemasons,[16] and the U.S. government. In March, U.S. president George Bush told the Slovenes and Croats that they wouldn't reward secessionists. U.S. secretary of state James Baker visited Yugoslavia on June 22 and said that the United States favoured Yugoslav unity. The North Atlantic Treaty Organization[17] also released a statement saying it wouldn't intervene in a Yugoslav civil war. Of the major countries, the Soviet Union, China, Britain, France, Sweden, Denmark, Italy, Greece, Romania, Poland, and Hungary all endorsed unity. Only Austria and Germany were anxious to recognize the breakaway republics.[18] This basically gave the invitation for Milosevic to force the recalcitrant republics back in line. He believed he'd be rewarded for not allowing them to secede. The Serbs in Croatia proclaimed their own autonomous region. On June 5, Slovenia

and Croatia agreed to a loose federation of sovereign republics. However, they soon did an about-face and both declared independence.

○ INDEPENDENCE: THE BREAKUP OF YUGOSLAVIA

On June 27, Serbia invaded Slovenia but withdrew a week later. The
war was mainly fought over Slovenia's seizing control of border cross-
ings with Italy, Austria, and Hungary. Because there was no Serbian
minority and it was too far away from Serbia and supplies, the army
soon left. The United States and Russia dumped the matter into the laps
of the Europeans, who responded with diplomatic pressure. With the
breakup of Yugoslavia so obviously under way, the European Union
established the Badinter Commission of Jurists, under French judge Robert Badinter, to advise on the breakup of Yugoslavia and to outline the
conditions for recognition. The Commission advised that Slovenia and
Macedonia (which declared independence in November 1991) be recognized as well as Croatia, but only if assurances were made for democratic principles, national minorities, and border protections. Bosnia,
which declared independence in 1992, could also be recognized, but only
after a referendum. Kosovo was considered invalid because it wasn't a
recognized republic. However, under the Nickles Amendment, the
United States cut off all aid to Yugoslavia to end the repression of Albanians. There were many congressmen who believed and still believe
that sanctions are the best way to go. They are a minority though.

Serbia demanded that borders be changed in order to protect ethnic
Serbians in the various regions. In January, a group of Serbia's leading
opposition figures initiated the formation of a Pan-Serbian Council for
National Salvation, which called for either an integral Yugoslavia with
no republican borders or a united Serb state of Serbia, Montenegro,
Bosnia-Herzegovina, and parts of Macedonia.[19] Croatia entered secret
talks with Serbia to divide Bosnia between them and the Muslims. The
talks soon broke down, and war between Croatia and Serbia began in
July. The EU announced it would recognize Croatia and Slovenia after
undergoing pressure from Germany, Italy, and Austria—and providing
that Croatia passed cultural autonomy laws.

While the rest of the federation was slowly falling apart, the Coordi-
nating Council of Albanian Political Parties in Yugoslavia agreed to
coordinate self-defence and make contingencies for a provisional
government. The Albanian Christian Democratic Party and several other
associations advocated a union with Albania. In response, army and police units distributed weapons to Kosovo Serbs, and Serbian volunteer
fighters entered Kosovo after calls from the Serbian Peony Association
for protection of the Serbs. In September 1991, a referendum with an
87 percent turnout voted 95 percent in favour of independence.

As war raged and became inevitable with Bosnia, the Serbs cleared areas of other ethnics seen as strategically critical for Serb interests (e.g., East Slavonia and Krajina in Croatia and eastern and northwestern Bosnia). This involved terror killing, caused tens of thousands of refugees to flee, and led to the use of concentration camps.[20] The revival of Serb nationalism led to a revival of the Chetniks—at least, that was what the paramilitaries called themselves. They were responsible for a disproportionate amount of killing and ethnic cleansing. Vojislav Seselj, the leader of the ultranationalist Radical Party, claimed to be the legitimate successor to Mihailovic. So did Vuk Draskovic, the leader of the Serbian Renewal Movement. The Bosnian Serbs insisted that they would form their own republic. Bosnian Muslim leader Alija Izetbegovic responded by saying they would turn to Muslim countries for help and asked the UN for a peacekeeping force and the European Union for recognition. Milosevic stirred up Bosnian Serb fears about being a repressed minority in a Muslim country, hoping they would join Serbia. As the refugee problem grew in Croatia, the UN sent in 14,000 peacekeepers.

Bosnia declared its independence on February 29, 1992 (after a referendum that the Bosnian Serbs boycotted) and the Bosnian Serbs declared their own republic (the population of Bosnia at the time was 17% Croat, 31% Serb, 44% Muslim, 5% "Yugoslav"—mainly the children of mixed marriages—and 3% gypsies and Jews). By early April both the European Community (EC) and the United States recognized Bosnia. The Serbs soon seized a village and began the war there, even though they claimed to have no territorial ambitions.

The Serb leadership was convinced that the EU would not get involved. The UN sponsored a series of sanctions and arms embargoes and froze Yugoslav assets. Sanctions have been used as an international political tool for centuries. An alternative to diplomatic protest and outright military intervention, sanctions signal disapproval of the actions of the country on which they are imposed. Sanctions may be more than economic. They can involve cultural and sport participation, diplomacy, transportation and communication, military (i.e., arms sales), trade, or criminal justice (i.e., international justice tribunals). Since the Cold War, the UN has imposed sanctions against such countries as Yugoslavia, Iraq, Libya, Liberia, Somalia, Haiti, and Rwanda. In some cases they have worked; in others they have not been effective. In some cases sanctions have drawn the people closer to their leadership in an us-versus-the-world scenario. In other cases real hardship has been visited on the innocents within the country. In Iraq, for example, many have died from starvation and disease while the leader Saddam Hussein is still no closer to being toppled from power. The sanctions in Yugoslavia were strictly enforced by the European nations through both NATO and the Western European Union.

Milosevic claimed he couldn't control the army and pressed China and Russia to recognize the Federal Republic of Yugoslavia, which was created from Serbia and Montenegro on April 27, 1992. The international community refused to recognize this new state and denied it Yugoslavia's seat at the UN. On May 5, the Yugoslav army relinquished its command of 100,000 troops in Bosnia, creating in fact a Bosnian Serb army. Thus, Milosevic could claim that Serbia was not involved. The Bosnian Serbs had always gone their own way, and Milosevic used it to his full advantage.

While all this was going on, in May 1992 an underground government led by Ibrahim Rugova was elected, but it was declared illegal by the Serbs and prevented from convening. Rugova, the former chief of the Kosovo Writers Association, leads the Democratic League of Kosovo (LDK). A quiet-looking bespectacled man, he argues for passive resistance. He wrote: "We would have no chance of successfully resisting the army. In fact, the Serbs only wait for a pretext to attack the Albanian population and wipe it out. We believe that it is better to do nothing and stay alive than be massacred."[21]

Meanwhile, the Bosnians grew impatient for UN help. Although the UN set up humanitarian air lifts to Sarajevo, many Bosnians believed that the UN was on the side of the Serbs. Soon Canadian peacekeepers were replaced with French (Catholic), Ukrainian (Orthodox), and Egyptian (Muslim) troops to show that the UN took no sides. In September the UN took the added step of expelling Yugoslavia from the General Assembly, the first time that had ever been done. Milosevic provided help for the nationalist Serb campaigns in Bosnia and Croatia while ousting his political rivals and seizing full control of the media at home. Radovan Karadzic, leader of the Bosnian Serbs, and Mate Boban, leader of the self-proclaimed Croatian Community of Herzeg-Bosna, signed an agreement to cantonize the country.

The Muslims in Bosnia seemed to suffer especially during this war. They were forced from their homes, placed in concentration camps (where most deaths resulted from poor hygiene, starvation, and beatings), and murdered, and many women were raped (some were even impregnated by the Serbs in order to humiliate the Muslims). These types of atrocities had not been seen since World War II. Muslims who weren't uprooted were forced to fly white flags outside their homes, had fourteen-hour curfews, weren't allowed to congregate on the street, were banned from wearing uniforms, and had restrictions on cars and telephones. Libraries, museums, and archives were favourite targets of the Serb gunmen, as were civilian targets, hospitals, and schools. The favourite tactic was to capture a town, seize the weapons, cut off the electricity and water, and force the inhabitants to sign over their homes and lands and leave. If they didn't, a few were shot and a few houses were bombed; the rest were taken to detention camps. Karadzic claimed that this was ethnic shifting, not cleansing, and that it was designed to save lives. To be fair, however, the Croats and Bosnian Muslims were guilty of their own atrocities. They too had camps. Croatia dumped thousands of Muslim and Gypsy refugees into Bosnia. But by far the most atrocities can be laid at the feet of the Serbs. Karadzic, trying to appear conciliatory, told the UN that he would close the camps if the UN forces would take the refugees to Bosnia (a vain attempt to get the UN to help with the ethnic cleansing). In 1993, the United Nations set up the first international war crimes tribunal since Nuremberg to investigate the growing number of complaints (this was mainly an effort on the part of the UN to appear to be doing something, anything, about the slaughter).

The EC by this time was divided. France, a traditional ally of Serbia, didn't want to use force. François Mitterand, extremely reluctant, was known for being pro-Serb. France's position changed, however, with the election of Jacques Chirac in 1995. England, which had supported Tito during World War II, didn't want to use force either. Only Germany endorsed the use of force. In fact, it was accused of wanting to create a Fourth Reich by Serbia. The Greeks lost trade and tourism as a result of the conflict and feared that the Turks were trying to create a Muslim barrier between Greece and Europe (Albania, Bosnia-Herzegovina, Kosovo, Macedonia, and Bulgaria). Hungary supported Slovenia and Croatia, formerly part of their empire. On the other hand, Russia was a traditional Slavic ally of Serbia and saw parallels with its own breakup. It also wanted to avoid making any move that would lead to U.S. involvement in Eastern Europe.

In 1993, the Croats and Muslims began fighting over the 30 percent of Bosnia not being held by the Bosnian Serbs. By 1994, however, they had signed an accord to end their war. The UN created six safe areas for the growing number of Muslim refugees. In December, Milosevic ordered human rights monitors from the Conference on Security and Cooperation in Europe[22] to leave Kosovo. Milosevic, realizing that Serbia had become an international pariah, broke ties with the Bosnian Serbs and left them high and dry for rejecting a peace plan.

The Bosnian Serbs, without their leader in Belgrade, took more than four hundred peacekeepers hostage. When the supreme military commander in the former Yugoslavia, French general Bernard Janvier, met with the commander of the Bosnian Serb army, General Ratko Mladic, he agreed to wage no air strikes in return for the release of the peacekeepers. This eventually led to the massacres in the safe area of Srebrenica from July 11 to July 13, 1995. Mladic and his army surrounded the city and massacred over eight thousand men, women, and children while the UN troops did nothing. Karadzic and Mladic were eventually arraigned on charges of genocide for this action.

In late September, the basic outline of a peace plan was accepted. In November, Milosevic, playing the peacemaker, represented the Bosnian Serbs in peace talks. In December, the Dayton Peace Accord was signed by representatives from Bosnia-Herzegovina, Croatia, and Yugoslavia and witnessed by the Contact Group (an international group founded in 1994 to find a way to end the war; it was made up of representatives from the United States, England, France, Germany, and Russia) and the EU special negotiator. In the Accord, Bosnia was split between the Bosnian Serb Republic (Republika Srpska) and the Federation of Bosnia (Croats and Muslims representing 51% of the land). The Accord provided for the following: a cease-fire and a withdrawal of all troops, a multinational military implementation force under NATO, boundary demarcations, free elections, a new constitution, granting refugees the right to return home, aid and reconstruction, and a UN international police force. As a result of that war, 250,000 had been killed and 2.7 million refugees had been driven from their homes. The latter were eventually allowed to return, with the right to claim their rightful property or ask for reasonable compensation. Several thousand Serb refugees from the Krajina region of Croatia began to arrive in Kosovo in August 1995. The government of Albania protested this resettlement vigorously. In 1996, Yugoslavia was recognized by the EU but not by other countries, including the United States. In March, Karadzic urged his Serbian countrymen who were about to leave Sarajevo to cause mischief, and they did so before leaving. The UN peacekeepers were slowly replaced by NATO forces (known as IFOR, or Implementation Force) as this war came to a close.

The Serbs failed in all their objectives. They couldn't keep the federation together, and they failed miserably in creating a Greater Serbia. Nor did they inherit any of Yugoslavia's global assets or club memberships. Milosevic took the blame for it. He had betrayed the Bosnian Serbs. But he still managed to hold on to power. In fact, he used his new international prestige to full advantage. He took over the only independent television station in the country, attacked the opposition as anti-peace, purged his own party, strengthened his party's coalition with his wife's party, co-opted small business owners into contributing to his party, and gave monopolies to his loyal supporters for the importing of consumer goods.[23]

KOSOVO: LEADING TO A CRISIS

The Kosovar Albanians were extremely disappointed that the Dayton Accord made no mention of their predicament. If the world community had glimpsed beyond Bosnia, it would not have been difficult to ascertain the burgeoning tensions of Kosovo. Having lost three wars he'd started himself, Milosevic needed a convenient scapegoat on which to blame the failures of the Serb nation to take its historic place as leader of the Yugoslavs. And because Kosovo was a province of Serbia, he felt that the international community had no business there. He hadn't pursued Serb claims in that province during the wars with the other republics in view of having to fight on a second front. However, with the wars over, the economy in ruins, and calls for his resignation growing, Milosevic had to turn to Kosovo and raise the spectre of nationalism once more—if for no other reason than to ensure his own political survival. In late 1996 and early 1997 this is what he needed desperately, especially after 113 days of street demonstrations against him by hundreds of thousands of Belgraders.

If nothing else, Milosevic is a master at exploiting the weaknesses of his enemies, and he exploited the West's hesitation to its maximum. As the French and English appeased Hitler and gave him most of Czechoslovakia in the Munich Pact of 1938, Milosevic saw a cringing West reluctant to get involved—a West that would allow him to do as he pleased inside his country. After all, had he not survived three wars without a loss of power? Serbia, moreover, could claim legitimate sovereignty to Kosovo. Milosevic understood the power of fear and knew how to use it. He counted on war, the ultimate condition of fear, to unite the Serbs around him.[24]

In order to appear conciliatory, Milosevic agreed with Rugova to end the six-year Albanian boycott of state schools in 1996. However, with the fall of the Albanian government in 1997 following a financial scandal that the people blamed on the government, the Albanian army dissolved and Kosovars bought guns for the KLA, or Kosovo Liberation Army (an independence movement founded in 1993, which Milosevic describes as drug runners and arms smugglers).

The so-called KLA was from the start a shadowy, neurotically covert group of terrorists by any standards. Rumour had it that affluent Muslims were funnelling money to it—from Saudi Arabia, Iran too. The KLA was the immediate pretext Milosevic needed. Since early 1995 a succession of car bombings, ambushes, attacks on police stations, and assassinations had completely mystified the Belgrade government. In April 1996, the KLA sent a letter to the BBC World Service claiming responsibility for killing several Serb civilians and policemen in the Decan and Pec regions of southern Kosovo. But to this day that letter was suspected to be a forgery by a band of Serbs who wanted to exploit the KLA's rhetoric of liberation through massacres and violence in order to clamp down on Kosovo.

On October 29, 1997, huge demonstrations by students led to attacks on Serb policemen and officials and pro-Serb Albanians. In February 1998, Serbian police attacked and killed people connected with the KLA, which resulted in a groundswell of support for the organization. That summer the Serbs fought back, and 250,000 Kosovar Albanians fled the fighting. Milosevic used the existence of the KLA to justify his program of ethnic cleansing.

In March and again in September 1998, the UN Security Council adopted an arms embargo on Yugoslavia and called for a political settlement. However, the arms embargo kept the non-Serbs powerless. By July, the KLA controlled one-third of Kosovo. Serbian paramilitary volunteers, including many "ethnic cleansers" from the Bosnian war, organized themselves into the Serbian Defense Guard. The Pentagon played down the chances of NATO actually becoming involved in Kosovo, which led to the Serbs attacking the town of Orahovoc one day later. In September, Serbia announced that the campaign against the Albanian separatists was over, but by the end of the month the Serbs had brutally massacred many Albanians in Drenica. In October 1998, Richard Holbrooke, the American architect of the Dayton Accord, met with Milosevic and got him to agree to reduce the number of troops in Kosovo and allow the presence of a verification force from the Organization for Security and Cooperation in Europe (OSCE). At the time, Milosevic was willing to let NATO troops monitor the cease-fire as was proposed by the French, British, and Germans; but the United States did not agree, thinking that Congress would not allow U.S. troops in Kosovo.

In January 1999, Enver Maloku, an aide to Rugova, was killed by eight Yugoslav army soldiers. Kosovar Albanians in retaliation killed several Serbian policemen. International monitors stopped the army from attacking. On January 14, forty-five Albanians were massacred in cold blood at Racak. Milosevic refused to let the war crimes investigator from the Hague, Canadian Louise Arbour, and her team enter the area. He also expelled U.S. ambassador William Walker for saying the Serbs were behind the slaughter. NATO demanded that Serbia withdraw its military forces from Kosovo, let Arbour in, and reinstate Walker. Milosevic agreed but claimed the dead were KLA members killed in battle.

The stage was set for peace talks. On February 6, a two-week-long series of peace talks was held at a fourteenth-century château in Rambouillet, near Paris. The meeting was co-chaired by French foreign minister Hubert Vedrine and British foreign minister Robin Cook with three mediators: Christopher Hill from the United States, the Austrian Wolfgang Petritsch for the EC, and the Russian Boris Mayorsky. The Kosovars at first refused to sign, and the talks hit a stalemate. The Germans, British, and French sent peacekeepers into Macedonia in case of a call to arms. Now it just might have happened that if the United States had sent its own peacekeepers, perhaps they could have intervened and stopped the coming war. Perhaps. Nonetheless on March 18, 1999, the Kosovars signed the Rambouillet Accord. All was in readiness. The ball was in Milosevic's court. Was he preparing for peace? Hardly. Cunningly, he had used the weeks between the conference opening and the Kosovar signing to build up his troops from 4,500 to 18,000.

NOTES

1. The Byzantine Empire was the successor state to the Roman Empire. It had a Roman political tradition, Hellenic culture, and Christian beliefs. The Orthodox Church was created when it split from the Catholic Church in 395. It rejected the jurisdiction of the Pope and did not agree with the findings of the eighth ecumenical council (Council of Church Authorities) over the determination of which were orthodox and which were heretical practices. The division between the two became permanent after 1054. By the 1200s the empire, having suffered major losses to the Turks and Venetians, broke into independent states for a time and finally fell to Venice. In 1453 Constantinople fell, signalling a final curtain to the empire. (The Roman Empire had lasted only eighty years after the split in 395.)

2. Warren Zimmermann, "The Demons of Kosovo" in *National Interest*, no. 52, Summer 1998, p. 3.

3. The Ottoman Empire was founded in the late thirteenth century by the Ottoman Turks, who were ruled by the descendants of Osman I until the fall of the empire in 1918. During the early phases of the empire, they expanded quickly into the Byzantine Empire, Bulgaria, Serbia, Kosovo, and the Balkan peninsula. The Ottomans later conquered major sections of Hungary, Transylvania, Wallachia, and Moldavia. The sultan was answerable only to God and was limited only by canonical law. After the clergy and Janissaries (i.e., soldiers who as children were taken from their parents as tribute from enslaved Christian lands and sent to Turkey, where their names and faith were changed) came to power, corruption became rampant. The slow disintegration of the empire dates from the early eighteenth century. The Russo-Turkish War cost it much of its European holdings. By the end of World War I, the Ottoman Empire was no more.

4. The term *Islam* is Arabic for "submission." It encompasses an entire way of life for many of the world's inhabitants, being a set of beliefs and a way of worship that provide rules for culture, law, the economy, government, and social systems. As a religion, it is prevalent from Africa to Southeast Asia. It began in the Middle East as a series of revelations revealed to the Prophet Mohammed (570–632) by the Archangel Gabriel. Soon after Mohammed's death, factions began to appear. The two main factions are the Sunni and the Shi'a. The Shi'a were originally supporters of Ali, Mohammed's cousin and son-in-law. The Sunni form at least 90 percent of the Islamic religion. The split between the two is the equiva-

lent of the Catholic-Protestant split in Christianity with the Shi'a as the Catholic and the Sunni as the Protestant.

5. The Austro-Hungarian Empire was created in 1526 by the merger of Austria and Hungary under the Habsburg dynasty. The empire grew to a vast size and was virtually self-sufficient. However, the minorities were not all treated equally according to the imperial policy of divide and rule. The heir to the throne, Francis Ferdinand, planned to create a third South Slavic partner within the empire before his assassination in 1914. The emperor soon declared war on Serbia, and the conflict drew in many different countries, leading to World War I. Forced to surrender in 1918, the empire was divided into separate countries through the Treaties of Versailles, Trianon, and St. Germain.

6. Albania itself was Roman Catholic in the north and Orthodox in the south and central regions. The society was also divided between two tribes: the Gegs in the north and the Tosks in the south. Most Albanians are Sunni Muslims with 25 percent belonging to the Bektashi, a Shi'a order. Albania was conquered at various times by the Byzantines, Serbs, Bulgarians, and Venetians. By the late nineteenth century Albanians living in Romania, Bulgaria, and Turkey began forming patriotic societies. Greece, Serbia, Montenegro, and Bulgaria have all claimed Albania.

7. Ramadan Marmullaku, *Albania and the Albanians* (London: C. Hurst and Co., 1975), p. 26.

8. Aleksa Djilas, *The Contested Country: Yugoslav Unity and Communist Revolution, 1919–1953* (Cambridge, MA: Harvard University Press, 1991), p. 44.

9. Relations with the USSR were not formally restored until 1956 after Soviet premier Nikita Khrushchev apologized for Stalin's excesses.

10. Ivo Banac, "The Fearful Asymmetry of War: The Causes and Consequences of Yugoslavia's Demise" in *Daedalus*, vol. 121, no. 2, Spring 1992, p. 145.

11. Arshi Pipa, "The Political Situation of the Albanians in Yugoslavia with Particular Attention to the Kosovo Problem: A Critical Approach" in *East European Quarterly*, vol. 23, no. 2, June 1989, p. 163.

12. Alexander Rose, "No Surrender Is a Central Theme in Serb Folklore" in *National Post*, May 29, 1999, p. E4.

13. Laura Silber, "Milosevic Family Values" in *New Republic*, no. 4415, August 30, 1999, p. 24.

14. Janusz Bugajski, *Nations in Turmoil: Conflict and Cooperation in Eastern Europe* (Boulder: Westview, 1993), p. 21.

15. Shkelzen Maliqi, "The Albanians of Kosovo: Self-Determination through Nonviolence" in *Why Bosnia? Writings on the Balkan War*, eds. Rabia Ali and Lawrence Lifschultz (Stony Creek, CT: Pamphleteer's Press, 1993), pp. 333–34.

16. The Freemasons (or the Fraternal Order of Free and Accepted Ma-

sons) was a secret society that aimed for morality, fraternity, charity, and obedience to the law of the land. The group arose during the Middle Ages. Its members were frequently used as scapegoats and considered to be involved in alien conspiracies, especially by totalitarian states.

17. NATO consists of Belgium, Canada, the Czech Republic, Denmark, France, Germany, Greece, Hungary, Iceland, Italy, Luxembourg, the Netherlands, Norway, Poland, Portugal, Spain, Turkey, the United Kingdom, and the United States. The European Union (EU) includes most of these countries: Austria, Belgium, Denmark, Finland, France, Germany, Greece, Ireland, Italy, Luxembourg, the Netherlands, Portugal, Spain, Sweden, and the United Kingdom.

18. Sabrina Ramet, *Nationalism and Federalism in Yugoslavia 1962–1991* (Bloomington: Indiana University Press, 1992), pp. 253, 265.

19. Hugh Poulton, *Balkans: Minorities and States in Conflict* (London: Minority Rights Publications, 1991), p. 20.

20. Michael C. Williams, "Ties That Bind" in *The World Today*, vol. 55, no. 5, May 1999, p. 4.

21. *Economist*, April 3, 1999, p. 21.

22. The Conference on Security and Cooperation in Europe, which became the Organization for Security and Cooperation in Europe in 1994, was made up of a number of states to promote democracy, human rights, and security. The current membership includes: Albania, Andorra, Armenia, Austria, Azerbaijan, Belarus, Belgium, Bosnia-Herzegovina, Bulgaria, Canada, Croatia, Cyprus, the Czech Republic, Denmark, Estonia, Finland, France, Georgia, Germany, Greece, the Holy See, Hungary, Iceland, Ireland, Italy, Kazakhstan, Kyrgyzstan, Latvia, Liechtenstein, Lithuania, Luxembourg, Macedonia, Malta, Moldova, Monaco, the Netherlands, Norway, Poland, Portugal, Romania, Russia, San Marino, the Slovak Republic, Slovenia, Spain, Sweden, Switzerland, Tajikistan, Turkey, Turkmenistan, Ukraine, United Kingdom, United States, Uzbekistan, and Yugoslavia (suspended in 1992).

23. International Crisis Group, "South Balkans: Serbia: The Milosevic Factor," February 24, 1998 (www.crisisweb.org/projects/sbalkans/reports/yu01main.htm).

24. Aleksa Djilas, "A Profile of Slobodan Milosevic" in *Foreign Affairs*, vol. 72, no. 3, Summer 1993, p. 88.

3

THE WAR IS NASTY, BRUTISH, AND SHORT

Nor can a great deal be expected from the media. Reporters rely on the controlled handouts of the State Department, Pentagon and NATO, seeing their duty as one of adding colorful details to official intimations of Serb atrocities. Thus, the observation of a NATO press relations officer that a freshly plowed field, seen from 30,000 feet up, might be the site of a massacre, has been disseminated as news.
—journalist who was later fired from his job

War was not immediately inevitable. True. But President Clinton and the Pentagon were eager for it from the start. So was Madeleine Albright in the U.S. State Department.

BEFORE YOU GO TO WAR YOU WILL FIRST SIT AND TALK

A negotiated settlement, it seemed, was still possible under the Rambouillet Accord. It was hoped that something could be worked out along the lines of a U.S.-backed, three-year interim autonomy agreement. A referendum would then be held a year or two later.

No one was talking about sending in troops or dispatching bombers arbitrarily. But bombing threats against Yugoslavia were being made off and on in the event that Milosevic refused to sign at Rambouillet. The Serbs felt they were being marched to the negotiating table at gunpoint. Then, too, the Kosovars sent a negotiating team that irked the Serbs—it was not so much Mr. Rugova's Democratic League of Kosovo (the moderate part); rather, the other Albanian opposition groups and five unruly and disdainful members of the KLA.

Compared with the Kosovars, the Serb side presented a united front. But that hodge-podge front also appeared perfectly rigged. All were cronies of Milosevic, including a motley mix of ethnic Muslim Turks and Egyptians and Gypsies. These minorities felt an independent, ethnic Albanian Kosovo would trample on their rights, the rights only a united Yugoslavia would be able to guarantee them.

Besides, Milosevic desperately needed to take his peoples' minds off the economic ruin of their country. War with the Kosovar Albanians seemed to be the easiest fix. Did the Serbs push the Albanians into a corner so they would have to fight back, thus justifying Serbian aggression? It seems, in part, that this is quite likely. Their rights eroded, their people kept poor and isolated in a Yugoslav version of apartheid, Albanians by and large had no choice but to fight back. Over the coming weeks, reports trickled abroad of Serbian troops amassing on the Macedonia-Kosovo border. Heavy fighting with the KLA erupted. And it was confirmed that tens of thousands of bedraggled refugees were in flight toward Albania and Macedonia. Anti-aircraft batteries were discovered by overhead satellite reconnaissance to be studded all over Yugoslavia, and all the main roads in Kosovo were blocked. The UN High Commissioner for Refugees listed 20,000 homeless since the signing of the accord at Rambouillet.[1]

The world had been monitoring the situation closely. As the violence escalated, the UN passed a number of resolutions aimed at curbing the fighting. In September 1998, Resolution 1199 condemned the violence and demanded a cease-fire, improvement of humanitarian conditions, the allowance of international monitoring, and the safe return of refugees. A month later Resolution 1203 established verification forces and urged Yugoslavia to accept them. Operation Eagle Eye was established to assess Yugoslavian compliance with these resolutions in coordination with the OSCE. Flights were instituted to monitor the situation through the Kosovo Verification Co-ordination Centre. Before the Kosovo Verification Mission pulled out on March 19, its members noted a buildup of Serbian forces. By mid-March, the outflow of refugees had grown and the attacks by Serbian forces against KLA forces had become more frequent. The emptying of towns and villages, the burning and looting of homes, the confiscation of identity papers, and the reports of atrocities also grew more relentless.

Milosevic didn't seem to care about the Verification Forces. At least the Serbian forces in Kosovo didn't. They were flagrant with their abuses. And Milosevic continued to arrogantly believe that the international community wouldn't involve itself in a domestic Yugoslav problem. After all, Kosovo had been a part of Serbia since the creation of the second

Yugoslavia. It would be as likely for the UN or NATO to intercede, he no doubt believed, as it would if Quebec were to try to secede and Canada put a halt to it by force of arms. It was an internal matter, pure and simple, and therefore Yugoslavia's business, no one else's. In an interview with the *Guardian Weekly* in late December 1998 he tried to convince the writer that he had only his nation's best interest at heart. When responding to a statement made by the chief spokesperson for the U.S. State Department, James Rubin, in which he said that Milosevic was the problem in the Balkans, Milosevic said: "My duty is to protect the interests of my people and my country, so if it is a problem for somebody, I must tell you I can only be proud of my role."[2]

On the other hand, Milosevic must have known in his heart that the international community would eventually do something—there were compelling reasons for the West to react. Milosevic had already managed to stay in power after fighting and losing three wars that he'd started himself. This time the scapegoat was to be the Kosovar Albanians. If he managed to rid himself of as many as was physically possible and draw in the West, he might stay in power indefinitely, then search for another scapegoat to blame. He may have reasoned that as long as the country was in chaos, his countrymen would rally around the government and support him. The West was doing him a service by interfering in domestic Serbian politics. It thus became a perfect target and another convenient scapegoat. On February 1, 1999, Yugoslavia called for an emergency session of the UN Security Council, asking it to prevent NATO forces from bombing Serbia. To those who had seen something of Milosevic's tactics in past years, it was clear that a major offensive was afoot. Playing the victim was always Milosevic's best strategy, and he was going to play it to the hilt. He gathered up his troops and embarked on a wholesale ethnic cleansing of Kosovo. And he was going to call NATO's bluff.

But was Milosevic the only one to blame for this situation?

The international community, especially NATO, seemed more than willing to go into Kosovo. And what of the provisions that were offered at Rambouillet? The Interim Agreement for Peace and Self-Government in Kosovo of February 23, 1999, had various articles. It sought the establishment of a democratically elected government within Kosovo that would allow self-government, but not actual independence, for at least three years before a vote was to be cast. As a sign that the Yugoslav government was serious, the agreement made several demands: there would be an end to force and a withdrawal of Serbian forces, the refugees would be allowed to return home, all citizens would have the right to access to international assistance, martial law could not be declared, all prisoners would be freed, there would be no prosecution for crimes except violations of international humanitarian law, and an independent media must be guaranteed. Once these provisions were undertaken, a new constitution for Kosovo would allow for Yugoslavia to control territorial integrity, the market, defence, foreign policy, customs, federal taxation, and federal elections. The agreement also set up a 120-seat assembly, led by a president and two vice presidents, with provisions for Serbs and other minorities to be represented. The assembly would be responsible for financing Kosovo institutions, budgets, and education; for picking judicial candidates, and for promoting local self-government (in the form of communes). The constitution also established an independent multilevel judiciary.

The proposed constitution set out a number of human rights and freedoms. It allowed for the national communities to preserve their national, cultural, religious, and linguistic identities (through allowance of their language, education in their own language, contacts with representatives of their community both abroad and within Yugoslavia, the use of national symbols, preservation of historical and cultural sites, no discrimination in health and social services, freedom of religion, freedom of the press, and jobs in the public service). The agreement also provided for humanitarian assistance, reconstruction, and economic development by various countries.

All this seems straightforward. However, the rest of the document contained provisions about which the Serbs had serious misgivings. The proposed police system was to be supervised and monitored by the Organization for Security and Cooperation in Europe (OSCE) Implementation Force, which was to be given unrestricted movement and access and was to monitor and inspect all law enforcement activities. The OSCE was also to supervise elections. In addition, NATO was to establish a force to support the Kosovo Force (KFOR) to ensure compliance.[3] The force would stay in Kosovo for three years leading to a referendum, after which Kosovo would decide its own future.

The Serbs could not accept these last provisions. They saw them as international interference. Although the leadership had proven itself unwilling to stick to promises in the past, they could not allow the OSCE and NATO to come into Kosovo and threaten its sovereignty there. Was this the point of Rambouillet? The West must have known that Serbia would not accept this. No Serb leader would or could let Kosovo go and not expect to be thrown out of office immediately. For Serbia to allow Western powers into the country to practically assume all security and law enforcement would be taken as a sign of Serbian weakness and would cause Milosevic's own people to turn against him. It would have been political suicide for him to accept these agreements. And what was to prevent that occupation force from trying to change Kosovo into a Western-type democracy that could eventually overtake Serbia economically and politically? Then again, the West had no reason to believe that

Milosevic would have actually implemented any of the provisions without international monitoring. Moreover, it seems that the Western powers didn't really expect Milosevic to sign the agreement. The United States, for example, would never allow foreign peacekeepers onto its own territory, no matter the cause. Was this the West's excuse to go into Kosovo? Was it a pretext for war? Was it, like Milosevic's tactic with the Kosovars, meant to give the final push so that the Serbians would fight back and justify international intervention? It was no secret that the West was only able to get Milosevic to move back into his own section of the former Yugoslavia after the end of the wars in Croatia and Bosnia. His own sense of political survival led him to abandon the Bosnian Serbs when they needed his backing to continue their war of expansion in Bosnia. The reward offered by the United States to bring Milosevic to international justice didn't work.

The Russians, too, reiterated their opposition to a peacekeeping force under NATO command. Moscow had wanted the OSCE, of which it was a member, to be in charge, so that a Russian contingent could be included.

It was profoundly unbelievable—this whole scenario at Rambouillet. Seven days and nights were to pass; the participants stayed on different floors and did not meet. The harsh truth be known now: in the course of these seven days, the only headway made was the consumption of 400 bottles of the finest French wines. Secretly, U.S. secretary of state Madeleine Albright flew to Rambouillet and talked to the Kosovar Albanians. She confronted them with three choices. Should the Kosovars decline to sign, they risked losing American support; if they signed, however, and the Serbs didn't, that would allow the Americans to bomb the Serbs; and finally, if both sides signed, which suited U.S. policymakers well enough, NATO could introduce the peacekeepers. Meanwhile, Americans and Russians met in the wings, with the Russians being cajoled into accepting the principle of a NATO, rather than an OSCE, deployment. Thus, the Kosovar Albanians decided to accept the Rambouillet Accord—and so did the KLA.[4]

But still the war had to be justified on the home front. Democratic governments just can't go to war without reason. The humanitarian tragedy was graphic; that helped. There were pictures of crying children, of bereaved mothers, of frightened men and women, of squalid refugee camps. The media's graphic coverage created a groundswell of support for the West to do something. Still, the public in the West was reluctant to have its soldiers killed to protect the refugees. Their leaders had to create a real need for them to become involved.

The use of historical analogies is always a good place to start. Milosevic, for one, is a master of it. He appealed to the 600-year-old tradition of Kosovo to stir his people into supporting his actions in placing the

Kosovar Albanians under a system of apartheid to stop their independence yearnings. As with Saddam Hussein during the Gulf War, Milosevic was portrayed by the Western media as Hitler. This is a particularly effective analogy, for who can support a Hitler? Never mind that Milosevic had no overarching plan to take over the world, that he didn't intend to wipe the Albanian people from the world stage, or that he was only working within the internationally recognized boundaries of his own state. The analogy was an effective one. It would stir people up just enough for them to clamour for action.

And so the West acted.

○ EVERYONE HAS A STAKE IN THE ARMED CONFLICT

What about the ordinary Serb? Did he or she really know what was going on? Most interviews with the ordinary man on the street cast doubts. The media in Serbia is controlled by Milosevic and his party. The only independent station was closed down in late March 1999. Milosevic has for years painted a picture of a Kosovo in which the ordinary Serb is a victim of racial discrimination—Albanians take all the jobs; Albanians force honest Serbs from their homes; Serbian fields are burned; Serb women are raped and their men beaten; not even a Serb child is safe from the threat of attack. Terrorist groups, funded by drug smugglers, are waging a war of genocide against the peace-loving Serbians. They are told the Albanians have a good life and want to stay in Kosovo, not leave as refugees. They are told that Albania is behind all the instability and that Yugoslavia has no choice but to defend itself. The media claimed that the West had made them all targets. No Serb could be safe, according to this view. No wonder the Serb people feel victimized; they couldn't understand why the West felt the need to bomb them. They weren't told about the misery of the Kosovars. They didn't know that refugees were crowding the roads trying to escape the fighting. They were only told that the government was fighting terrorists, not the Albanian people as a whole. They didn't know that ordinary Kosovars were being beaten and tortured and held in jail for months for even the slightest connection to the KLA. They didn't know that many Kosovars were unemployed and that Serbs held all the civil and state jobs. Ordinary Serbs had been kept in the dark.

In mid-March, the Kosovo Liberation Army, under the leadership of the young Hashim Thaci, signed the Rambouillet Accord, no doubt because it promised eventual independence for Kosovo. Milosevic rejected it out of hand. Now there was no reason for the West not to go into Kosovo. But before we begin that discussion, let us look at the KLA, this new entity that seems to hold all the cards in Kosovo.

The Kosovo Liberation Army, or Ushtria Clirimtare e Kosoves, was founded in 1991 by brothers Adem and Hamza Jashari (both were later murdered along with forty-nine other members of their family). Its basic tenet involves the formation of a Greater Albania. Its leaders have all spent years in prison for advocating separatism. It is split between one fascist group made up of descendants of Albanians who fought the Serbs eighty years ago, and most of the KLA leaders in exile who led militant separatist movements to integrate with Albania.[5] Many of the present leaders came out of Pristina University. In fact, the current leader, Hashim Thaci, attended the university and got his start in the student union. Because 70 percent of the Albanians are under age thirty, the KLA has managed to recruit widely from this demographic group. Although they are led by ideologues, the movement has attracted peasants, farmers, students, intellectuals, and other people from nearly every stratum of Kosovar society. At the core of the movement were a few hundred ethnic Albanian soldiers trained by the Yugoslav army. Thousands of emigrés returned home to train for the KLA. They had opposed the Serbs and moderate Albanians, especially those led by Ibrahim Rugova. Much of their money had come from the large Albanian emigré population. But as Milosevic and many Western governments claim, at least part of their money is generated from drug smuggling. Then again, this is not the first guerrilla organization to use drug money as financing. Groups like the Irish Republican Army (IRA), the Shining Path in Peru, the Chechens in Russia, and the Mujahedin in Afghanistan all have used this method to raise funds.[6] Most of the weapons used by the KLA had come from Albania, where the army depots were looted after the fall of the Albanian government. Although they seem to be the main party that the West is now dealing with, not so long ago the KLA were little better than terrorists. In 1998 the U.S. special envoy to the Balkans, Robert Gelbard, told Yugoslavia that the KLA were outlaws and that the United States condemns outlaw terrorism. This, akin to the unfortunate declarations of Western powers saying they wanted Yugoslavia to stay united, practically gave Milosevic a green light in Croatia and Bosnia. It gave him a rationale, just what he needed to destroy the KLA.

On March 24 the NATO forces, made up of contingents from the United States, Britain, Canada, France, Germany, Italy, the Netherlands, Belgium, Denmark, Norway, Portugal, Turkey, and Spain, launched an air strike against targets in Serbia and Montenegro, backed by frigate and destroyer forces in the Adriatic Sea. Just imagine: on one side stands a formidable military alliance of the world's mightiest nations, equipped with state-of-the-art weaponry and emboldened by moral affirmation of a great humanitarian cause; on the other stands a small and poor Balkan country.

NATO's stated goal was to stop the Serbian war machine and force compliance with the Rambouillet Accord. Most of the countries involved supported intervention. Britain, the most bellicose, demanded that bombing operations commence at once. The air war mainly involved planes from the United States, Britain, France, Germany, Spain, the Netherlands, Portugal, and Canada. However, the involvement of the Dutch, Norwegians, and Turks was to take in refugees. The main targets of the air war were army communications, roads, railways, oil refineries, and bridges—anything to cut off Serb access to Kosovo and to knock out army supply lines. No sooner did war erupt than President Clinton took to the national airwaves, announcing to all Americans—surely not the first blunder of his career—that he would not send ground troops into Kosovo. Milosevic might have caved in at the outset of the air operation if he hadn't heard this piece of news. Instead, he held out, thinking that the American public would eventually tire of war and demand peace.

Tactically, the bombardment of Yugoslavia might well go down as the most expensive military campaign, bomb for bomb, in history. The chairman of the U.S. Joint Chiefs of Staff, General Henry Shelton, could easily boast that 90 percent of the bombs dropped were precision-guided, compared to only 9 percent in the 1991 Gulf War, a fact that (though this cannot be verified at the present time) significantly reduces the number of casualties among innocent civilians. The cost of the missiles and bombs was astronomical. One cruise missile (like the Tomahawk) fired from a ship or submarine runs $1 million, and an air-launched cruise from a B-52 is double that amount. A Hellfire missile fired from an Apache helicopter costs about $42,700. A laser-guided 2,000-pound bomb dropped from a radar-evading F-117 costs $26,000, whereas unguided bombs fired from B-1 and B-2 bombers run only $600 each.[7] Any one of these "smart" bombs was often used wastefully to obliterate nothing bigger than a truck, not to mention the ubiquitous Serbian decoys.[8] It actually cost $700 million to send twenty-four Apache helicopters from Germany to Albania. The U.S. Congress was prepared to approve the Clinton administration's request for $6 billion to finance the war and offered up to $10 billion if it proved necessary.[9] The United States bore the brunt of the outlays, unlike in the Gulf War, where countries such as Saudi Arabia and Japan had contributed the lion's share of the military expenditure.

THE BOMBING OF SERBIA AND ITS AFTERMATH

In the first forty days of the air operation, newspaper headlines across the world lambasted the "tragic misapplication of air power by politicians," arguing for a ground war. In effect, most observers had been advocating the use of ground troops. Bad weather had significantly hampered the air operations at the outset, but in the end NATO's technological edge proved very effective.[10] Yugoslavia's formidable air defences were not so formidable anymore; the Russians, moreover, had known this all along. Russian military observers knew that the U.S. military had the capability of using computers and information operations that involved cyber attacks on Serbia's air defence network; cyber warfare was not discussed much by strategists and commentators and talk show hosts on radio and TV.[11] (Most media commentators know very little about it, although kids in North America play laser tag at theme parks everywhere.) The Americans admitted this much months afterward.[12] On top of this, the media and press underestimated the devastating effects of psychological warfare techniques known as PsyOps (short for Psychological Operations). Some of the planes scattered leaflets and flyers designed to turn the Serb soldiers against their leadership. It actually worked. Yugoslav soldiers did not surrender in droves like the Iraqis did a few years earlier. Nevertheless an unprecedented number of desertions from the Yugoslav army may be attributed to psychological warfare, a technique that affected the morale of the Serbian soldiers.

Yet it was not morale that caused Montenegro to declare neutrality during the war. NATO, however, had indeed targeted Montenegro; Yugoslav military installations were on its territory. The Montenegro leadership denounced the attacks as a smoke screen. Yet no one was fooled, for what this leadership really wanted was to blame Milosevic for it all. Milo Djukanovic, in Podgorica (Montenegro's capital city), appeared to be balancing on a razor's edge. Half of the Montenegrins actually supported Milosevic, but Djukanovic had decided to throw in his lot with NATO, playing a perilous game of brinkmanship. As a result, he created one of the world's strangest anomalies: Montenegro became a republic at peace within a country at war. From the outset Djukanovic kept on denouncing the NATO bombing and publicly called Milosevic insane. By war's end he had accepted more than 80,000 refugees from the Serbian province of Kosovo.

With NATO unleashing a deadly fusillade, Serbia cut off ties with the United States, Britain, Germany, and France, all of which were seen as the chief aggressors. Russia, which had been opposed to the bombing, was livid in its condemnations, arguing that Moscow's opinion was disregarded, expelling its NATO representative, and shortly thereafter withdrawing its military students from NATO countries. Moscow suddenly sought a resolution in the UN Security Council to stop the bombing— and lost by a vote of 12 to 3 (with China and Namibia rallying in support of the Russians). It is not surprising that protests by ethnic Serbs took place all over the world. (Surprisingly, though, Monica Lewinsky's Russian publisher cancelled the former White House intern's book tour.)

Despite the best intentions of the bombers, the air war caused the Serbs to hasten their expulsion of the Albanians and the war against the KLA before the air war could intensify. On March 25, over sixty-five men, women, and children were massacred by Serbian soldiers in Bela Crkva.

The next day, two hundred Serbian paramilitaries gathered up the men, told the women and children to leave for Albania, and massacred the people they'd taken prisoner and those who refused to leave in Suva Reka. Most of the houses were burned; many women and children who were hiding in a restaurant were killed. There were reports that Zeljko Raznatovic's (known as Arkan[13]) Tigers and the paramilitary group known as the White Eagles were carrying out ethnic cleansing here as they did in Bosnia. These are only two examples of outrage. Other atrocities beggar description.

On March 26 the first wave of refugees arrived in Albania, a country reeling from its own poverty and ill equipped to handle a flood of new mouths to feed. As the refugees crossed the border, the Serbian police confiscated their identification papers, making it hard for them to return.

To the Serbians, the bombing was an international crime of the first magnitude. Demonstrators clogged the streets in every town and city. Many demonstrators wore T-shirts with targets emblazoned on them, burned the flags of coalition member states, and shouted slogans against the "North American Terrorist Organization." Rock bands played pro-Serbian tunes. The anger was almost palpable.

Tales of rape and slaughter soon began to permeate Western airwaves from the Kosovo refugees. The knock at the door in the middle of the night. The terse words of insult and anger telling a family they had to leave or be killed. The long, cold, hungry journey as bombs rained from the skies and gunfire crackled around them. The smell of burning houses and rotting corpses of their fellow Albanians on the side of the road, and no time to stop and give them a proper burial. The separation of children and parents, of husbands and wives. And the awful uncertainty of not knowing if loved ones were alive or dead, of perhaps never knowing. The terror of seeing people you know and love cut down by Serb bullets. Having everything of value taken away—possessions, heirlooms, identity papers, the deed to one's house—one was suddenly left with nothing. A person's identity was erased in the twinkling of an eye, as if it had never existed. Men and boys over age fifteen were slaughtered like sheep before their parents' eyes. Why? Because they were able-bodied and potential fighters. Women were detained by paramilitaries and police. They were repeatedly violated and tortured if they refused to submit; sometimes murdered. The terror went on for days.[14] One now sings ballads about the wells of Kosovo that became clogged with the dead and their excrement: both human and animal. Many Albanian villages were completely despoiled; the people from there were told never to return.

A major American embarrassment occurred on March 31 when three American soldiers were taken by Serb forces near the Macedonian border. The three servicemen—Christopher Stone, Steven Gonzales, and Andrew Gonzales—claimed they were taken when they mistakenly crossed the Macedonian border into Kosovo. The three were shown, battered and bruised, on Serbian television. Their imprisonment remained a major sticking point for over a month until American religious and political leader Jesse Jackson flew to Belgrade to meet with Milosevic to negotiate their release. Jackson had previously negotiated the release of hostages in Syria, Cuba, Kuwait, and Iraq. In return, Jackson praised Milosevic for agreeing to the release and condemned the NATO bombing.

In early April, Ibrahim Rugova, the moderate Albanian leader, was shown on Serbian television talking with Milosevic. He looked very uncomfortable and was obviously not speaking freely. He was later released in May from Yugoslav custody and flew to Rome.

As the refugee crisis worsened, hundreds of refugees were flown to Turkey and Norway. Later, they were sent further afield with many going to the United States and Canada. The vast majority of the refugees took up residence in Albania, Macedonia, Montenegro, Bosnia, and surrounding countries. They joined a sad and surprisingly long list of refugees and displaced people around the world. According to the latest figures from the United States Committee on Refugees (1998), there were over 30 million refugees worldwide, mainly Sudanese, Palestinians, Afghans, Iraqis, and Columbians. Of these, less than a million returned home in that year.

The NATO preoccupation with not having any casualties among its soldiers led to many accidents. The warplanes were ordered to fly extremely high so that they could avoid being shot down by Serbian anti-aircraft guns. As a result, they couldn't always verify their targets completely. On April 12, NATO attacked a passenger train, killing ten Serb civilians. On April 14, a NATO pilot, thinking a column of vehicles were soldiers who had set fire to surrounding villages, bombed civilian refugees in a convoy. Seventy-five men, women, and children were killed. Forty-seven bus passengers were killed when NATO planes bombed a bridge near Luzane on May 1, and more were killed when the ambulances trying to save the wounded were bombed themselves. Two days later another bus was shelled near Savine Vode, killing twenty. On May 7, cluster bombs (which are forbidden by the Geneva Convention) were used to bomb the town of Nis, which had no military or police presence, killing twenty civilians. A week later, refugees were bombed near Kovisa, killing eighty-seven. On May 20, the Dragisa Misovic Hospital in Belgrade was bombed, resulting in the destruction of the neurological ward and severe damage to the children's and gynecological wards. The next day, a Kosovar village was bombed by accident and seventy-eight were killed, fifty-eight wounded. A refugee camp was mistakenly bombed a week later. There was even an incident in which NATO jets accidentally struck Sofia, Bulgaria's capital, and one in which they dropped bombs on the Albanian side of the border.

The number of accidents was very low considering the number of sorties flown and the number of missiles launched. Deaths from "friendly fire" and "collateral damage" are prevalent in all wars. But these incidents show that unlike in the Gulf War, the reality of "smart" bombs and other such weaponry is no longer like a video game. Real people die, real innocents die. Milosevic made much of these accidents. He claimed that NATO was deliberately attacking hospitals, cultural and historical monuments, monasteries, kindergartens, and refugee camps. He also claimed that civilians and refugee columns (fleeing the bombing, not Serbian aggression) were being targeted for destruction by the blood-thirsty West. And the people of Serbia, by and large, believed him.

○ Chemical and oil refineries were also targeted, and the resulting de-struction let loose clouds of toxic gases that might have serious health risks for the population at large. Electricity and water sources were also destroyed, leading to hardship for many innocent Serbians. The bombing of many factories has thrown thousands of Serbians out of work, raising serious questions about their ability to survive a harsh winter. In mid-winter of the year 2000, it was discovered that lethal cyanide polluted the Danube to the extent of killing whole clusters of fish, and the cyanide poi-soning of this main waterway was flowing to the Black Sea in alarming proportions.

The most serious accident, in international terms at least, was the bombing of the Chinese embassy in Belgrade on May 8. NATO forces claimed that they had meant to bomb the Federal Directorate for Supply and Procurement and blamed the accident on an out-of-date map and faulty information (later the CIA took responsibility, saying that its maps were not consulted before this bombing run was recommended). Three were killed and dozens injured. The leadership of China was outraged. Widespread public demonstrations broke out all over China, which the Chinese government allowed. The Chinese people were told that Amer-ican troops had deliberately bombed and killed Chinese territory; they were told nothing of the situation of the Kosovar Albanians. After the demonstrations had served their purpose, the government reined in the participants and aired President Clinton's apology on Chinese television. The bombing set back efforts to end the war, cost NATO a lot of credi-bility, and further damaged U.S.-Chinese relations. However, the prag-matic Chinese decided they needed the support of the West, so things eventually got settled. The United States has since made restitution to the families of the victims, and both sides are negotiating a settlement on damages done to both embassies (the American embassy in China was damaged during the demonstrations).

The Russians were still fuming over their lack of control of the situation. They couldn't use their Security Council veto, and they seemed powerless to affect the outcome of the war. Russia had said it couldn't condone the bombing of Serbia. The West didn't seem to mind that. The marginalization of Russia was one of the Western countries' biggest mistakes. Insiders in Washington arrogantly believed that Russia could no longer be a threat. Never mind that they still commanded a vast nuclear arsenal—most experts believed that Russia's spiralling-out-of-control economy and domestic problems precluded it from any serious involvement in Kosovo. Others who were more cautious feared that this could reawaken the slumbering Russian bear and lead to an escalation in anti-Western sentiment in Russia. On April 20, however, Russia announced that it wouldn't break with the world powers over the Kosovo situation. The Russians surely realized that their lack of political muscle did not imply that they could be eliminated from brokering the situation. Realizing too that they couldn't prevent the war from happening, Moscow was ready to put a quick end to it. Diplomatic missions to Serbia and the NATO countries were undertaken at fever pitch. Russia wanted some just consideration for the Serbs. Otherwise, the peace imposed would amount to a one-sided agreement against Slavic brethren. Germany, in a show of greater common sense than any other nation gave, insisted that any peace plan should include contingents of Russian peacekeepers. Although the Albanians would have none of this, the Serbs were adamant. The lessons of the Bosnian war had shown that peacekeepers of the same religion or ethnic group worked best during wars of ethnic hatred.

On the whole, the Russians proved unreliable. Most Serbs were disappointed that the Russians did not come to their aid. They had expected the Russians to come down hard, diplomatically at least, and cut ties with the NATO countries while demanding an end to the bombing. The fact that Russia did not do so gave Milosevic pause. If he couldn't count on the Russians, who was he to rely on? Despite the fact that the Yugoslav parliament voted to join a union with Russia and Belarus on April 12, the Russians made no overt moves to help Serbian interests.

Even though Milosevic announced a cease-fire and claimed the KLA was defeated in mid-April, the war dragged on. NATO forces continued the bombing, destroying the headquarters of the Serbian Socialist Party and the state television station. Vuk Draskovic, an opposition leader, responded to these developments by saying that the government was lying to the people and that Serbia might have to live with the presence of armed peacekeepers.

Sanctions and an oil embargo were added to the air war in early May. Serbia had already faced sanctions during the Bosnian war, and some argued that they were a major reason for Serbia's eventual capitulation. In this case, trade and travel sanctions were imposed. There is reason to suspect that sanctions only manage to hurt the innocent members of society, rather than the leadership. Leaders like Milosevic can use sanctions to stir up the population by blaming hardship on the West. Weapons embargoes are, of course, a vital part to ending a war, but the restriction of trade can often lead to humanitarian tragedy.

By May 6, Russia and the West had agreed on terms to set up an international armed force to guarantee the safe return of refugees. Russia had at last agreed to all five NATO principles for an end to the war: an end to the violence, withdrawal of Serb forces, the return of the refugees, an international security force, and a political settlement. Russia now brought considerable political and diplomatic pressure on Serbia to settle the conflict. Viktor Chernomyrdin, the Russian statesman, was sent to Serbia and got Milosevic to agree to settle the war within the framework of the United Nations. There was also the promise that Serb forces might be allowed back into Kosovo once peace had been established; that was the most dangerous stab at NATO.

In early May, Yugoslavia went to the International Court of Justice (ICJ) at The Hague to accuse NATO forces of genocide and demand that they stop bombing. In order to prove that he could be reasonable, Milosevic pulled a few troops out of Kosovo, but not enough to make any difference. By early June, the ICJ had rejected Yugoslavia's petition. By late May, Serbia was picking fights along the Albanian border. As a response, NATO boosted peacekeeping numbers and a standby military force was put in place. By now, Britain—as hawkish as ever—was pushing for ground troops and low-flying air attacks; the Germans were only in favour of continuing the air attacks; meanwhile, the Italians, Greeks, Hungarians, and Czechs wanted to halt the bombing. The alliance seemed to be coming apart at the seams.

In an unprecedented move, and one that was bound to exacerbate matters, a sitting head of state was indicted for war crimes. Slobodan Milosevic (along with Interior Minister Vlajko Stojiljkovic, Army Chief of Staff General Dragoljub Ojdanic, Deputy Prime Minister Nikola Sainovic, and President of Serbia Milan Milutinovic)[15] was charged with several counts of war crimes: the deportation of 740,000 Albanians as a crime against humanity; two counts of the murder of hundreds of civilians (one as a crime against humanity, and the other as a violation of the customs of war); and the persecution of Albanians on political, racial, and religious grounds as a crime against humanity. The war crimes tribunal is a spinoff of the International Court of Justice, created during the Bosnian war. The chief investigator, Louise Arbour, a Canadian who has since left the tribunal to become a Canada Supreme Court justice, and her team of seventy investigators went into the field to gather information.[16] Arbour has argued that because Milosevic is the head of the Yugoslav army, he is indictable. Whether he ever comes to trial is another matter entirely. Like the Nuremberg Trials,[17] it is doubtful that the actual individuals who committed the atrocities will ever come to trial. Instead, the leaders are the targets. Justice might take a while. The tribunal itself has never been adequately funded. Most of the suspects are hiding in Yugoslavia or in the Republika Srpska (the Serb Republic in Bosnia). Although the United States has put a $5 million bounty on Milosevic, it appears unlikely he'll ever be brought to trial. In Yugoslavia, the government immediately stated that the indictments were meant to conceal NATO crimes in the peacekeepers' genocide against the Serbian people.

In order to prosecute these crimes, the International Tribunal needs the following: eyewitness accounts, forensic evidence (e.g., bullet cases, DNA, blood), and intelligence linking the crimes through the chain of command (e.g., spies, satellite radio and telephone intercepts). The amount of evidence, not the number of victims, has become the most important criteria for the tribunal experts. Scotland Yard, the Royal Canadian Mounted Police, the FBI, and police agencies from Germany, Denmark, France, Holland, and Switzerland are all taking part in the investigation.[18]

On May 29, Yugoslavia accepted a peace deal. It was partly in keeping with the ill-fated Rambouillet Accord, but it differed significantly. (The reader will find reference to it in an appendix to this book.) NATO wanted a clear personal statement from Milosevic before stopping the air raids. In response, Yugoslavia accepted a G8[19] proposal to the UN Security Council that agreed with the five NATO conditions for the end of the war. The European Union and Russia sent representatives President Martti Ahtisaari and Viktor Chernomyrdin to Belgrade to ensure they signed the agreement. Igor Ivanov, the Russian foreign minister, followed up with calls for an international presence in Kosovo. In the meantime, Britain and the United States were not so secretly finalizing plans for a ground invasion code-named Operation Bravo for 300,000 NATO troops. It was for an invasion of Serbia. One of the invasion entry points was to be from Hungary in the north, one of the newest members in the NATO alliance. A further invasion code-named B-Minus was to be launched into Kosovo with British, American, German, French, Spanish, Belgian, Canadian, Dutch, Italian, and Polish troops, scheduled for the first week of September.

AT LAST, A PEACE AGREEMENT

On June 9, a military agreement was signed by NATO and Yugoslavia. It called for the full withdrawal of Yugoslav forces. The agreement, named the "Military Technical Agreement between KFOR and Federal Republic of Yugoslavia and the Republic of Serbia," dealt with the deployment of a peacekeeping force, the end of hostilities, and the withdrawal of Yugoslav forces. Within 24 hours of signing, the army had to withdraw from the northern part of the province and all military flights had to come to a full stop. Within 48 hours, records of all landmines and booby traps had to be handed over to KFOR. Within 72 hours, all aircraft and anti-aircraft weapons were to be removed from Kosovo. The forces were given six days to leave the south and eleven days for a full withdrawal. In return, 50,000 KFOR troops would move into Kosovo and divide the province into British, French, Italian, German, and American sectors. On the following day, when proof of Serbian withdrawal was presented to NATO, the air war came to an end. Despite NATO bluster, Serbian forces had managed to hide and use decoys successfully enough to avoid major damage. Shortly thereafter, Milosevic gave an impassioned speech while standing before a bombed-out bridge, calling for national unity and rebuilding.

The KFOR troops entered Kosovo soon afterwards in accordance with Operation Joint Guardian. The Russian troops, perhaps as a final thumbing of the nose at the West's refusal to take Russia seriously, drove into Pristina before NATO's troops. The incident outraged the West. Ivanov had promised them that the Western troops would go in first. He quickly stated that it was all a mistake. The Russian Defence Ministry gruffly stated that it wasn't. The British, Germans, and French quickly set up zones of occupation, with the Italians and Americans coming in later. By June 20, all Yugoslav military and police forces had left Kosovo. The seventy-eight days of bombing were over.

As in all wars, propaganda played a large part in this one. Truth, as the adage goes, was and always will be the first victim of war. Milosevic, a master of the art of distortion, claimed he had a clear conscience. He stated time and again that all he wanted was for all the communities in Kosovo to be equal and that Albania and the narco-terrorist KLA were the cause of all the problems. He claimed that many of the refugees seen on Western television were paid actors. Besides, he often said, the refugees' plight was caused by the NATO bombing. There were no reports in the Serbian media about Serbs killing Albanians. Small wonder the ordinary Serb on the street had no idea why NATO would be bombing Belgrade, so he resigned himself to believing in Western aggression. Stories circulated in Belgrade following the signing of the peace accord that peace emissaries Ahtisaari and Chernomyrdin had threatened to level Belgrade to the ground if Milosevic didn't agree to peace.[20] NATO was described in the media as the big loser. In a speech on June 10, Milosevic stressed that Serbia hadn't given up Kosovo and that the territorial integrity of their borders had been guaranteed by the G8 and the United Nations. In fact, Milosevic even claimed a sort of Pyrrhic victory, saying that the Belgrade delegation at Rambouillet had adopted an Agreement for Self-Government in Kosovo-Metohija that clearly acknowledged the

presence of the international community under the UN banner in Kosovo.[21] He appealed to his people's fear, and it worked, for a while at
least. As Anthony R. Pratkanis and Elliot Aronson write: "Fear appeals
are powerful: they channel our thoughts away from careful consideration
of the issue at hand and toward plans for ridding ourselves of the fear."[22]
With the war on, thousands of children and twice as many adults would
be out in the streets of the main cities, dressed in Serbian tricolour, or
just waving the Serbian colours, showing targets on their butts where
NATO forces might direct their hits, defying the Americans, challenging
the Europeans.

It was all show, all pretension. What fickleness, what gullibility. Immediately after the defeat, rallies were taking place all over Serbia again.
First for Milosevic; then against him. The people, after all, can't be duped
for long. Serbia had lost the war. No Pyrrhic victory, this. The Serbs had
capitulated. Outside of Belgrade, some of the Yugoslav towns like Nis
and Pirot were being run by opposition groups. Milosevic's supporters
were fewer and fewer in number, his propaganda machine unmasked.
He was slowly seeing his tight grip on the country weaken. One day,
surely, it would slip through his fingers completely; that is, when the
realization of total defeat became apparent.

With no footing except in the support of his army, and perhaps some
gangsters tied to his son Marko, his liquid assets in far-off China, Milosevic's power would have vanished like smoke if the NATO coalition
had made that the prime objective. But the coalition powers did not.
Had they not acted in the same way with Saddam Hussein? Herein lies
the ultimate irony. Are we to assume therefore that NATO struts about
with a solid yellow stripe of fecklessness on its armor? Was the force of
such arms not enough to be rid of Milosevic?

On a number of occasions I spoke with the Canadian ambassador for
humanitarian affairs, Raphael Girard, Canada's special envoy on the Kosovo crisis. He confirmed that because the Russians had withdrawn all
support, any ground war would eventually have resulted in Milosevic's
capture. Milosevic may have been as fearful of a ground war as many
were in the West. Possibly Milosevic's feints and strategems and bluffs
had been called (so he thought); crazy or not, he would know when to
cut his losses. For he came out of it with only minor blemishes, his rep-
utation as a sublime blackguard intact, still inspiring awe—such was his
luck, such the flexibility of his insidious mind, that he was bound to
succeed in the art of survival.

The West, on the other hand, was guilty of its own propaganda. Every
day briefings by the NATO leaders became glowing reports of NATO
victories. Grainy pictures with no context became the evidence of mass
graves and burned villages. Atrocities were reported, only to be later
discredited. Bombing mistakes were downplayed with quick apologies;

scads of statistics followed showing that it only happened once every so often (meaning once in a blue moon), and that was deemed a very acceptable number. War zone reporting is always a dangerous occupation, and few journalists were able to report from the front lines. The use of the Internet and the cell phone were very important for those few who actually managed to get the reports out.

ANGLOCENTRICITY

The coverage of the events had a distinct Anglocentric tone, which one does not find so much in the overall NATO command. The French might always rant about the growing hegemony, unilateralism, and isolationism of a "hyperpower" United States. I myself have argued throughout this book that there is much truth to this; but French braggadocio, when it comes to war, should not be taken too seriously. What I mean by *Anglocentric* (Anglo and American) is a media coverage and NATO military planning dominated by these two countries (Britain and the United States). Most disturbing to me indeed is the British attitude toward the campaign. Steeped in arrogance and overconfidence (a smokescreen for their past colonial blunders and present economic insecurities?), the British still like to believe themselves as supreme in war as they are in the writing of the mystery novel. In reality, however, Jamie Shea's rundown of the operations on CNN was nothing short of vapid and evasive. Retired British majors and generals were always on hand for comment. The persistence of the British to see themselves in the limelight of the EU and of NATO amounts to frivolity. For such a third-rate power to send a fleet to the Falklands might not have been entirely absurd in the early 1980s. True enough; had the daunted Argentinian air force been in possession of many more (French-made) Exocet missiles, London's armada would have been rapidly expedited to the bottom of the sea. The British relied heavily on American support and logistics. And the same holds true today.

The Brits clamoured for a ground war in Kosovo, but the truth of the matter is that a ground campaign would have proved unmanageable for the British army. It was all later revealed in the British press. British soldiers had to borrow guns from other KFOR personnel because theirs malfunctioned. They complained constantly about confused lines of command; their radios frequently broke down (the Serbs could hear what was being said); and they were totally unprepared for nighttime fighting—there just wasn't enough night vision equipment to go around. "We were fortunate that an inadequate system was not put to the test," complained Brigadier Adrian Freer, Commander of 5 Airborne Brigade. "If aught' were to go wrong, we'd be dead meat" was his usual complaint.[23] And what if the Serbs had resisted?

WHAT IF IT HAD ACTUALLY COME TO A
GROUND WAR?

Effective as the American technological edge was, it may have been no less an unmixed blessing for the Americans that it never came to a ground war. The Yugoslav soldier is touted as one of the toughest in Europe. (But that is beside the point.) To diminish casualties among its combat troops, NATO would have to rely heavily on Apache helicopters in any ground assault. Incidentally, the U.S. army seemed to be more willing to suffer casualties in training and in getting these machines to Albania, whence the ground assault could be launched, than in real battle operations. At least three Apaches went down with their crews while in training. This set a bad standard for the soldiers. The Pentagon had spent $15 billion over the past two decades to make the Apache the most lethal and least vulnerable attack helicopter in the world—a real tank killer! What's more, it can fly in the kind of rainy, cloudy weather that was grounding so many jets in the first month of the Kosovo air campaign, and it is capable of attacking enemy troops deep behind their lines. The irony: the Apaches never flew in Kosovo.

First the Apaches were supposed to arrive in Macedonia, where a NATO base had been set up in Skopje. But Macedonia was reeling from the influx of hundreds of thousands of refugees, and the Macedonian government rejected them. When they finally got to Albania, they were mired in a sea of mud "so thick that one military intelligence officer sank up to her chest. Soldiers were ordering thigh-high fishing boots from home."[24] The base at Tirana had to be rebuilt at a cost of $480 million. And it took twelve long days for twenty-four Apaches to fly from Germany to Albania. The inclemency of the weather must have hampered some. But it was the French who were blocking the Apache landing ramp at the Tirana airport with a refuelling depot, and they adamantly refused to budge for an entire week. It was also feared that the Apache deployment might result in casualties as high as "50 percent within days."[25]

Furthermore, it takes a considerable amount of time to train specialist crews to fly the Apaches. The Yugoslavs had ample time to disperse before the Apaches arrived. The densely wooded mountain passes of Albania and Kosovo were shelter for any number of scattered Serbs with shoulder-fired, surface-to-air missiles. In the Iraqi desert this had not posed a threat. In rugged Afghanistan, on the other hand, Soviet "Hind" helicopters were vulnerable to the heat-seeking, shoulder-fired Stinger that lay in ambush unseen, in a gorge or a bend of a mountain slope. At $14.5 million the Apache may be the world's best combat helicopter, but nothing could give a guarantee against "a little bullet in the big sky shot by some lucky Serb with an AK-47 or, worse, a shoulder-fired SA-7 projectile."[26] The Apache was just too risky to use.

The results of the war in Kosovo were many and varied. In terms of human lives, 6,000 Serbian soldiers were killed and 2,000 (that is the last estimate by the Belgrade government) Serbian civilians died. Over 100,000 Albanians were killed; 600,000 were displaced within Kosovo, and 800,000 were driven out into other countries (443,000 into Albania alone). Serb refugees began to move out of Kosovo as soon as the war ended, fearing retaliatory attacks by the Albanians. Most of them ended up in Serbia and in Bosnia. The cost in psychological terms is equally devastating. The horrors of war will live in this region for generations—neither forgotten nor forgiven. Families have had their homes taken from them, many dwellings have been burned, many occupants never returned from abroad. Fathers, husbands, sons—many families have no one left to sit at the head of the table. Children have been orphaned, parents have been left childless. Women suffered the horrifying ordeal of rape and debasement. Yet return they must to a life and a culture that place a stigma on a dishonoured woman. In Kosovo and in Serbia many are out of work, because there has been damage to industrial complexes. Many will go hungry during the winters ahead. Humanitarian aid organizations are already at work, to be sure, but it will take years to rebuild the infrastructure and the harmony of shattered human lives.

NOTES

1. See UNHCR, Reports for May 1999, Geneva, Switzerland.

2. Lally Weymouth, "I Can Only Be Proud of My Role" in *Guardian Weekly*, January 3, 1999, p. 11.

3. http://www.monde-diplomatique.fr/dossiers/kosovo/rambouillet .html ("Interim Agreement for Peace and Self-Government in Kosovo"—the Rambouillet agreement).

4. *Literaturnaya Gazeta*, July 16, 1999; see also *Washington Post*, July 13, 1999.

5. Chris Hedges, "Kosovo's Next Masters?" in *Foreign Affairs*, vol. 78, no. 3, May/June 1999, pp. 26–28.

6. Eske Wright, "A Balkan Version of the IRA?" in *New Statesman*, vol. 128, no. 4431, April 9, 1999, p. 17.

7. *New York Times*, May 2, 1999.

8. Flying at 20,000 feet, it is difficult to distinguish a farmer's lorry from an armored vehicle.

9. CNN news broadcast, June 7, 1999.

10. Newspapers and talk shows were not the only media critical of the air war. The London-based think tank the International Institute for Strategic Studies, in its publication *Strategic Survey*, prematurely stated it was a strategic failure. See the May 1999 edition of this quarterly.

11. *Voennaya Pechat'* (Moscow), September 1999, vol. 8, p. 36.

12. "Computer Warfare Used in Yugoslavia" in HistoryChannel.com, December 1999. See the Pentagon web site on cyberwar.

13. Arkan is a gangster/warlord who has been indicted for war crimes in Bosnia. He led an 800-man-strong ultranationalist army known as the Tigers. He and his men had been accused of looting, torture, rape, and murder. Before the Bosnian war, Arkan was an assassin for the Yugoslav secret service during the 1970s. He is also wanted in seven European countries for armed robbery and murder. Incredibly wealthy from his past dealings, he established his own party, the Party of Serb Unity, and won a seat in Kosovo's legislature. He and his young pop singer wife, Ceca, became very popular celebrities in Serbia. Carl Honore, "Serbia's Pretty-Boy Psychopath" in *National Post*, May 29, 1999, p. E11.

14. Not that rape is a characteristic of the Balkan wars only. The rape of innocent women and children during war is as old as war itself. In modern times, thousands of German women were raped by the Russians in 1944. During World War II, the Japanese army used Korean, Chinese, Filipino, Indonesian, Burmese, and Dutch women as "comfort women" to "entertain" their troops in what has been termed the Rape of Nanking. But rape may have been most blatantly used during the Bosnian war. It took place often in public and involved several men either in conjunction with invasion or in detention centers. Some women were forced into brothels and others into "rape camps," where they were kept and violated until they became pregnant. Sometimes the rapes were videotaped and shown on Serbian television. The Muslim women were then said to be Serbians and their Serbian rapists were announced as Muslims or Croats. Today, there are innumerable children living in Bosnia who were born of such atrocity. Many of these children were rejected by their mothers. Countless others were aborted. See Catherine N. Nicarchos, "Women, War and Rape: Challenges Facing the International Tribunal for the Former Yugoslavia" in *Human Rights Quarterly*, vol. 17, no. 4, 1995, pp. 656–57.

15. Others under investigation include: Frenki Simatovic (a former ethnic cleanser, now chief of Serbia's Special Forces of State Security), Lubinko Cvetic (deputy head of security in Kosovo), Momir Bulatovic (former president of Montenegro, now prime minister of Yugoslavia), Colonel General Nebjosa Pavkovic (commander of Serb forces in Kosovo), Mirko Marjanovic (prime minister of Serbia), Lt. General Radomir "Rade" Markovic (head of the Yugoslav secret police), General Sreten Lukic (head of police in Kosovo), and Zoran Sokolovic (interior minister of Yugoslavia). See Carl Honore, "The Most Wanted Men in Serbia" in *National Post*, May 29, 1999, p. E11.

16. The main problems they faced were the contamination and dis-

turbance of burial and massacre sights by refugees eager to find loved ones, soldiers trying to cover up the crimes, and reporters trying to report the war. They also faced booby traps and mines.

17. The Nuremberg Trials against Nazi officials took place after World War II. Many considered it an example of victor's justice because the winners of the war were equally guilty of massacring innocents (e.g., the Russians had massacred thousands of Polish officers in the Katyn Forest; the Allies had firebombed Dresden, killing hundreds of thousands of civilians; and the United States had firebombed Tokyo and dropped nuclear bombs on Hiroshima and Nagasaki). Sebastian Junger, "The Forensics of War" in *Vanity Fair*, October 1999, p. 142.

18. Ibid.

19. The G8, or Group of 8, is made up of the world's richest industrialized nations: the United States, Japan, Germany, Britain, Italy, Canada, France, and Russia.

20. International Crisis Group, "South Balkans: Back to the Future: Milosevic Prepares for Life after Kosovo," June 28, 1999 (www.crisisweb .org/projects/sbalkans/reports/kos25main.htm).

21. Ibid.

22. Anthony R. Pratkanis and Elliot Aronson, *Age of Propaganda: The Everyday Use and Abuse of Persuasion* (New York: W. H. Freeman, 1991), p. 162.

23. BBC World Service, January 3, 2000.

24. *The Times*, July 23, 1999.

25. *Washington Post*, December 29, 1999.

26. Ibid. Apparently none of the Apache pilots were used to flying with night-vision goggles; some were inexperienced, and at times during training there was a complete loss of radio contact because of the high mountains. The following is a ludicrous scenario of engagement of the battle plan: "to zip through the mountains at 90 miles per hour. Bomblet-spewing ATACMS tactical missiles would have already pummeled the enemy troops along the flight path. Dart-filled rockets would deal with the remnants. Six rescue helicopters would be 10 minutes away. Five Apaches would fly a feint close by. A half dozen Air Force jets would provide protective cover. Like a mosquito darting for blood, each Apache would stay in the battle zone a mere five minutes, with its infrared jammer turned on to throw off incoming missiles" (ibid). Sounds more like a Nintendo game or a scene from *Star Wars* than serious combat reality.

4

AFTERMATH: THE MORE THINGS CHANGE, THE MORE THEY STAY THE SAME

Such subtle covenants shall be made,
Till peace itself is war in masquerade.
                                                    —Dryden

NATO bombs did the trick, but made the situation worse.

Before NATO's air war began, 2,500 people had died in fighting (mostly KLA partisans and Serb soldiers). By the end of the bombing, 10,000 (mostly Albanian civilians) were dead. Before the war 230,000 had become refugees, and at the end of it 1.8 million were displaced, including 860,000 outside Kosovo's boundaries. Most have returned now, although 150,000 Serbs and Roma (Gypsies) managed to flee the province for good.[1] Yugoslavia has sustained bombing so devastating as to have driven its infrastructure back fifty years. Indeed, precision bombing has turned Yugoslavia virtually into a Third World country. Yugoslavia was not quite that in Tito's day nor before the wars at the close of the millennium. NATO filled the void left behind in Kosovo and has thus become something akin to an interim colonial administrator, a caretaker. In a patriarchal, vendetta-driven society, what hope can one hold out for self-government, now or in the foreseeable future? Violence and plunder are familiar features again. People can be accosted and killed for as paltry a reason as belonging to the wrong ethnic group. Virulent hatred is as alive today as it was at the beginning of the war. Could that be what the NATO powers wanted to achieve?

Meanwhile, Milosevic broods in his office in Belgrade, unimpeachable from within, unreachable from without. He has successfully gathered his minions about him. The War Crimes Tribunal can't try him. He has joined Saddam Hussein in a rogue's gallery of global villains. Both men are symbols of the powerlessness of Western coalitions. There was a time, not long ago, when global policemen could remove, say, a Noriega from power in Panama, or some other authoritarian despot, be it a drug kingpin or an embezzler of gargantuan sums. The "good guys" don't employ tactics like that any longer. Heroic Westerners, who no longer play sheriff, are loath to send out hit squads to eliminate their enemies (only the Israeli Mossad does that, I would say). No, we in the West sit back, almost mum, waiting for that "one step over the line" that will justify force beyond that mandated by our superior culture. How many times do these villains need to step over the line? I'm reminded of an old joke from the Reagan era, when a line in the sand was drawn for Libya's Qaddafi. When he crossed it, we drew another, farther back, then another, and another, and still another, taunting him at each turn to cross a new line. We were rapidly running out of lines. How many times will Hussein be bombed? And Milosevic? Milosevic could carry out a coup d'état in Montenegro. He could incite violence in Vojvodina. And the West will hem and haw until it finally intervenes. Certainly, putting a price on his head is hardly enough of an inducement. Protests don't seem to work anymore. The opposition in Serbia is hardly able to take over; policymakers in the West lament that this opposition is far too divided. So things have not changed that much.

KOSOVO: MISERY AND HATRED—
THE BYPRODUCTS OF WAR

No sooner had the war stopped than old problems resurfaced. For example, the KLA, although seen as a freedom force by the Kosovar Albanians, would need to be disarmed or there could be no peace between Albanians and Serbs. Land mines and booby traps dot the rugged landscape. Thousands have been maimed or killed from such explosives. Rotting corpses of humans and animals have contaminated the drinking water. Hundreds of thousands of people are homeless. Epidemics were rife in the immediate aftermath. And retaliation by the hate-filled Albanians is pervasive. Again, the cycle turns.

What kind of leadership would the Kosovars need? They probably don't care right now. They need electricity, water, and their homes rebuilt before they can worry about elections and representative government. The Albanians are quite willing to let the UN or NATO help them survive the first winters. Winter is always a real threat. Most Albanians have insufficient shelter. They live in tents or amid bombed-out ruins, covered with leaky roofs. They are seen travelling in rickety tractors. The United Nations High Commissioner for Refugees (UNHCR) and other

Western agencies are in a flurry to provide enough shelter from the ice, snow, and falling temperatures that winter brings. The cities are expected to swell with multitudes fleeing from the countryside. The city of Pristina has already seen a doubling of its population. A myriad other problems will soon conspire. Will there be enough electricity? Water? Food? Many refugees believed that the Western agencies would rebuild their homes right away, but the start of massive reconstruction only began in the spring of 2000. Instead, relief agencies are helping Kosovars winterize their homes and creating collective shelters across the province. Logistics is a nightmare; the real fear persists that the agencies will run out of supplies before anyone is guaranteed adequate shelter. And if the already overloaded and overworked electricity plants fail, there are more life-threatening perils. As it currently stands, the UN refugee agency is providing 56,000 shelter kits (including plastic sheeting, tools, and timber) and plans to distribute 30,000 tents, 60,000 stoves, more than 1 million blankets, 550,000 mattresses and 183,000 hygiene and kitchen packets.[2] Kofi Annan has appealed to the international community to help reconstruct electricity networks, waterworks, and hospitals as soon as possible.

Realistically, it could take a decade to resettle and rebuild Kosovo. One needs only to look at Bosnia. It took years to rebuild, and the work is nowhere near done. In Bosnia, with its 2 million refugees (20,000 are still missing), I witnessed a ravaged infrastructure, scant law enforcement, scant history of democracy, lawless blood feuds, a social order predicated on male machismo and patriarchy, little if any safety for returning refugees, three irreconcilable ethnic groups, no major political party that enjoys support from all three, a nickel-and-dime commerce, no independent judiciary, no success in apprehending war criminals—all this makes for a bleak future. On the other hand, the warring parties are separated, the troops have gone back to civilian life, electricity has been restored, homes have been repaired, airports have reopened, planes are flying, trains are running, gross domestic product and wages are up, a new currency is out, new auto plates have been issued, and there is freedom of movement.[3] Many of the same conditions exist in Kosovo. These are not insurmountable problems. The basics are all there.

Yet thousands of ethnic Albanian prisoners languish in Serbian prisons. A greater number have "disappeared," perhaps incarcerated somewhere, perhaps massacred. Countless families have been forced to pay bribes to Serb officials to secure the release of their loved ones. Hundreds of Serbs and Roma have been abducted by Albanian groups too, their fates unknown. The Society of Political Prisoners and international agencies such as Amnesty International and the International Committee of the Red Cross have raised the issue repeatedly with Western governments, and some pressure has been brought to bear. The Yugoslav government must be forced to release information on Albanian prisoners; and the Albanian authorities must bring pressure to bear on groups holding Serb and Roma prisoners, or at least account for their whereabouts.

The fact that guerrillas still hide in the mountains and highlands is also a threat to the peace process. Former KLA members who want to continue to drive out all the Serbs continue to operate their deadly cat-and-mouse games with the authorities and international peacekeepers alike. Threats, kidnappings, murders, arson—all the tactics of people desperate to have their country back and expel every last Serb and Roma, no matter their innocence. Old people, who form a majority of the Serbs left behind, face harassment and violent death (more on this in the pages ahead). In addition, General Agim Ceku, former chief of staff for the KLA and current head of the Kosovo Protection Force, has stated time and again that the Serbian government maintains its secret service and paramilitaries in Kosovo. Perhaps this is the case. It would certainly fit Milosevic's profile of lying. He agreed to take the troops out of Kosovo, but this is hardly the first time he broke his word. Serbians now vent their anger that they lost Kosovo. Some are just mad enough to go back and cause a disturbance.

The general chaos of the situation, where several forms of government and authority exist all at once, has led to real fears of the rise of organized crime in the region. The EU, UN, and the international community have watched crime spread quickly across Eastern Europe and the former Soviet Union in the wake of the fall of communism. Market capitalism is not spreading rapidly enough, and organized crime has quickly moved in to fill the economic vacuum. In Kosovo, the criminal element flourished under Serbian rule as the people needed the black market to procure enough essentials to survive. Before the war, it was virtually impossible to infiltrate these organizations. After the war, with the Albanians mistrusting nearly everyone, it will be impossible to curb the tide. With the economy battered and the refugees unruly, a black market flourishes on an uneven playing field and provides bare necessities and a few luxuries.

The environment is literally besmirched in the entire Balkan peninsula. Petrochemical fires from bombed factories and oil refineries sent tons of toxins into the atmosphere, notably in Pancevo and Kragujevac in Serbia. The bombing of the Pancevo Petrochemical Complex was especially troubling. Thick clouds of cancer-causing chemicals drifted over the area and downwind, containing several thousand times the level of safe exposure. The bombing of bridges and the runoff from chemicals spills from destroyed manufacturing plants have poisoned and blocked rivers, and that has caused problems not just in Yugoslavia but at points downstream. The Danube River has become virtually impassable, resulting in major problems along this main shipping route. Groundwater is slowly being polluted from chemical runoff and seepage. A number of transformer stations that were heavily damaged had contained deadly polychlorinated biphenyls, or PCBs. One litre of this substance can pollute one billion litres of water. In one attack in Belgrade, 150 tons were released into a canal with only partial cleanup achieved. Heavy metals like mercury, cadmium, chromium, copper, and zinc were released as a result of factory bombings. The use of graphite bombs caused the short-circuiting and collapse of the electricity grid across the country. Many heating plants were destroyed. As winter approaches, there will be massive felling of trees in the countryside, which will lead to the loss of forests and the attendant troubles of spring runoff and soil erosion. Some 2.5 million hectares of land have not been planted. The spectre of malnutrition and hunger looms large beyond the main cities. Cluster bombs have become no less a problem. When exploded, they burst into tiny bombs, 5 to 10 percent of which did not detonate. These clusters of clusters continue to pose a threat to both humans and animals. In late July, a UN team investigated the environmental damage done to Serbia, Montenegro, Kosovo, Macedonia, and Albania and warned of future health problems—miscarriages, birth defects, fatal nerve and liver diseases, and the like.[4]

Another major health risk stemming from a tampered environment is the use of depleted uranium bullets by the allies. Uranium 238 left over from the production of nuclear bombs was given to weapons manufacturers to create these bullets. They were designed during the 1970s—to be used against Soviet tanks; they would generate searing heat that would ignite fumes and ammo inside the tanks. These were first seen in Iraq in 1991, throwing up clouds of dust and debris that travel up to 26 miles. The fragments left behind are also particularly deadly. The resulting radioactivity would take at least 4.5 billion years (roughly the age of the solar system) to lose even half of its radioactivity. The Clinton administration refuses to say where these bullets were employed, but it is estimated that 3,000 to 4,000 were fired during the Kosovo conflict.[5] So the potential health risk for the people of Kosovo is indeed staggering, suggesting there might be birth defects and cancer for decades to come.

The return of hundreds of thousands of refugees from neighbouring countries and from within Kosovo itself has created some concerns. Many have returned to find their homes either destroyed or occupied by other returning refugees. Paramilitaries had forced people out of their homes as the Serbian forces began to withdraw. The mass exodus of Serbs and Roma into Serbia and surrounding countries wreaked havoc everywhere. Many ethnic Serbs had nowhere to go; they were turned away from the big cities or forced back into Kosovo, where they faced the fury of the embittered Muslim Albanians.

The lot of the Kosovars is truly a difficult one, but it is improving.

Because there has been so much lawlessness, there is the question of safety (providing a safe home for them); documentation (many had their papers taken by Serbian forces when they fled, and the replacement of these papers has caused delays in processing); the destruction of infrastructure, income, and social security; reconciliation (between the refugees and the remaining Serbs and Roma); information (as to the programs and options available to them); and time and distance to overcome the trauma of their experiences.[6]

The evidence of mass graves and the murders of thousands of ethnic Albanians is also a stumbling block to peace and stability in the region. The War Crimes Tribunal, under new chief prosecutor Carla Del Ponte (who replaced Louise Arbour when she took her place in the Supreme Court of Canada), has had more than it can handle investigating the thousands of bodies found in mass graves. There are hundreds of sites that still need to be dug up. Three hundred forensic experts from fourteen countries have performed the grisly task of sorting through bodies and evidence. Of course the returning refugees only wish to bury their dead. Not willing to disturb their dead, the refugees at times have made it exceedingly difficult for the investigating teams to carry on with their work. So the teams stopped working on October 31, 1999, for the winter. It was then announced that the forensic doctors were going to bring more charges against Milosevic from evidence they'd gathered.

Such is the mission that the United Nations Mission In Kosovo (UNMIK) carries. It has four main priorities: to ensure that humanitarian needs are met; to guarantee essential public functions; to establish the foundations for an economic recovery; and to lay the framework for some form of democratic self-government. A heady task. The whole enterprise is led by Bernard Kouchner, former French health minister and founder of the Médecins Sans Frontières (which won the 1999 Nobel Peace Prize for its work in war-torn countries). Along with the 700-strong OSCE Mission in Kosovo, which has identical priorities, UNMIK has been excessively slow in getting its act together. International criticism forced it to make a statement that NATO would have to restore law and order until UNMIK could stand on its own feet, with its own police force and civilian administration. Belgrade has repeatedly criticized the mission, saying that it has expanded its powers and suspended Belgrade's control over the region. Indeed, trying to raise the spirit of the Kosovars will be a Herculean task. Right now, UNMIK must focus on providing basic services.

On September 3, 1999, the UN at long last took the initiative by declaring the German mark (arguably the strongest currency on the continent) Kosovo's official currency of choice and a customs service to allow trade by money rather than barter.

To back up UNMIK, a large number of international peacekeepers have been dispatched throughout the region. Kosovo has been divided into five zones run nominally by French, Italian, British, German, and American peacekeepers. Peacekeepers of other nationalities have been divided among these sectors. The peacekeeping units were created by the NATO Military Technical Agreement of June 9, which covered the agreement between NATO and Serbia. The international deployment of NATO troops was to ensure compliance of the agreement on both sides. Because United Nations mandates have proven insufficient in the past in the former Yugoslavia, NATO was the only organization able to fulfil the mandate and the only organization with the military support platform capable of deploying soldiers at a moment's notice. NATO's rapid deployment force, consisting of members of the European military and the U.S. Marine Expeditionary Unit, were capable of deploying within 24 hours. NATO also had a far superior base of operations, which had previously been set up in Bosnia under SFOR (Stabilization Force) and in Macedonia (under a UN mandate that ended in February–March 1999). As a result KFOR, or Kosovo Force, was deployed. This force evolved from the humanitarian forces deployed in Albania and Macedonia under Operation Allied Harbor, which provided infrastructure for the refugee crisis and a platform for the rapid deployment of NATO forces in the provinces.

The most controversial peacekeepers are the Russians. The Albanians don't want them there, fearing they will support the Serbs. Russia, with strong backing by Germany, demanded permission to dispatch its own units. The West begrudgingly but wisely agreed and divided the Russian peacekeeping units between the American, German, and French sectors. Moscow later indicated it will maintain these units notwithstanding a heavy financial strain on an already mortgaged Russian economy. On August 23, Albanians in the city of Orahovac, about 30 miles southwest of Pristina, blocked Russian peacekeepers who had been sent to replace a Dutch contingent. The Kosovars were fearful the Russians would protect Serb criminals who had been involved in recent war atrocities. Orahovac was also the scene of repeated demonstrations. Although both the United States and Russia asked the Albanians to allow the peacekeepers access, the protestors erected a tent city along a barricade to keep the troops out. KLA political leader Hashim Thaci strongly supported the blockade. On October 24, two months after the barricades went up, over 4,000 Albanians gathered together and reaffirmed their resistance to a Russian presence. German and Dutch peacekeepers confirmed that they would not remove the barricades by force.

Formerly commanded by British general Mike Jackson, KFOR, as of October 8, came under the command of German general Klaus Reinhardt. Reinhardt became the first German to command a NATO mission abroad. He quickly reaffirmed KFOR's focus on rebuilding civil society in Kosovo. Despite assurances from several quarters that violence is on the wane in Kosovo, NATO resolved to bring in more troops to maintain order throughout the province.

The creation of a virtual Kosovo protectorate by the United Nations has caused much consternation in Belgrade. Although by law Kosovo is still a part of Yugoslavia, it has a separate administration and is a de facto independent state under international supervision.[7] Two past examples indicate that this is not a new occurrence in this part of the world. The 1878 Treaty of Berlin made Bosnia and Herzegovina a protectorate of the Austro-Hungarian Empire, although it remained a part of the Ottoman Empire. The Austro-Hungarians provided security, stability, and economic growth. In a more recent example, the UN Transitional Administration for Eastern Slavonia controlled civil affairs and offered protection to the Serb community as the area changed hands from Serb to Croatian administrative rule.[8] UNMIK therefore faces the problem of setting up a government and working with the administrative facilities already in place.

To that end, the United Nations sponsored the creation of a transitional government subordinate to the UN administrators of the province and set up by Sergio Vieira de Mello, the outgoing interim UN administrator. However, the main problem with the creation of this government was deciding who would sit on it. To understand this selection process, let us consider the dynamics of Kosovo's culture and its local politics.

There are more than fifteen Albanian political groups, each demanding a place in the ruling of Kosovo. The struggle for the hearts and minds, and, most important, the votes of the Albanian people can, and often does, turn nasty. Hashim Thaci, who heads the KLA's political directorate, wants independence but is willing to accept an interim protectorate. Known by his KLA associates as Commander Snake, he is known for his forceful personality. Although convicted in absentia by Yugoslav courts for terrorism, Thaci wants to be leader of the province and even helped in the creation of a provisional government with Ibrahim Rugova and Rexhep Qosja. However, the KLA is still plagued by accusations that it repeatedly assassinated prominent Albanians who opposed it.

Ibrahim Rugova, a literary critic turned politician, leads the largest party—the Democratic League of Kosovo. He founded the party in 1989. It was Rugova who set up a parallel government for the Kosovar Albanians during the years of Serbian rule in the 1990s. Rugova's pacifism kept Milosevic from attacking during the wars with Croatia and Bosnia, but it proved ineffective when Milosevic needed another scapegoat for his domestic problems and chose Kosovo. Drawing most of his support from the urban educated, Rugova was seen as too mild by the KLA. His party began to lose support as it tried to monopolize power. Rugova is himself described as "aloof," "autocratic," "narrow-minded." A seemingly mild-mannered man, his belief in nonviolence may have sprung from the deaths of his father and grandfather. They were headstrong men whom Tito had liquidated just days after Rugova was born, an event that came on the heels of an uprising in 1945. Rugova's prime minister (in exile, in Bonn), Bujai Bukoshi, broke with Rugova in 1995. Both he and Rugova kept a low profile during the war.

A third major player on the Albanian scene in Rexhep Qosja, a man of letters who leads the United Democratic Movement that was founded in 1998 as a coalition of seven parties (Albanian Democratic Movement, Parliamentary Party of Kosovo, Albanian Unification Party, Albanian Liberal Party, Albanian National Party, Greens, and Albanian Republican Party).

Other parties in the unofficially elected parliament of 1998 include: Albanian Christian Democratic Party of Kosovo, Social Democratic Party, Liberal Party, People's Movement of Kosovo, Democratic Union Party, and the National Movement for the Liberation of Kosovo.

Each of these parties has a stake in Kosovo's future. The Transitional Council includes two members of the political successor to the KLA (Thaci and Xhavit Haliti), two members of the Democratic League of Kosovo (including Rugova), two United Democratic Movement members (Rexhep Qosja and Mehmet Hajrizi), two independents (Veton Surroi and Blerim Shala), two Serbs (Bishop Artemije Radosavljevic of Raska-Prizren, who is the head of the Serbian Orthodox Church in Kosovo, and Momcilo Trajkovic of the Serbian Resistance Movement, a former governor of Kosovo), and two other minorities (Numan Balic of the Bosnian group Democratic Action, and Sezair Shaipi of the Turkish Peoples' Party). Rivalries between Thaci and Rugova have accounted for the fractiousness of the nationalist movement. Essentially, Thaci wants to be the ruler of Kosovo himself. Rugova received a boost to his candidacy for leadership when Albanian premier Pandeli Majko visited Kosovo in the summer of 1999 and recognized Rugova as president. Nevertheless, Rugova declined to attend the first meeting of the Council. The reason was simple: he felt that his party was underrepresented. The second session was postponed to allow the Serbs sufficient time to grieve the Gracko massacre of fourteen Serbs. Thaci then skipped a meeting on August 21. The Council finally met on September 1 to form a commission to assist in efforts to enhance security throughout the region.

The major obstacle to an enduring peace in Kosovo is the increasing violence against Serbs and other minorities by the Kosovar Albanians. When the war ended, many Serbs left Kosovo for fear of reprisals. It is ironic that those who were involved in the wartime atrocities probably left with the Serb army. This means that the Serbs who remained were innocent. Those who did leave did not lose their valuables or have their property deeds seized, as did the Kosovar Albanians. Uprooted, they were left to fare for themselves, having suffered the same indignities as the Albanians, though not on the same scale, and not nearly risking their lives to the same degree. Nonetheless they were forced to deal with murders, kidnappings, forced expulsions, burnings, looting, harassment, and intimidation—daily and weekly.[9] Nor were they welcomed with open arms by their kinsmen in Serbia, who saw the refugees as a further drain on their already overstretched resources. In fact, Milosevic started sending the Serb refugees back to Kosovo. Those who refused to return were labelled traitors; those who did were conveniently offered fuel, food, and medicine. He even blocked aid to them as refugees so they might feel more compelled to go home. The KLA, on the other hand, denied any responsibility for these expulsions and intimidations—though it seems unlikely the KLA was uninvolved. KFOR and UNMIK were faced with this incongruous situation. In due course, UNMIK, UNHCR, and OSCE jointly set up an Ad Hoc Task Force on Minorities to coordinate protection efforts. The new secretary general of NATO, George Robertson, restated that the goal of NATO and the UN is to create a multiethnic Kosovo.[10]

At the time of this writing, 25 percent of Kosovo's Serbs have fled. The United Nations has asked for more international help to protect civilians. Back in July 1999, fourteen Serbs were shot to death in the fields of Gracko while trying to bring in the harvest. They had asked for peacekeeping protection, giving ample warning that violence could happen, yet their voices had gone unheeded. The KLA denied any involvement. Bishop Artemije, however, stated time and again that Thaci encouraged these reprisals of terror. The incident prompted an angry Kouchner to say, "The world did not intervene to make Kosovo safe for revenge and intolerance." Two days later, Belgrade demanded a meeting of the UN Security Council to examine ways to stop the ethnic violence and demanded that Yugoslav forces be allowed back in to protect Serbian cultural sites. This last demand was quickly turned down. In consequence, in only six weeks after the air war, seventy Serbs and over seventy Albanians had been killed in similar revenge attacks. By the end of August, it was estimated that nearly all the Serbs in the province had left along with the other minorities. But U.S. general Wesley Clark, NATO's military commander, downplayed these incidents by saying that Serb refugees were beginning to return to their homes, while Milosevic kept insisting that the Yugoslav army be returned to Kosovo. Meanwhile, the Kosovo Serbs held rallies for three days and organized a march on Belgrade to protest the government's indifference to their predicament. It was not until late October that the United Nations set up a bus service, offering a safe passage to those who wished to leave the province. The UN also opened up to all victims of the war a rehabilitation centre replete with medical and psychological support staff. Presently a Housing and Property Claims Tribunal is dealing with the thousands of property disputes that have arisen. German lawyer Leopold von Carlowitz was put in charge to organize the Tribunal.

Only elderly Serbs remain in Pristina today. The are generally housebound, frightened to leave lest they be attacked. And indeed they are harassed and threatened if they so much as step outside their door. One helpless old woman was strangled in her own bathtub. The U.S.-based Adventist Development and Relief Agency delivers food to twenty-five Serbian homes a day.[11] In late October, false lists of Serbian war criminals were posted by the banned KLA and members of the Kosovo Protection Force. On October 27, a NATO-led convoy of Serbs from Orahovac leaving Kosovo for Montenegro was attacked by Albanians after Serbs began showing the three-finger salute, symbolizing Serb nationalism. German and Dutch peacekeepers were forced to fight off the crowd and then take refuge in a nearby peacekeeper station. Fifteen people were injured, and fifteen vehicles were burned.

The Roma were for the most part unfairly stigmatized along with the Serbs. They were perceived as collaborators by the Albanians and were likewise driven out. Ironically, before the war the Serbs persecuted these Gypsies for sympathizing with the Albanians. The Gypsies traditionally have been persecuted throughout the ages, yet Yugoslavia is home to the largest Roma population in Europe. However, their treatment by the Albanians is only one example of the intolerance they face in modern Europe. More than one hundred Roma actually drowned trying to flee Kosovo in a ship on the Adriatic Sea. Many Roma now live in refugee camps. The Jews (we shall return to the subject of Jews and anti-Semitism in the concluding remarks), who helped the Albanians, are also being driven out, for they are either mistaken as Serbs or presumed to be collaborators. Thaci at least wanted to appear conciliatory to the West and ordered the KLA to protect Jewish residents of Kosovo.

The Gorani are a group (about 12,000) of Albanian-speaking Muslim Slavs who the KLA thought provided the secret service information on the army. They have endured their share of discrimination. The Roman Catholic Albanians (about 10% of the population) were likewise not closely associated with the KLA, and they have suffered for it. It may be naive to believe that Islamic fundamentalism lies at the heart of the Kosovo-Albanian movement. But to believe it to be untrue because the Kosovo Albanians are both Muslim and Christian is equally naive. The Albanian Muslims are first and foremost Muslim, and their ties are bound up with an Islamic movement abroad, even though that movement need not be identified with the radical and fundamentalist kind.

Among the "guilty" who are being harassed are Albanian collaborators who worked with the Serbian police and paramilitaries. Most of them left with the army; those who are caught are executed by the KLA even though that is forbidden by the Geneva Convention. Worse, those who are even suspected of being collaborators are also harassed. In isolated cases they are killed. This is a type of frontier justice, to be sure.

Some Western European countries have rejected asylum applications from Serbs and Roma, exacerbating the situation further. Italy, for example, closed its borders to refugees, especially the Roma, in view of the number of Gypsies already in Italy. The United States, on the other hand, agreed to take in 4,000 Serbs.

Many Albanians saw this behavior as fair and legitimate. The Serbs and collaborators were getting what they deserved, the Albanians maintained. As already argued in previous chapters, in their world the value of the vendetta is still regarded as appropriate. Where there is no law and no authority, a family will often take the law into its own hands. As in the United States, many of the bomb-throwing Albanians are children who are recruited so they won't be harshly sentenced if and when they are caught. Even children feel the hatred of their elders toward their "enemies."

Consider the following graphic illustration of mutual hatred: Valentin Krumov was a Bulgarian UN worker on his first day on the job in Kosovo. Krumov was walking the streets of Pristina when someone asked him the time of day in Serbian. He replied in that language and was immediately swarmed by a group of young men who beat and then shot him, leaving him to die on Mother Teresa Street. The young man had been oblivious to the fact that Slavic aid workers, like Bulgarians and Poles, never dared to speak their own language lest they be mistaken for Serbs.[12]

Albanians were not the only ones taking part in attacks. Serbs also engaged in revenge killings and kidnappings to protest their treatment by the Albanians. Peacekeeping forces often had to step in to halt retaliatory strikes and did their best to stop the fighting. But the feuds continued unabated. This never-ending cycle kept repeating itself.

A symbol of the continued ethnic hatred has been the city of Mitrovica. French peacekeepers have kept the city divided, much like the city of Berlin at the height of the Cold War. Albanians live in the south and Serbs in the north, divided by a bridge manned on a full-time basis by peacekeepers. In early August 1999, fully 1,000 Albanians clashed with KFOR soldiers trying to gain access to the Serbian part of town. Since then, clashes and riots have become commonplace. At night, each side plays loud patriotic songs trying to drown out the other. So far, more than one hundred people have been hurt in fights with the peacekeepers.

Soon after the end of the war, the KLA was urged to disband and turn in its weapons. The Western allies wisely agreed that the existence of the KLA would only inflame the hatred of the Serbian population, who regard them as terrorists. Under an agreement with NATO, the members of the army cannot wear uniforms, show insignia, or carry weapons. The United States warned repeatedly that the liberation army would lose Western support if its members failed to disband and turn in their weapons. Several deadlines were not honored, but eventually the KLA did hand in over 10,000 weapons by late September. In early September, however, hundreds of weapons were found hidden in a village near the Albanian border. Caches of weapons probably exist all over Kosovo. But the fact that weapons were turned in was a symbolic gesture and made a significant impact on Western public opinion.

The new political wing of the KLA, the Party for Democratic Progress of Kosovo, has taken over as a provisional government. However, the population has become disenchanted with the movement. The average Kosovar is generally fed up with all the violence that is singularly attributed to this army. Recent surveys have shown that Thaci would be defeated by a margin of at least four to one in an election against Rugova.[13] The party has also been accused of intimidating and assassinating political opponents and running roughshod over local politicians and institutions. These complaints come not only from the other Albanian parties but from Western diplomats and members of the KLA. Members are accused of taking over the best apartments and houses and driving fancy cars. The chief problem with the new provisional government is one of legitimacy, given the fact that no one was elected. Inclusivity of all political parties and minorities (and therefore accountability to them) is the other major problem. Besides, the majority of such terrorists have no proven diplomatic skills or even a modicum of political experience.[14]

Another aspect of the dissolution of the KLA was the creation of the Kosovo Protection Corps. Thaci had vowed that after the war the KLA would split into a police constabulary, a civil administration, a defence force, and a political party. NATO and the army originally agreed on a 3,000-member corps that would be permitted to bear arms and would include a helicopter unit, an honour guard, bodyguards, and a small "quick reaction" unit. Kosovar Albanians saw this as a first step to building a Kosovo army that would prevent Yugoslavia from reinvading. On June 27, the KLA agreed to disarm and demobilize in exchange for setting up a national guard–like outfit to help with reconstruction. Although Russia opposed all but the complete dismantling of the army, Western governments agreed to the solution. The head of the new corps is Agim Ceku, the former head of the KLA military. Most of the 3,000 active and 2,000 reserve members are former KLA, with 10 percent allotted to the Serbs and other minorities. Serbs and Albanians were both to be trained to handle civil security crises. On September 22, Madeleine Albright defended the conversion of the KLA into the Protection Corps as consistent with developing a civil society in Kosovo. The United

States, Britain, France, Germany, and Italy approved of the plan. In October, a 16-man team consisting of 10 Albanians, 3 Serbs, 2 Bosnians, and a Kosovo Turk were sent to France for a 31-and-a-half-week training course by French Civil Securities. Final training will be undertaken by the Organization for Security and Cooperation in Europe, which plans to have each officer accompanied by two UN personnel. The first graduating class of 173 will include 8 Serbs, 3 Bosnians, 3 Romas, 3 Turks, and 39 women. Eventually the OSCE will train 6,500 police officers over two years. In addition to the Protection Corps, the UN is training a police force consisting mostly of Albanians.

The Kosovar Serbs have repeatedly said that they will never accept an independent Kosovo, threatening instead to create their own defence force and to resign from the Transitional Council. In late August 1999, fearing violence by the Albanians, the Serbs urged the UN to create five safe havens in Kosovo to last for five years. The Albanians were adamantly averse to this, arguing that it was the first step toward partitioning the province. Moderate Serbs began boycotting the Council from the moment the KLA was transformed into the Protection Force and have appealed to Belgrade for leadership. On October 18, after a meeting in Gracanica, moderate Serbs declared that they would impose self-rule in areas where the Serbs predominate. Six days later they set up a new political organization and dropped plans for a Serb Protection Force. Bishop Artemije is the head of the new council; the secular head is Momcilo Trajkovic, whose mandate is to protect the Serbs and help refugees resettle in Kosovo according to UN resolutions.

What are the alternatives for the future of Kosovo? With so much division, it seems as if nothing can be done. Simply put, the Albanians refuse to be a part of Serbia in view of all that has taken place. Kosovar Albanians could become an international protectorate with republican status equal to Serbia and Montenegro, but that means staying with Serbia. Or Kosovo could be partitioned, but that would vindicate the ethnic cleansing undertaken by the Serbs, and each side would vie for the most productive lands. An interim international protectorate is what the Kosovars have now, and it seems to be the best alternative in the face of so much ethnic hatred.[15] Like Germany and Japan after World War II, the West could very well occupy Serbia and compel this state to adopt democratic institutions and enforce liberal democracy.[16] This, however, is somewhat far-fetched; it would be expensive and cost allied lives, leading to a confrontation with Russia. Exchanging populations (like the Greeks and Turks did in 1923, as Pakistan and India did in 1947) or occupying Kosovo and expelling all Serbs would likewise reward ethnic cleansing—hardly a realistic proposition.[17] The Serbs have suggested dividing up Kosovo on ethnic lines to protect themselves. But the West has rejected this out of hand. On October 13, Kofi Annan made it clear that the UN would not endorse an independent, but rather a multiethnic, Kosovo.

Still, nothing short of complete independence is what most Kosovar Albanians are seeking. The United States has come around in support of independence. The Europeans and Russians are skeptical, believing it could trigger a war in Macedonia or Bosnia. On September 23, NATO secretary general Javier Solana stated that for the sake of political stability in the Balkans, Kosovo must settle for less than independence. The Kosovar Albanians might accept this, but eventually they will want full independence, especially if Milosevic stays in power. Independence is also supported by a large Albanian diaspora (600,000 in Europe and 300,000 in the United States and Canada). If they bring their considerable numbers (and influence, if any) to bear in the West, "independence" might become an option again.

The West has approved a new Marshall Plan for Eastern Europe.[18] On May 10, 28 foreign ministers and 17 international organizations approved a recovery program called the South Eastern European Development Initiative. On June 10, the Stability Pact called for cooperation among the EU, United States, Russia, Japan, the Balkans, Turkey, and other countries; regional and international organizations; and financial institutions. At the Sarajevo Summit in July, $2 billion in aid was announced, but it was stipulated that Serbia will receive no international aid as long as Milosevic remains in power. A European Reconstruction agency headquarters was set up in Thessaloniki, Greece, with an operational centre in Pristina. On July 28, the leaders of Albania, Bosnia, Bulgaria, Croatia, Macedonia, Hungary, Romania, and Slovenia met to discuss mutually beneficial projects. On July 29, the Stability Pact met in Sarajevo. Forty leaders from the Pact and most Balkan countries discussed the German-inspired Pact for Southeastern Europe signed in June, which pledges the governments there to promoting Western-style reforms and living peacefully with neighbors, sets up permanent panels to settle border conflicts, and promotes minority rights and economic cooperation. In Kosovo, the EU and World Bank will bear the main responsibility for reconstruction.

Many international companies see the opportunities for contracts as a commercial boom. Soon after the war ended, many companies sent representatives to study possible areas of reconstruction. By rebuilding factories, these corporations could ultimately control vast amounts of Kosovo's future earning potential, leading to a type of economic colonialism.[19] It could also mean jobs for millions of Europe's unemployed.

But what of Serbia, the present international pariah, and what of its leader?

SERBIA: UNDER MILOSEVIC'S THUMB

Before NATO's bombs fell, most of Serbia's factories had been idle for as long as ten years; 400,000 people were out of work, a brain drain had taken the best minds to Western Europe, and Milosevic had sold off most of the national resources to his cronies. Since the war, the infrastructure is in ruins (including heating stations, power plants, and water sewage treatment facilities), another million people are unemployed, the average income is $48 per month, there is increased inflation, and Serb and Roma refugees clog the country.[20] The war cost Serbia over $95 billion, making it the poorest country in Europe.

A sense of naiveté is peculiar to Serbian ways. The Serb has a sense of drama, of unrequited grief and sorrow; there is unrelenting pathos in the Serb psyche. One writer described it thus: "The sweep of Serb national history from the Middle Ages until the present day broadly encompasses a long, seemingly cyclical tale of freedom, betrayal, enslavement or exile, patient servitude, and, finally, a struggle of liberation. In the end, so their chroniclers and poets teach, only unity among Serbs can prevail over the outsider."[21] The outsider role can be played by anyone. Currently it is an Albanian Muslim, but it could easily be a Westerner, a German, for example. The Serb has a very fine sense of victimization, pervasive to a fault. The poignancy evoked by the word *outsider* relative to the native Serb seems quite apropos, similar to *ausländer* in German folklore. For *outsider* denotes not only an outlander (a stranger, a foreigner) but an alien, something akin to a barbarian. When Serbian children returned to school in September 1999, they were subjected to periodic lectures on NATO's aggression. This came in the form of letters from education Minister Jovo Todorovic, who told them that many of the best students in Serbia had been slaughtered in the bombing. No mention was made of the Kosovar Albanians; nothing was said about what they had suffered. The Serbian schoolchildren were told nothing about Kosovo or Belgrade's role in events there. The public was only told that Serbia was stopping Albanian terrorists, that the Albanians hated all Serbs, and that these "outlanders" were being helped by international "barbarians" bent on destroying mother Serbia.

Tough times lie ahead now. Most Serbs turn to the black market for food. Pensions and wages have not kept up with the cost of living. Nostalgia for socialism, for Tito, is returning. Even the army has been protesting about its pay in arrears. In the first winter after the war, shortages in heat and electricity became commonplace. Food shortages were on the rise. The value of the dinar had fallen. A sweeping malaise like this can spill over. But why do the Serbs not rise to topple their government? Part of the explanation is that of civic duty. Like their Slavic cousins, the Russians, Serbs essentially fear chaos, so they will put up with a lot from their leaders. To the average Serb, government is something to be feared; it is a necessary evil, arbitrary and severe.[22]

Cleavages are slowly widening and threatening to tear the country apart. Rural residents are angry at the loss of Kosovo, and urban residents are glad the bombing has stopped. Soldiers are angry with the elite for whom they believe Milosevic sold them out. As for the city dwellers, they have had their fill of so much war.[23]

However, the conditions in Serbia may lead to future problems. Between World War I and World War II, Germany experienced social agitation by radicals, mass unemployment, inflation, and humiliating peace treaties. The rise of Hitler was directly a result of these conditions. When he became powerful, he was appeased by the French and British, leading to the Munich Pact of 1938 that sacrificed most of Czechoslovakia to Germany. In Serbia, the same conditions exist. Milosevic was appeased by the Western governments before the war. Now the economy is poor, and sanctions have crippled foreign trade. If the West is not cautious, Milosevic could one day convince the people of Serbia to rise again and drag the entire Balkans into an unstable future. Montenegrin president Milo Djukanovic probably stated it best when he said that Milosevic "has elevated to absolute perfection the means of governing by manufacturing crises."[24] All his rhetoric has put the opposition parties on the defensive, and NATO's inability to stop attacks on ethnic Serbs in Kosovo has given him a powerful weapon at home.

Many people have compared Milosevic to Nicolai Ceausescu, the former dictator of Romania. Both ruled with an iron hand. Both were willing to cling to their wives' apron strings. Both were slaves to a personality cult. Both discriminated against ethnic minorities (in Romania the discrimination was very pronounced against the Hungarian and Jewish minorities). Both repressed their opposition and refused to carry out crucial political and economic reforms. Both engaged in nepotism, lining their own pockets with the nation's riches. In Milosevic's case, his son Marko runs the town of Pozarevac like a private fiefdom, manages Yugoslavia's largest nightclub and restaurant, and controls a monopoly on the importation of cigarettes and alcohol through duty-free shops. Rumour has it that he safeguards the family endowment in South Africa and launders money through Cyprus, Israel, and Greece. Milosevic's daughter Marija is a staunch supporter of her father's party, which is reflected in the news broadcasts aired by the radio station she owns.[25]

Milosevic and his wife may one day share the fate of the Ceausescus. In December 1989, the Romanian army and security police killed hundreds of protestors. Eventually the army turned against the secret police. The Ceausescus, Nicolai and his wife, Elena, were caught trying to leave the country, much in the same way as King Louis XVI and Marie Antoinette tried to flee during the French Revolution. Like their royal counterparts, the Ceausescus were given a show trial and then executed on December 25, 1989. In Serbia, the shortages of food and heat in the winter could also lead to a mass uprising, exactly what Milosevic doesn't want. Although he's lost the support of the church, the old Communists, the purged leaders of the Socialist Party, and Serb refugees, he still endures and resumes his repression of dissidents in Serbia.

If he did leave the country, he would have very few options. The recent extradition trial in London for General Augusto Pinochet, the former Chilean dictator, shows that the world will no longer protect dictators. China may be a possibility. It is rumoured that a good portion of the Milosevic family fortune has been relocated there. But the resulting problems with the United States may not be worth the trouble for Beijing. Milosevic is also close to Belarus leader Alexander Lukashenko, and may try to seek asylum there.

Despite all this, the resolution of conflict in Kosovo is a prerequisite for democratic change in Serbia, and only Milosevic has the authority to negotiate an agreement. There is no one else strong enough to do it. Much like his participation in the signing of the Dayton Accord to end the Bosnian war, Milosevic is the only credible negotiator. Only he can rally the people behind a resolution through his strict control of the media. Only he can force through the constitutional amendments needed.[26] If the West is, figuratively speaking, forced to go to bed with Milosevic, it would lose credibility overnight—but everything becomes an option in politics if the opposition can't get itself elected. Opposition forces within Serbia continue to fight for his ouster. They have organized mass rallies and demonstrations demanding his resignation. But political infighting and the need to distance themselves from Milosevic's accusations that they are merely tools of the Western allies have divided them. Most of the Serbian public are too concerned with everyday life and their own survival to support opposition parties that they feel are too busy fighting each other to fight Milosevic.

But before we discuss the opposition tactics, we should first examine the political parties of Serbia. The main political party in the country is the Socialist Party run by Milosevic. It was formerly the Communist Party and has changed very little since the fall of communism. Regular purges of the ranks ensure that the party is completely loyal to Milosevic. A closely allied party is the Yugoslav United Left, a coalition of twenty-three left-oriented parties run by Mirjana Markovic, Milosevic's wife. This party is more hard-line left than the Socialists. The League of Communists–Movement for Yugoslavia is also a left-leaning organization. An extreme right-wing party that is allied with the Socialist Party is the Serbian Radical Party, led by Vojislav Seselj, the former "ethnic cleanser" and second most popular politician in Serbia. His party rose from the Chetnik movement and the paramilitaries who slaughtered innocents in

Bosnia and Croatia. It has a nationalist and xenophobic platform that seeks the creation of a Greater Serbia and the expulsion of 300,000 "illegal" Albanian immigrants from Kosovo. The party generally appeals to the least educated and the lowest paid segments of society, but its insistence on restoring law and order and fighting corruption has brought it support from the army and police.[27] Seselj has accused the democratic opposition, independent media, and human rights workers of being traitors.[28] Milosevic let Seselj and his party into the government in order to show the West that he is the lesser of two evils and that if the West demands elections, the alternative is worse than he is. Milosevic can then say that he is a moderate holding back the ultranationalist.

Another strong party in the parliament is the Serbian Renewal Movement led by Vuk Draskovic. A former deputy prime minister (along with Seselj), Draskovic and Seselj were kept at each other's throats by Milosevic and played off of each other. Draskovic is a major opposition member, but he has lost much of his credibility in switching his allegiance back and forth between the government and the opposition. He is a well-known journalist and novelist (he is the spitting image of the rakish Rasputin), the one-time owner of the only independent television station. A former dissident who endured torture at the hands of the Serbian police, he turned on his liberal associates and joined the government as an informer. (These Judas qualities are also strangely in line with Russia's Rasputin.) He helped set up the paramilitaries during the Croatian and Bosnian wars and has declared that NATO wants a Greater Albania. An opportunist just like Milosevic, he has kept his cards to himself. While supporting the opposition, he has also declared that there is no alliance of the opposition. When the main opposition coalition, the Alliance for Change, demanded that Milosevic step down and be handed over to the War Crimes Tribunal, Draskovic suggested that Milosevic become a figurehead ruler until elections were called and that he (Milosevic) be given immunity to ensure his cooperation. Draskovic has also stated that any transitional government must include both supporters and opponents of Milosevic.

On a rainy day in the fall of 1999, a truck ran into Draskovic's car, killing his brother-in-law and two bodyguards. He, miraculously, emerged unscathed. An attempt on his life? (What, Rasputin again?) Who sent in the assassins? Milosevic decidedly needs a Draskovic charisma around him. Like a loose cannon Draskovic threatens the opposition's chances for success. And singlehandedly he could undermine the movement for democratic change.[29]

There are over 180 political parties in Serbia, but only a few can be discussed here. The opposition includes not only political parties but the multiethnic trade union UGS Nezavisnost, student unions, and the church. To stop opposition at the university level, Milosevic politicized

all universities in 1998, making all academic posts political. The largest
and most active opposition coalition is the Alliance for Change. The
Democratic Party is led by Zoran Djindjic, a former mayor of Belgrade
who once supported Radovan Karadzic, the former leader of the Bosnian
Serbs who is now sought for war crimes. The party is nationalist but still
wants democratic government and a market economy. It has denounced
both the KLA and Milosevic. The Civic Alliance of Serbia is anti-war and
liberal, and it seeks to defend minorities. The Social Democracy Party
led by retired general Vuk Obradovic calls for justice for the atrocities
committed in Kosovo. The G-17 is a group of economists led by Mladjan
Dinkic who call for major economic reforms and the replacement of Milosevic with a caretaker government. The Yugoslav Action Group is made
up of sixty nongovernmental organizations that oppose Serbian nationalism and ethnic cleansing. New Democracy is an alliance of grass roots
organizations. Former general Momcilo Perisic formed the Movement for
Democratic Serbia to demand Milosevic's ouster and democratic change.
Other lesser-known parties include: the Christian Democratic Party of
Serbia, the Social Democratic Union, the Democratic Party of Serbia, the
Democratic Alternatives Party, the Progressive Party, and the Congressional (Christian) National Party.

In 1996, three of the main political parties—the Serbian Renewal
Movement, the Democratic Party, and the Citizen's Alliance—formed a
coalition called the Zajedno and won the elections. When Milosevic an-
nulled the election results, the coalition eventually fell apart after the
Democratic Party and Citizen's Alliance boycotted the new elections. Recently, many of the opposition groups have joined together in the Alliance for Change umbrella group. The frontrunner to lead the group is
Dragoslav Avramovic, an aging former World Bank economist. Members
of the group have led countless rallies against Milosevic but have so far
failed to cause a major uprising despite a long summer of protests. In
late October, the Alliance for Change met in Budapest to discuss options
and elections. They also met with U.S. officials, urging them to drop
economic sanctions against Serbia. They claim major support among the
Serbian people and have stated that poll results show 80 percent of the
people wanting a change. The group also agreed to expand their movement to include other parties, including the Serbian Renewal Movement.

Although many in Serbia do want a change, it's not clear that they
necessarily support the opposition groups. Many Serbs feel that they
won't unite and that internal rivalries, egos, and compromises with the
government have weakened their appeal. Many Serbs blame all leaders
for their problems, not just Milosevic. Many fear the demonstrations will
lead to civil war. However, the Kosovo Serbs have turned against Milosevic and strongly support the opposition. Momcilo Trajkovic, the
leader of Kosovo's Serbian Resistance Movement, has even stated that

Milosevic must leave if Kosovo is to remain multiethnic and part of Serbia. The opposition is basically rudderless in a sea of social upheaval and finds it hard to agree on most issues. There is little access to the media, and Milosevic has done his best to convince his people that the opposition is working with the United States to take Kosovo from them. Still, there is no gainsaying that the opposition has organized a series of well-attended rallies for change.

On June 29 a massive rally by 10,000 Serbs occurred in Cacak. In mid-July, a 5,000-strong crowd gathered in Subotica to demand Milosevic's resignation. On July 22, 100 army reservists demonstrated demanding back pay. On August 2, 6,000 protested south of Belgrade. After moves against the opposition were undertaken by the government on August 17, 25,000 protested in Nis the next day. On August 19, 150,000 demonstrated in a massive opposition rally in Belgrade attended by many of the opposition members and clergy. The government had tried to defuse the demonstration by promising early elections, but that promise didn't keep the crowds away. Several town councils have also demanded that Milosevic step down, including Becej and Belgrade. The Serbian Orthodox Church has even spoken out against Milosevic. Bishop Artemije and others have repeatedly demanded he leave office. Yugoslav generals have warned that the army will quash politically inspired violence. Still, the rallies have continued. NATO ought to become involved as well, although NATO support should not be so overt as to give Milosevic political ammunition. Pressuring banks and large companies not to support Milosevic's government; pressuring oil and gas suppliers to be paid in cash, not IOUs, from the government; giving the army a show of support if the government resolves the situation in Kosovo; offering financial aid to help the Serbs build democratic institutions—surely these would be steps in the right direction.[30]

It's possible Milosevic could turn his attention to the Sandzak, an area of land that straddles Serbia and Montenegro and is 54 percent Muslim (with the rest of the population being made up of Serbs, Montenegrins, Croats, Jews, Gypsies, Hungarians, and Albanians). The Muslims are ethnically Slavic, but that would probably not stop Milosevic. Serbia denies that the Muslims are an ethnic minority but claims that they are Slavs pure and simple. In the past, coercion and discrimination have marked Serbian relations with the region and Belgrade has done nothing to stop it. During the Croation and Bosnian wars when ethnic cleansing took place in the Sandzak, over 17,000 people left the area. The area has no general interest in secession, although Milosevic has accused Muslim National Council founder and head of the Party for Democratic Action, Sulejman Ugljanin, of agitating for separation. That may just be enough to turn the Serbians against the Muslims of the Sandzak.

Another potential target is Vojvodina. Like Kosovo, Vojvodina is a province of Serbia where Serbs make up 54.4 percent of the population, Hungarians 19 percent, Croats 5.4 percent, and the rest of the population consists mainly of Slovaks, Romanians, and Ruthenian/Ukrainians. A mosaic of cultures exists on the former southern border of the Austro-Hungarian Empire because in the 1800s the Hapsburgs wanted to settle different national groups there to create a bulwark against the Ottomans. Large numbers of Serbs migrated there to escape Ottoman domination. The Treaty of Trianon of June 4, 1920 (which split up the remains of the Austro-Hungarian Empire), gave Vojvodina (Vajdasag, in Hungarian) to Yugoslavia. During World War II, Hungarian troops invaded and recaptured it, causing the deaths of several thousand Serbs. After the war, the Serbs killed about 40,000 ethnic Hungarians in retaliation. Since then, the Hungarians have been careful not to provoke the Serbs. Between 1946 and 1989 Vojvodina was an autonomous province, until Serbia decided to change that arrangement. After the fall of communism, several political parties were formed in the early 1990s, including the Democratic Community of Vojvodina and the Vadusag Hungarian Democratic Community. In July 1991, Belgrade began to make a number of discriminatory dictates for the province. Serbian was declared the sole official language, and the electoral boundaries were changed so that fewer Hungarians were elected. Later that summer the Serb authorities created the Association of Hungarians for the Homeland of Serbia and Yugoslavia, saying that the Democratic Community Party didn't represent the Hungarian population and was trying to create rifts with the Serbs because they wanted minority self-government. The Democratic Community has the support of the far-right Hungarian Justice and Life Party, which wants one-third of Vojvodina returned to Hungary. Since 1991, 40,000 ethnic Hungarians have fled for their lives. During hostilities in Kosovo, Vojvodina's Magyar-speakers who sought sanctuary in Hungary said they were subjected to brutality and harassment by Serb policemen. However, these Magyars are generally dreaded and rejected in Hungary for having been raised and reared in Serbia. On August 20, the Democratic Union of Vojvodina's Hungarians, the Alliance of Vojvodina Hungarians, and the Vojvodina and Hungarian Civic Movement came together to form the National Council of Vojvodina's Hungarians. To be a Vojvodina Hungarian is like being in a no-win situation, far worse than being an East German who comes to West Germany. It is more like being a Sicilian or a Calabrian who goes to live in Siena or Torino in northern Italy.

Would Milosevic turn against the ethnic Hungarians? His recent statements seem to suggest an inclination to blame the leader of the League of Social Democrats of Vojvodina, Nenad Canak, for fomenting separatism. If he moves against Vojvodina he runs the risk of involving Hungary, the neighbour to the north. Hungary is now a member of NATO; if it is attacked NATO must retaliate, hence the risk of further bombing.

MONTENEGRO

What about turning on Montenegro? We discussed this mountainous land and its recalcitrant leader, Djukanovic, in the previous chapter. Montenegro is Serbia's strange and lonely partner in the federation of Yugoslavia. Formed in 1482, it is a small country (population: approximately 680,000) with a tradition of warrior princes and clan life. It reminds one of Corsica, a land half-tied to France whose glorious sons produced a Napoleon Bonaparte, France's greatest emperor and lawgiver. For centuries Montenegro was ruled by a series of *vladikas*, that is, princes who were also bishops in the Orthodox Church. It was never completely conquered by the Ottomans, and this has been a point of pride for the Montenegrins. The last struggle of the Ottomans during World War I caused the king to flee to France (in a surprising move, Milosevic allowed the remains of this last king, Nicholas I, and his wife, Milena, to be returned in 1989). Montenegro was independent between 1910 and 1918 until it became part of the Kingdom of the Serbs, Croats, and Slovenes in 1918. The independent Montenegrin Orthodox Church was absorbed into the Serbian church in 1918 (but was revived in 1993). The nationwide multiparty system in Yugoslavia grew out of the Montenegrin uprising of 1989 in which mass demonstrations unseated the entire communist leadership and replaced it with communist reformers and their sycophants. The Montenegrins and the Serbs share many close political and cultural ties including their faith, alphabet, and language. In fact, to the ire of many Montenegrins, many of them claim that they are in fact Serbs. This may be likened to the situation of east-bank Ukrainians (east of the Dnieper River) whose orthodoxy and history and culture have more affinity with the Russians. And many Ukrainians wish to return to the fold with Russia.

There are thus many within Montenegro who gravitate toward Serbia and hope to remain in the federation. The south supports Djukanovic; the north follows Milosevic. In the 1992 referendum, most Montenegrins voted to remain in Serbia. So, in their name, Serbia now seeks to check any bid for independence. The Yugoslav army is stationed in Montenegro but makes no move to take over. And what is there for anyone to take over—the presidential palace? During the war in Kosovo, Yugoslav forces engaged in limited ethnic cleansing of Albanians in northern Montenegro. In July 1999, Milosevic sent an additional 30,000 troops to Montenegro. In response, Djukanovic beefed up his police force as a counterweight to the garrisoned army. But policemen in an unstable Balkan setting are bought and sold like wares at an Oriental souk. Furthermore, Milosevic once adored and now utterly despises Djukanovic and is likely to want him out of office. On May 23, he fired Adoje Kontic, a Montenegrin prime minister, and replaced him with Momir Bulatovic, who loaths Djukanovic no less and is close to Milosevic. When Djukanovic defeated Bulatovic in the election for the leadership of Montenegro, Bulatovic roused his supporters and marched on Djukanovic's offices—and then, like a thief in the night, he managed to slip away before his crowd ran into the police.

Despite what Milosevic and other Serb leaders have said, Djukanovic doesn't necessarily have his sights on independence. He seems to support the territorial integrity of the federation, but only if democratization and liberalization are undertaken by the Belgrade regime. That is what he says. He curries favour with Washington, vaunts his prowess as a basketball player, and speaks loudly about democracy. In truth, he has ties to Montenegro's underworld and siphons off huge sums for himself to Zurich and Geneva from foreign assistance programs. He looks and sounds good to the West through this image and the public relations behind it. But he is as hollow and as knavish as the entourage of Milosevic in Belgrade. Montenegro is a highland basket case, its tourist and commercial ventures dead or dying in the wake of the war. The country's elected leadership may in all likelihood be duty-bound to mouth the usual liberal-sounding shibboleths. Those who support independence are few and far between, paying lip service to Westerners who need to hear it. They belong to a porous movement: the small Liberal Alliance of Montenegro.

On August 5, 1999, Montenegro approved a plan to dismantle the Yugoslav federation and make it a loose association of sovereign states. It has called for Yugoslavia to be renamed as well. In late October 1999, it took further steps to introduce the *deutschemark* as the republic's second currency, a prelude to introducing its own currency. But the economy of this region is such that the German currency would automatically be regarded as a second currency (it is a unit of account and store of value), for what merchant or bank could possibly reject it in a Europe where the Bundesbank almost sustains the entire European economy and the European Euro?

On October 22, Milosevic made the surprising announcement that he would allow Montenegro to leave the federation if the people decided to go. In meetings with ultranationalist and Socialist Party leaders on October 25, however, Serbia's vice premier, Vojislav Seselj, said that a split with Serbia could lead to a war between the pro-Serbia faction in Montenegro and the pro-Western government.

So far, the West has cautioned Djukanovic not to put the cart before the horse, fearing a bloodbath. The West also believes that the longer

Montenegro stays in the union, the sooner Milosevic will fall. But if Serbia were to move on Montenegro, would the West respond? Probably. But here one would definitely need to launch a ground war. The only problem, though: Who is the friend and who the foe in mountain terrain? It would be NATO's nightmare, winnable at a huge cost in lives. Montenegro, like the other republics that separated, has a history of independence and is just as worthy of becoming an independent nation.

MACEDONIA—CLAIMED BY MANY

A further threat by Serbia might be directed at Macedonia, its neighbour to the south. Although it was granted independence and spared the bloodshed of Croatia and Bosnia, Macedonia remains abjectly poor by Balkan standards. Surely Serbia would like to see it crawl back into the federation. It is one of the most mystifying nations in the world. Claimed by Serbia, Greece, and Bulgaria, it lies at a crossroads—racial, cultural, linguistic, historical—the stuff the Balkans are made of. Although it was a part of Yugoslavia not too long ago, it once belonged to Bulgaria between the Treaty of San Stefano and the Congress of Berlin. Bulgarians insist there is no separate Macedonian nation; there are just Macedonian-speaking Bulgarians. The Greeks make the same argument and consider Macedonia part of northern Greece. Currently led by the Internal Macedonian Revolutionary Organization–Democratic Party for Macedonian National Unity, the country's economy is in a free fall; its trade relations with its erstwhile trading partner, Serbia, have collapsed. Of course, the German mark constitutes a unit of transaction here too.

To exacerbate matters, one-quarter of Macedonia's two million citizens happen to be ethnic Albanians. And this non-Macedonian minority is in fact wooed by Greeks, Albanians, and Bulgarians—albeit they are despised by the Serbs. During the 1980s ethnic Albanians were severely repressed, although the repression eased somewhat with the demise of communism. Today Albanians have their own political parties and one-sixth of the seats in parliament but are still largely underrepresented in local government, law enforcement, and the military. The refugee crisis sparked by the Kosovo upheaval led to many Kosovars crossing the border into Macedonia. The government was uncomfortable with the number of displaced Albanians, fearing a possible uprising among its own population. The camps that were set up were poorly run and unhygienic. Refugees were mistreated by police and border guards. The Macedonians also shipped at least 40,000 refugees to Albania, Greece, and Turkey. Heavily criticized by the West, Macedonia responded by claiming insufficient resources. The tension between the ethnic Albanian population and the Macedonians has been steadily increasing. The Serbs may be intentionally exacerbating these tensions to pose as defenders of Macedonian sovereignty and integrity against alleged Albanian irredentists.[31] If the tensions escalate, Macedonia may find itself turning to Serbia for help. And if that happens, conflict will not be necessary. But if conflict were the answer, Serbia would draw the ire not only of the West but also of Bulgaria and Greece, involving itself in a larger conflict than it could realistically win.

CONSIDERATIONS FOR THE FUTURE

Milosevic may or may not turn to violence again. His country is still the subject of crippling international economic sanctions. The sanctions cut Serbia off from International Monetary Fund and World Bank funds, and the OSCE, UN, and EU have also blocked their trade preferences. This has basically cut the Serbian economy in half. The trade deficit is increasing by $2 billion a year, and the country staggers under a foreign debt of $12 billion.[32]

Many countries, such as Greece, France, Germany, Austria, Italy, Finland, the Slovak Republic, Russia, and the United Nations believe that depriving Serbia of international assistance will only feed the Serb people's sense of victimization and collective paranoia that the world is out to get them. Recently, EU foreign ministers have taken steps to ease sanctions against Yugoslavia, especially to Kosovo and Montenegro. One of these steps involves approving $5 million in fuel oil to be sent to Nis and Pirot, two opposition-controlled Serbian cities.[33] Germany and France want to provide humanitarian relief. Austria wants to repair the Danube bridges because the debris from their destruction is blocking the river. Hungary is now allowing Russian gas shipments through its borders into Serbia for humanitarian reasons.[34]

The Serbian opposition forces have also asked that the sanctions be lifted. Former Yugoslav premier Milan Panic stated after a meeting of opposition forces in Hungary that if Washington wants Milosevic, it should come and take him. "This is a Serb speaking . . . I know this is internationally unacceptable, but if you want him so bad, don't punish me, I am hungry, take him out, get him out, force him out, do something."[35] In this he is right. Milosevic and his cronies aren't suffering. It is the average Serb on the street who feels the effect of these sanctions. He or she will starve or freeze to death, not Milosevic. If we expect Serbs to rise, we are in for a disappointment. Only a few will fight; these few have no support. Milosevic has the majority, silent or not, and he will use the sanctions time and again to foster anti-American hostility.

Sanctions should be restructured so they affect only the leadership, not the ordinary citizen. If this is impossible, the sanctions could be eased as a list of conditions is accepted. Such conditions could include: (1) the removal of Milosevic and the establishment of a democratic government, (2) a commitment to political and economic reform, (3) a pledge to comply with the Dayton Accord, (4) cooperation with the War Crimes Tribunal, (5) the release of Kosovo prisoners, and (6) a negotiated division of all assets from the dissolution of Yugoslavia.[36] In return the international community could (1) release money for rebuilding, (2) open embassies, (3) let the IMF, the World Bank, and the European Bank for Reconstruction and Development go to work in the country, (4) unfreeze Yugoslavia's assets in Western countries, (5) increase foreign investment and trade, (6) establish an OSCE democratization mission, (7) begin talks to let the Serbs redeem the Yugoslavia seat at the United Nations, and (8) make the Serbs an offer of membership with the Council of Europe and with NATO's Partnership for Peace. However, the arms embargo and the travel ban on Milosevic and his henchmen (generals, police, and paramilitaries) who are guilty (or suspected) of atrocities should be kept.[37]

NOTES

1. Fareed Zakaria, "Keeping Kosovo" in *National Review*, vol. 51, no. 18, September 27, 1999, p. 22.

2. Peter Finn and R. Jeffrey Smith, "Kosovo's Homeless Shudder as Balkan Winter Threatens: U.N. Officials Race to Provide Temporary Shelter, Heat, Food" in *Washington Post*, October 19, 1999, p. A12.

3. Jacques Paul Klein, "Stopping the Whirlwind" in *The World Today*, vol. 55, no. 6, July 1999, pp. 7–8.

4. The facts and figures given in the paragraph were quoted from "War in Yugoslavia: Environmental Effects in Yugoslavia" in *The Bulletin, Quarterly Magazine of Regional Environmental Center for Central and Eastern Europe* at www.rec.org/REC/Bulletin/Bull84/EnvEffects .html (January 2000).

5. Scott Peterson, "The Trail of a Bullet" in *Christian Science Monitor*, vol. 91, no. 217, October 5, 1999, p. 1.

6. International Crisis Group, "Balkans: The Balkan Refugee Crisis: Regional and Long-Term Perspectives," June 1, 1999 (www.crisisweb .org/projects/sbalkans/reports/ba02main.htm).

7. International Crisis Group, "South Balkans: The New Kosovo Protectorate," January 2000 (www.crisisweb.org/projects/sbalkans/reports /kos23main.htm).

8. Ibid.

9. "Federal Republic of Yugoslavia: Abuses against Serbs and Roma in the New Kosovo" in *Human Rights Watch*, vol. 11, no. 10, August 1999 (www.hrw.org/reports/1999/kosov2/). See also *Politika*, October 17, 1999; *Duga*, October 20, 1999.

10. Robertson replaced former secretary general Javier Solana in Oc-

tober after Solana left to take a post as European Union foreign policy chief.

11. George Jahn, "Few Serbs Remain in Kosovo Capital," October 9, 1999 (dailynews.yahoo.com/h/ap/19991009/wl/yugoslavia_last_serbs_1.html).

12. Peter Finn, "Forces of Intolerance Threaten to Consume Kosovo" in *Washington Post*, October 13, 1999, p. A1.

13. Peter Finn, "Support Dwindles for Kosovo Rebels: Ethnic Albanians Dismayed by KLA's Violence, Arrogance" in *Washington Post*, October 17, 1999, p. A1. Many Kosovars I interviewed in Macedonia and at a Canadian Army base in Canada made similar complaints to me about the Party for Democratic Progress of Kosovo. Relief workers from several agencies corroborated these views in December 1999.

14. International Crisis Group, "South Balkans: Waiting for UNMIK: Local Administration in Kosovo," October 18, 1999 (www.crisisweb.org/projects/sbalkans/reports/kos28main.htm).

15. International Crisis Group, "South Balkans: War in the Balkans: Consequences of the Kosovo Conflict and Future Options for Kosovo and the Region," April 19, 1999 (www.crisisweb.org/projects/sbalkans/reports/kos20main.htm).

16. Daniel Jonah Goldhagen, "A New Serbia" in *New Republic*, May 17, 1999, p. 2 (www.thenewrepublic.com/magazines/tnr/current/goldhagen051799.html).

17. Richard Falk, "Reflections on the War," p. 4 (www.thenation.com/issue/990628/0628falk.shtml).

18. The Marshall Plan, or the European Recovery Program, was developed by the American general and statesman George Marshall in response to the economic crisis of post–World War II Europe. The Plan provided aid for Austria, Belgium, Denmark, France, Greece, Iceland, Ireland, Italy, Luxembourg, the Netherlands, Norway, Portugal, Sweden, Turkey, the United Kingdom, and West Germany. A total of $13.3 billion was spent between 1948 and 1951. The main purpose of the Marshall Plan was to guarantee that Europe would not fall to communism. Many have argued that there should have been a second Marshall Plan after the fall of communism to help the newly emerging countries of Eastern Europe. Brigitte Granville, "Time for a Rescue" in *The World Today*, vol. 55, no. 7, July 1999, p. 7.

0   19. Mark Boal, "The Peace Dividend: Businesses Are Waiting to Cash In on the Rebuilding of Kosovo," June 21, 1999 (www.salon.com/news/feature/1999/06/21/reconstruction/index.html).

20. International Crisis Group, "South Balkans: Transforming Serbia: The Key to Long Term Stability," August 12, 1999 (www.crisisweb.org/projects/sbalkans/reports/yu10main.htm).

21. Alexander Rose, "No Surrender Is a Central Theme in Serb Folklore" in *National Post*, May 29, 1999, p. E4.

22. John S. Rechetar Jr., *The Soviet Polity: Government and Politics in the USSR* (New York: Harper and Row, 1978), p. 45.

23. "Transforming Serbia."

24. *Dani*, August 13, 1999.

25. Steven Edwards, "Family Moving Fortune out of the Country" in *National Post*, May 29, 1999, p. E3. A separate source in Israel informs me that Marko's dealings with money sharks in Israel is no secret. Serbs have always found the Israelis to be trustworthy.

26. International Crisis Group, "South Balkans: Serbia: The Milosevic Factor," February 24, 1998 (www.crisisweb.org/projects/sbalkans/reports/yu01main.htm).

27. Ibid.

28. Justin Brown, "An Heir to Milosevic: Is He Better?" in *Christian Science Monitor*, May 25, 1999 (www.csmonitor.com/durable/1999/05/25/pls3.htm).

29. "Transforming Serbia."

30. International Crisis Group, "South Balkans: Serbia: The Milosevic Factor."

31. Violence increased in Macedonia in the new millennium. Street fights between Albanians and Macedonians are commonplace. In February 2000, four Macedonian policemen were gunned down. There are instances of rape and pillage, and gangsterism is rampant.

32. Janusz Bugajski, *Nations in Turmoil: Conflict and Cooperation in Eastern Europe* (Boulder: Westview, 1993), p. 135.

33. International Crisis Group, "South Balkans: Serbia: The Milosevic Factor."

34. William Drozdiak, "Cold Snap Could Cool Support for Milosevic" in *Washington Post*, October 22, 1999, p. A25.

35. Ibid.

36. Dusan Stojanovic, "Serbs, Montenegrins Discuss Future," October 25, 1999 (dailynews.yahoo.com/h/ap/19991025/wl/yugoslavia_montenegro_12.html).

37. "Transforming Serbia."

Refugees sit by a fire at a camp in Albania. Courtesy of Médecins Sans Frontières.

An old man eats bread that was just distributed. Courtesy of Médecins Sans Frontières.

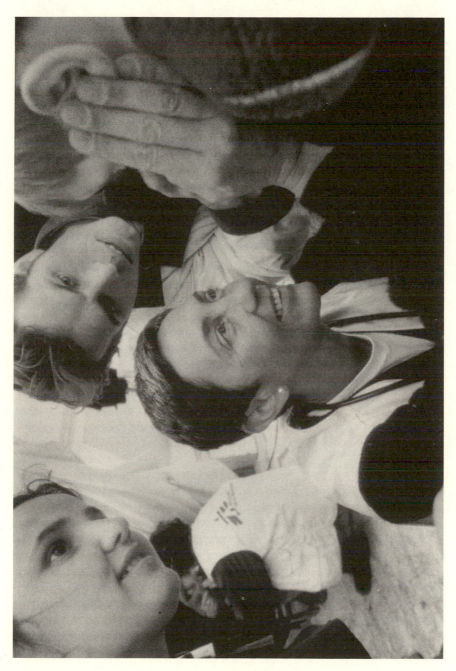

A member of the Nobel Prize–winning organization Médecins Sans Frontières examines a trauma patient. Courtesy of Médecins Sans Frontières.

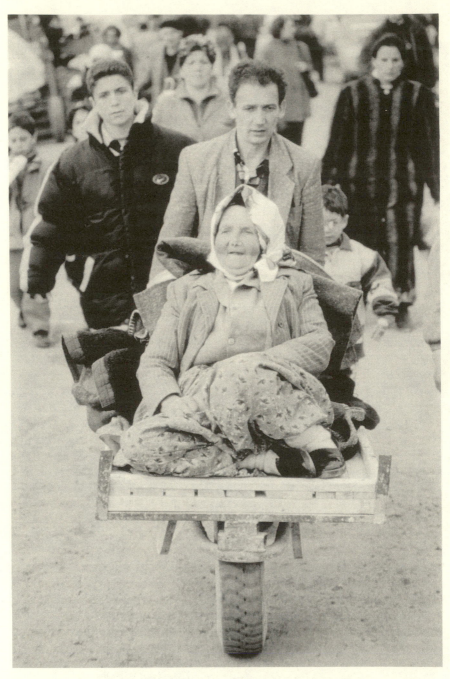

A Kosovar refugee is brought to camp in a wheelbarrow. Courtesy of Médecins Sans Frontières.

The face of horror and trauma: countless young Kosovar women were raped. Courtesy of Médecins Sans Frontières.

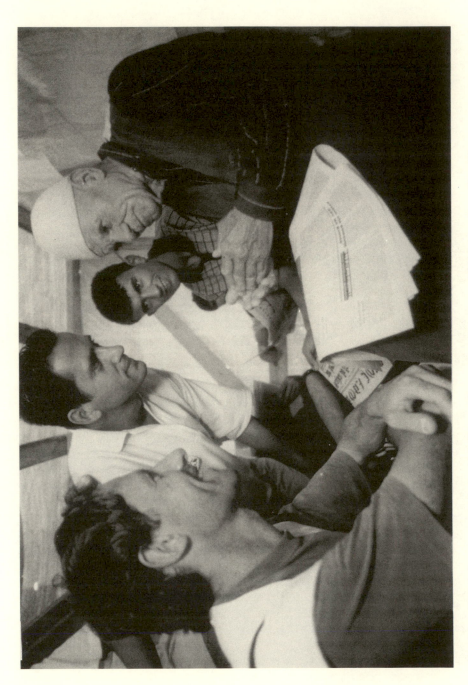

The old suffered the same psychological pain as the young. Courtesy of Médecins Sans Frontières.

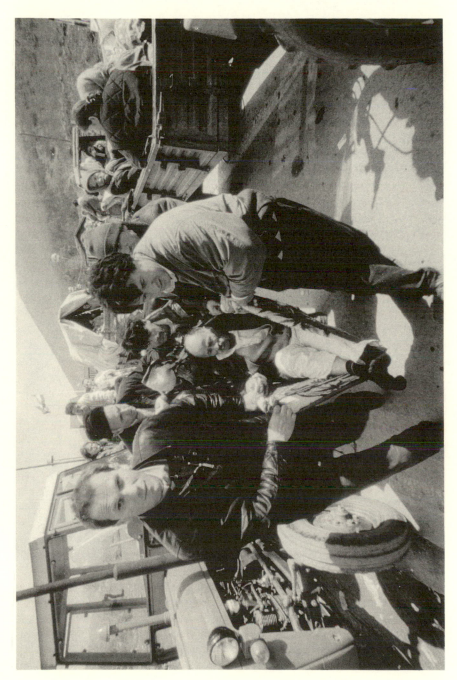

Volunteers bring an injured refugee into camp. Courtesy of Médecins Sans Frontières.

A Canadian soldier guarding a refugee compound. Courtesy of the Department of National Defence, Canada.

A Kosovar refugee embracing an army photographer, with tanks in the background. Courtesy of the Department of National Defence, Canada.

Serbs leaving home. Courtesy of the Department of National Defence, Canada.

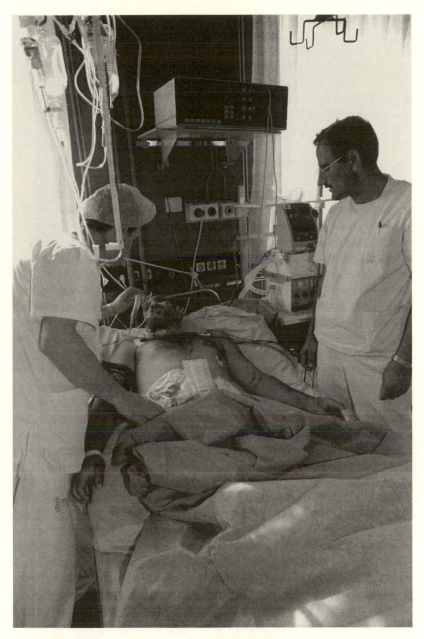

KFOR provides medical treatment when refugees return. Courtesy of the
Department of National Defence, Canada.

Most Kosovars were glad to be back, but many became lawless, setting out to murder the Serbs who stayed behind. Courtesy of the Department of National Defence, Canada.

A Serb frowning at the prospect of having to leave Kosovo. Courtesy of the Department of National Defence, Canada.

Serbs withdraw from Kosovo. Courtesy of the Department of National Defence, Canada.

5

INTERNATIONAL
RAMIFICATIONS

You remember de Gaulle's definition of NATO: "An organization, imposed upon the Atlantic Alliance, which amounts to nothing else than the military and political subordination of West Europe to the United States of America." In the meantime, I must admit I felt a little ashamed when, in Belgrade, having been asked why this president (Milosevic . . .) readily receives an American and not a Frenchman, a Serbian member of the democratic opposition answered: "At any rate, it's better to talk to the master rather than to his servants."
—Régis Debray, *Le Monde*, May 13, 1999

Kosovo, like no other place I know, has left an indelible imprint on the world conscience—more so than the current struggle over Chechnya. The destruction of Serbia's economy by NATO warplanes reverberated far beyond the Balkans. But war almost always has a loony logic. In the aftermath of ruin there comes a renewal, a time for reconstruction and development. It all seems benignly appropriate, like the yuletide season in December in America that sheds its spiritual meaning and goes commercial. In economic terms especially, that is good.

Not only was this the first time that NATO went to war, but it is unique in a number of other ways as well. The success of the mission in Kosovo furnished ample reason to justify humanitarian intervention to a vast segment of the world. NATO was rejuvenated; it had a new purpose, new confidence. NATO has a new look now. The poorer countries of Eastern Europe were more than supportive. They wanted to be trusted. Their desire reflected more than an effort to curry favour with an organization to become part of it some day. Those who wished to become part of it went all out to make themselves worthy of it—not, however, without being reticent about dastardly undertakings. Membership has its privileges, as the saying goes, but it carries a price. NATO membership, in and of itself, never will be the real goal of these nascent market economies. Getting into the European Union is. Economics rules Eastern Europe today, not ideologies or military alliances. And that is good too. Yugoslavia, if anything, must seem like an aberration. When a rough and infamous rogue brings danger into these countries' midst, intervention seems almost necessary to protect the ogre, as it were, from himself.

WAS INTERVENTION GOOD?

For humanitarian reasons, yes; for commerce, yes indeed. During the Cold War, such intervention would have been impossible. Certainly in the case of Kosovo, NATO would not have succeeded. The Soviet Union would never have allowed the Atlantic Alliance, led by the United States, to interfere in Eastern Europe, despite the fact that Yugoslavia was independent of the USSR. The fall of communism and the decline of Russian power opened the way for such interventions. Some are successful, some fail, some are downright impracticable—like the idea of NATO intervening in Chechnya. A major turnaround in America foreign policy also paved the way. For decades after the loss of the Vietnam War, Americans were reluctant to engage in large-scale military adventures. The isolationist view prevailed. "No intervention!" was the buzzword— unless America was guaranteed total victory with the full support of the people and the government; unless there were minimal casualties; unless there was a strict timetable.[1] A case in point is the U.S. invasion of Grenada. (Not Somalia, where it failed.) Once the United States became the undisputed world superpower, American policymakers reasoned that despite President Bush's avowal never to metamorphose his countrymen into "world cops," Americans had a right to a niche in the international system. Events in Iraq stand as a prime example of this new way of thinking. The American willingness to protect Kurdish safe-areas in Iraq is a first step toward interventionist thinking.

The United States, though, may have gone too far. Not by malicious or mischievous intent, to be sure. Rather, it was rivalry in the Security Council among the Americans, Russians, and Chinese that justified this particular action (Washington was convinced that the Russians and Chinese would use their veto power in the Security Council to block any bombing of Serbia). NATO and the EU are heavily dependent on the United States economically and militarily and therefore had little choice but to accept American participation in the war. A book written about Somalia in the late 1990s predicted just such a scenario. Thomas Weiss suggested that interventions to prevent starvation, forced migrations, violations of fundamental rights, and genocide could lead to a new doctrine by which "UN decisions would trigger humanitarian intervention subcontracted to coalitions led by major powers or deployed entirely by them. The UN would ensure accountability for such undertakings but continue traditional peacekeeping and humanitarian actions after them."[2]

Thus, there is a tension, if not an outright contradiction, between the rules of world order stated in the UN Charter and the rights articulated in the Universal Declaration of Human Rights. The Charter bans any force violating state sovereignty; the Universal Declaration guarantees the rights of individuals against oppressive states. When is intervention justified? Robert H. Jackson wrote that it may only be acceptable for the following: self-defense, consent (of the country involved), and "humanitarianism."[3] What does this last word mean? Human rights, international ethics, morality, and the individual and international law— admittedly, not long ago the only subjects of international law were states. This opens up another kettle of fish. If the international community can intervene in Kosovo, why not in Chechnya? or Tibet? or Kashmir? or Northern Ireland? Political realities come into play here to offset the hallowed principles of morality. And so the international system is really a sham. If an international army were to intervene in Russia, or China, or India, or Britain, it would risk escalation. If it intervened in Israel, it would draw the ire of a powerful Jewish lobby. Intervention can only become a tool of international diplomacy if it involves countries that aren't powerful, countries that are pariahs, countries that have no moneyed diaspora. In this light, diplomacy is nothing but a travesty.

If intervention is to work, regardless of the area, there has to be a set of laws to oversee it. Intervention must be based on legitimate and universal norms. The international community as a whole must decide under what circumstances intervention may take place. In the early days of the crisis in Kosovo, there was a lot of back slapping for a job well done. The West tried to find excuses not to intervene and went all out to appease the Serbs to get them to stop their actions in Kosovo. It is precisely delays such as these in Somalia, Rwanda, and Bosnia that cost hundreds of thousands of lives. There ought to be a set of conditions that, when broken, call for immediate intervention.

Indeed, Thomas Weiss has suggested a new doctrine on humanitarian intervention through the UN. First, he says, intervention should be timely and robust, or not occur at all. The longer the international community delays, the greater the death count. Second, essential goals must be clearly communicated; save the people first, worry about finding the guilty parties later. Also, identify priorities in helping those affected by the war. Third, prevention must be emphasized. If conflict can be circumvented, all the better. Fourth, human rights must be dealt with in a straightforward and clear manner. Fifth, make better use of humanitarians. Their services were created for a reason, so let them do their job. Sixth, do not be driven by the priorities of the media. The media have far too often sensationalised a story, and in order to please the public back home, governments have had to change their priorities—not always for the better. Seventh, do not overestimate regional organizations; use them wisely. NATO has proven that it is able to work effectively, whereas other regional organizations may not be as willing or able to do so. Eighth, perhaps the main thrust of the argument: accept that casualties are an inevitability of war and that long-range peace may require that people die. It's a decision no one wants to make, but sometimes there is no alternative.[4]

Some people may argue against intervention as a political tool. For example, Edward Luttwak claims that the purpose of war is to resolve political conflicts. However, no one wins decisively anymore. No longer can war be a zero-sum game. Intervention prevents wars from being played to their natural conclusion.[5] The players are separated and sent to their own corners by the international community, where their hatred is allowed to fester. Eventually, they'll face off again and again until no one is left standing. Imposed cease-fires give the combatants a chance to rest and rearm. There is a meager chance nowadays that the United States and Russia will become involved in these wars and go nuclear. Nor are peacekeepers reliable, argues Luttwak, because their main job is to stay alive. Peacekeepers, therefore, tend to appease the locally stronger force, tolerating its abuses while being unable to protect innocent civilians from being massacred.[6] A war, on the other hand, that is allowed to play through to its end will eventually ensure some closure, according to Luttwak. In Kosovo, the most important thing was to have zero casualties among the allied forces so as not to suffer a backlash at home that could ultimately justify outlays for expensive weapons.

The American general who oversaw the NATO air campaign, Lt. General Michael Short, in hearings before Congress said that concern about civilian casualties and collateral damage precluded a devastating blow that would have ended the conflict quickly. He stated that the allies (1) didn't want certain targets hit, or (2) specified times for target hits when civilians were not present. Instead of ending the conflict in one fell swoop, as it were, the war dragged on for eleven weeks. Short said he would have liked to go straight to Belgrade to capture Milosevic, and the war wouldn't have been necessary after that.[7] If that had happened, how many innocent people could have been saved in the long run? What Luttwak posits is controversial; his views on playing war through to its end may appear bloodthirsty and cold, but they make sense. To date, wars in the Falklands, Iraq, and the former Yugoslavia have really not been settled; they could spring back up at any time.

Intervention thus seems to be more acceptable after the events in Kosovo. The International Institute for Strategic Studies, in its annual report of 1999, asserted that intervention can be validated by nations around the world despite opposition from such countries as China, Russia, France, and Israel.[8] Furthermore, as intervention spreads across the globe, it has a way of scaring dictators and despots into rethinking their strategies. With the United States ready to intervene for the "little guy," international politics will likely never be the same again.

No sooner had the war in Kosovo come to an end than President Clinton said that in the future Americans would intervene to stop wholesale racial and ethnic slaughter. This Clinton Doctrine would soon face a major international test, one that underscored the need for a set of operational rules to be written down regarding intervention. But intervention to stop aggression is no less than aggression itself, which is outlawed by the UN Charter and international law. In addition to shredding the UN Charter and perverting the purpose of NATO, Clinton violated at least two provisions of the United States Constitution. Under Article I, Section 8, of the Constitution, Congress, not the president, holds the power to declare war and to punish offenses against the law of nations. After all, there is a world of difference between a monarchy or dictatorship and the presidency of a constitutional republic. A king may use his army as he pleases; an American president would have no such unlimited power. Also, under Article VI of the Constitution, treaties are not considered mere scraps of paper; they are part of the supreme law of the United States. Walter J. Rockler, a former American prosecutor at the Nuremberg War Crimes Tribunal, wrote a scathing indictment of both President Clinton and the American Congress that appeared in the *Chicago Tribune* on May 23, 1999: "these days a supine Congress, fascinated only by details of sexual misconduct, can hardly be expected to enforce constitutional requirements."

What was the reaction to the war in Kosovo across this planet, where communications move so rapidly?

EAST TIMOR

The small nation of East Timor, half of an island in Indonesia, has been fighting for independence for decades. Formerly part of the Portuguese empire, it gained independence in 1975. Soon thereafter, Muslim Indonesia invaded and repressed the predominantly Catholic population. Indonesia exculpated itself for the blatant aggression by citing the civil war that raged in the province between the pro-Indonesian group

Apodeti and the Revolutionary Front of Independent East Timor. After the Apodeti were defeated, Indonesia attacked. In four years one-third of all East Timorese were dead. Twenty-four years of brutal Indonesian rule resulted in 200,000 deaths. The first pro-Indonesian militias were set up by Indonesian leader Suharto's son-in-law, General Prabowo Subianto, in the 1980s to keep pro-independence forces from gaining strength. Finally, in 1999, a UN-sponsored independence referendum was held. Despite threats from the militias, there was a 99 percent turnout at which 78.5 percent voted to break away. Almost immediately, the militias charged that the UN had rigged the vote. The same thing happened in 1992 when the UN organized elections in Angola that led to a civil war. This bodes ill for upcoming UN-sponsored elections in the Western Sahara.

In East Timor, before the votes could even be counted, the militias began gruesome assaults across the small nation of 800,000. Thousands of refugees were soon in full flight. They took to the hills (at least 600,000) or escaped to West Timor (130,000). Many were forced to sign papers at gunpoint saying they supported autonomy from Indonesia. Towns and villages were razed. At least 30,000 people were butchered. As in the Balkans, young men were snatched from their families and simply "disappeared." No one was safe. Catholic priests were murdered by the militias, and nuns were raped. Why? Because they allegedly promoted independence. Even the head of the East Timorese Protestant Church was beheaded in a refugee camp in West Timor.

Was this a new development? Could it have been predicted? Without a shadow of a doubt. In the year before the vote, the militias and the Indonesian government had been quietly trying to get UN workers, pro-independence supporters, and journalists out of East Timor. Given the situation and the strength of the militias, the international community should have foreseen the violence.

What was the world's reaction? Did anyone witness Christians from the West leaping into battle to save the East Timorese population? Was this the Asian version of Kosovo? Hardly. Threatening immediate sanctions and feeble finger-wagging were all that came from a mighty and complacent West while a life-and-death struggle raged. Portugal alone stood out. It had always tried to keep East Timor high on its list of priorities ever since it was taken over by the Indonesians. Portugal had made many an appeal to the West for more effective measures. Tardily the United Nations raised itself up from hibernation and perfunctorily threatened Indonesia with sanctions. The IMF and the World Bank announced they would link loans to peace efforts in Indonesia—the first time these institutions had ever done such a thing. Countries doing business with Indonesia procrastinated and made excuses about sanctions not working and about igniting a war that would destabilize the region.

After all, business is typically more interested in profit than in human lives. Further, the United Nations, the United States, and other major powers affirmed that they would go into East Timor only with Jakarta's permission.

Now, did NATO ever deign to ask Milosevic if it should enter Kosovo? A rather disheartening scenario as the bloodletting spiralled!

Finally, President B. J. Habibie, on September 12, gave the peacekeepers permission to enter East Timor despite earlier denials by Indonesian ambassador Makarim Wibisono. On September 15, the United Nations Security Council authorized an international force. Indonesia pulled out its troops as soon as the peacekeepers arrived. Led by Australia (whose troops formed the bulk of the peacekeepers), the 7,500-strong force entered the *abattoir*. Other countries likewise sent contingents (the United States only provided logistical support—so much for the Clinton Doctrine!): Portugal, the Philippines, New Zealand, Britain, Canada, France, Thailand, Singapore, Fiji, South Korea, Bangladesh, Pakistan, Malaysia, China, and Russia. The pro-Indonesian faction was unhappy and threatened the peacekeepers, specifically lambasting Australia and claiming that its troops wanted to take over the country.

With trouble at home, Habibie soon resigned and was replaced by Abdurrahman Wahid. With trouble also possible in the Aceh province in northern Sumatra, the South Moluccas islands, and West Papua and their independence movements, the Indonesian government had no choice but to let East Timor secede. In fact, the government approved the results of the East Timor referendum, and it has become the world's newest country. On October 26, the United Nations took control of East Timor. More than 9,000 troops were dispatched to replace the force initially sent to restore order. Thousands of international police were also sent in. But the country is in ruins. There is wholesale devastation: hundreds of thousands are in refugee camps in West Timor, and thousands more are hiding in the mountains. There is inadequate shelter, and starvation is a threat.

Why were there delayed reactions? The answer is straightforward. Indonesia is a major trading partner in Southeast Asia. Indonesia is the fourth most populous nation in the world. Indonesia is a power to be reckoned with in the region. Economics, not human rights, are genuinely at stake here (never mind the Clinton Doctrine). No bombs were dropped, no air sorties took place. Yet evidence of mass graves patently shows that atrocities were committed, as in Kosovo. The racial argument might seem compelling. But the reader will remember that the United States had intervened in Haiti and Somalia. Perhaps the answer lies in "geographical propinquity," or, more simply, the notion of convenient proximity. After all, Kosovo is closer to U.S. interests in Europe. Strategically, Indonesia is an important country for the United States. It controls the Strait of Malacca and is a wall against the Chinese to the north. It has the largest Muslim population in the world and practices a tolerant version of Islam. Thus, it appears that the real Clinton Doctrine is that America will protect innocent civilians from bullies, but only bullies who don't count geopolitically.[9]

What's the difference, then? Certainly, the war in Kosovo was justified in terms of ending human rights abuses. But would the United States of a century ago have allowed other countries to send troops onto its territory? The United States of today didn't pass the United Nations Genocide Convention until 1988, for fear of Africans and Native Americans bringing charges. The same delaying tactic kept the government from bringing charges against Hussein in Iraq or Pol Pot in Cambodia.[10] It was also willing to allow carnage and war in other parts of the world to continue as long as its troops were fighting the "Communist menace." How many people have been killed in South and Latin America in U.S.-supported fights against Marxist and Communist governments or rebel groups?

Most Western countries have, at one time or another, expelled or exterminated entire ethnic groups in order to make their countries religiously, culturally, socially, or politically whole. The imperial legacy is likewise tarnished. The great game of one-upmanship in Southwest Asia between the Russians and the English has left its mark. The imposing of forced borders in Asia, Africa, and the Middle East by the imperial masters with no thought given to ethnic, racial, religious, or linguistic divisions has led to decades of border clashes and cross-claims. Australia was first colonized as a penal colony and the natives slaughtered by the English. Disease and superior weaponry killed millions in the conquered countries. Democracy, capitalism, and Christianity were imposed as the "superior" beliefs and systems of government. Indeed, Westerners have little to be proud of in their past.

Even today, the rise of right-wing parties in the West is proof that intolerance is alive and well. In Europe, racism has come on the heels of high unemployment and recession. Parties have risen to defend national integrity and to renounce the idea of a European Union. The United Kingdom has at least twenty known right-wing groups. The United States has extremely violent militias and neo-Nazis. Russia has over one hundred groups, and even Sweden, Norway, Denmark, and the Netherlands have fascist hate-mongers. Germany is home to many (approximately 100) of the most violent organizations in the world (there were over 12,000 attacks on foreigners in 1997 alone). France has over 40 groups, including the *Front National* under Jean-Marie Le Pen. Italy also boasts 60,000 members of violent right-wing associations. In Australia, the One Nation Party led by Pauline Hanson blames the country's woes on Asians and Aborigines. Right-wing radicals everywhere share a common antipathy for gay men and lesbians, for disabled people, black Africans, drug addicts, Jews (and other Semites such as Arabs) and generally all immigrants. The sheer number of hate-mongers is staggering.

The West's sudden show of sympathy for the rights of the Kosovars rings a bit hollow. The United States and its sycophantic supporters literally threw Yugoslavia (Serbia and Montenegro) out of the United Nations but did little in response to Talabani's ruthlessness in Afghanistan. Consider also Rwanda, Somalia, and Cambodia (remember the killing fields of the Pol Pot regime?). Those governments slaughtered and purged their peoples, so why weren't they also expelled? The United States certainly recognized Russia as the legitimate heir to the USSR. Why not Serbia and Montenegro for Yugoslavia? Witness the number of signatories of the Helsinki Accords of 1975. Back then there was a solemn call for respecting a nation's sovereignty. The parties pledged to refrain from the use of force and they recognized the inviolability of borders, territorial integrity, and noninterference in internal affairs.[11] The Helsinki Accords were meant to be binding on those who agreed to sign them. Yet the NATO states that signed broke the spirit and letter of Helsinki when they bombed Yugoslavia.

This is not to say that intervention was wrong in this case. The point is that the whole context of intervention, retaliation, and punishment should be looked at more closely. There will always be contradictions in the arguments we present. There will always be conflicting situations. Two or more situations are both similar and dissimilar in their incongruities. Moreover, my argument does not detract from the fact that the West is a far better place than any other on earth. There is, at least, in the Western liberal democratic tradition a respect for the "rule of law." And when the law is violated or policies are shown to be counterfeit, there is further recourse; there is always an opportunity to appeal and to contest. In Western diplomatic protocol, arbitrariness is increasingly a thing of the past. Today the Vatican apologizes for the Church's past treatment of Jews and other nationalities. Christian groups apologize to Muslims for the Crusades (for the Crusaders were really thugs and ruffians who raped and pillaged and burned in the name of the Almighty). These are steps in the right direction. They are strictly symbolic gestures, to be sure, but the gestures are appreciated.

THE UNITED NATIONS

The war in Kosovo demonstrated in a graphic way that the United Nations is badly in need of reform and restructuring. The fact that the United States completely bypassed the UN in order to get international justification to go into Kosovo was a telling move. Otherwise, China and

Russia would have vetoed. (Here, I must confess that I cannot blame the American policymakers. The veto has been used and abused for ideological reasons. Needless to say, this was not its original purpose.) For this reason many argue that the UN is feckless. The organization may have completely lost the capacity for independent action unless it is explicitly supported by a United States that forced it into Iraq and, along with the Europeans, pushed the organization into the first wars in Yugoslavia.

Moreover, the United States has tended, since the fall of the Soviet bloc, to dominate the Security Council and to press for many resolutions that are in its best interests. With Russia and China always foraging for U.S. dollars, many of these resolutions (the less controversial ones, that is) are usually voted in. And Washington is ever averse to paying for the UN. As a matter of fact, the United States could lose its vote in the General Assembly if it continues to default on the roughly $1.5 billion it owes in back dues. Some American analysts have held—and we are at a critical juncture on this one—that the United States should abandon the UN if it fails to follow Washington's lead. This would essentially turn the UN into an instrument of American interests and policies. A telling sign came on October 13, 1999, when Richard Holbrooke brazenly advised officials in Kosovo to follow American leads without worrying about UN reactions.

Most Third World countries resent UN intervention. It infringes on their sovereignty. They are suspicious of the main Western powers, a view that is shared by Russia and China.[12] Countries such as Russia, France, and China likewise oppose economic sanctions and the use of force that the UN has authorized in Iraq. Seen as corrupt, wasteful, and rife with fraud, the world body has taken some steps in downsizing and restructuring that have led, in some cases, to severe shortages in manpower and equipment. But the first steps have been taken.

Recognizing the need for reform, in 1995 the UN established the Open Ended High Level Working Group on the Strengthening of United Nations System. Kofi Annan, the sitting secretary general, has stated that the UN needs to develop faster responses to civil wars. Because the peacekeeping operations of the UN are the most crucial, perhaps even the most beneficial, something can always be done about this sphere of activity. There is much room for improvement in this area. Perhaps a permanent, independent UN force may be the answer. The UN could then dispatch forces into war-torn areas without having to wait for national contingents to gather from around the world.

Perhaps the greatest challenge is the reformation of the Security Council. It needs to have a more democratic feel. Most of the nonpermanent members of the Security Council would want more than five countries exercising the right of veto. The United States has proposed the inclusion of five more members: Germany, Japan, and one each from Asia, Africa, and Latin America and the Caribbean (suggesting India, either Nigeria or South Africa, and Brazil). However, there are many more who oppose the granting of a veto to five more members. Italy has proposed five new permanent members, ten from a pool of thirty who pay their UN dues and contribute to peacekeeping and participate fully, and ten from the rest of the members.[13]

There is no question that reform is essential to the United Nations if it is to survive in the twenty-first century. Otherwise it will acquiesce, reluctantly, to a United States dictating international policy for many years to come.

NATO

Having recently celebrated its fiftieth anniversary, NATO was in danger of becoming obsolete. It was originally created as a bulwark in Western Europe against the threat of the Soviet Union and Eastern Europe. With that threat gone, it seemed like NATO might have to be retired. But along came a war to give it a new lease on life, a raison d'être. It pulled its members together and showed that it could handle a crisis in Europe. Notwithstanding American support, the countries of Europe performed admirably. Most countries originally joined NATO to reduce their own military expenditures in favour of an increased presence of NATO forces in their states. In return, NATO would protect their borders from national security threats. The war in Kosovo underscored the technological gap between the European militaries and the American military. As a result, the EU is seriously looking at assembling its own military force.

With the constant threat of instability in Eastern Europe, the evolution of NATO as the international policing body has been an ideal way of resolving what at one time would have been impossible. The expansion of NATO into the former Warsaw Pact countries is inevitable. Eventually, all of Europe might be united under one organization. The Partnership for Peace, or the Euro-Atlantic Partnership Council, may be a step in that direction. It includes the nineteen members of NATO plus Albania, Armenia, Austria, Azerbaijan, Belarus, Bulgaria, Estonia, Finland, Georgia, Kazakhstan, the Kirghiz Republic, Latvia, Lithuania, Moldova, Romania, Russia, Slovakia, Slovenia, Sweden, Switzerland, Macedonia, Tajikistan, Turkmenistan, Ukraine, and Uzbekistan. All of them may one day join NATO. For this to come to pass, Lord Robertson, the current leader of NATO, stated after the war in Kosovo that Balkan stability is of utmost priority.

THE UNITED STATES

I take an ambivalent view of the United States. It is a country that both beckons and baffles, and it pursues policies that are not always correct in my view. But they are not incorrect either. It is far from me to agree with the dauntless skeptics and cynics of the American left such as Noam Chomsky and Edward Said, but these two academicians write with verve and wit. Professor Said, for example, is as capable of venting nearly as much anger on U.S. policies in Kosovo as he does on Zionism in Israel: "Clinton . . . should be indicted as a war criminal as much as Milosevic. Even according to U.S. law, Clinton violated the constitution by fighting a war without congressional sanction. That he also violated the UN Charter simply adds to the felony."

I need not belabour the American attitude toward Kosovo. Indeed, the pages of this book are filled with straight satire of the new Pax Americana. Washington did prove to all and sundry that it could fight a war with no military casualties on its side, except for inadvertent deaths. It did prove that high-tech weaponry was justified, to the immense relief of American weapons manufacturers and the Pentagon as they go looking for budget increases from Congress. The spectre of Vietnam has been quieted and put back in its grave. Moreover, Clinton's and Madeleine Albright's theories on intervention based on moral and strategic grounds have also been justified. And the Democratic Party scored big by supporting the war, while the Republicans suffered lamentably by opposing it. The only visible downside in America's victory has been the recurring upswing of the nation's sense of self-importance. Americans often claim they led the diplomatic and military effort in Kosovo and that their leadership was absolutely necessary to the success of the mission. This is true; but Americans cannot bring about a more lasting peace in Kosovo, any more than the Soviets could in Afghanistan. Revitalizing NATO was a big plus; but Americans were not alone in this, for the diplomatic efforts of the EU and Germany, not to mention Russia, were just as critical.

EUROPE

Britain and its rambunctious prime minister, Tony Blair, were chief advocates of the air war in Kosovo. Vis-à-vis the United States, the British leadership was sheepishly obsequious, almost to a fault. Blair, who enjoys a huge majority in Parliament, is known for an "ethical foreign policy" and is seen by the Kosovars themselves, more than any other leader, as being associated with the liberation of Kosovo. While touring a refugee camp he was cheered—nay, practically mobbed—by the Albanians. The Brits, certainly not the Germans (I can only make reservations for the French, but more about that will follow), were the most vocal members of the Western coalition, demanding that the bombing of Serbia continue until Milosevic caved in. If it please the reader, I would welcome a re-reading of the double entendre reserved for Britain, especially its pitiful pretensions to supremacy in arms and combat, in Chapter 3 of this book. Pax Britannica, as it were, is not dead yet.

As I have indicated elsewhere in this book, Germany's participation and the role played by the *Bundeswehr* surpass that of Britain. The Germans too were strongly behind their chancellor, Gerhard Schröder. This was apparent both during and after the war. After all, Germany has the greatest financial stake in a stable Eastern Europe. The Serbs, it must be recalled, especially hold the German (the Hun) in contempt. The history of World War II is ingrained in Serbian children every day. During the Bosnian wars Germany supported Croatia, which owes much of its newfound prosperity to trade with Germany. And German intelligence, according to a German program called *Monitor*, in late September 1999 supplied the KLA with grenades, monitoring devices, and commando and intelligence training.[14] Some of the finest KFOR peacekeepers appear to be German soldiers; they are reputed to be among the most professional. The Germans are credited with setting up one of the best hospitals in Kosovo for trauma and surgery. German military training has redeemed itself to the point that the *Bundeswehr* now possesses superb sapper teams, meticulously removing mines (with the incomparable German-made Leopard tanks) and doing the finest police constabulary work, including the messy task of disarming unruly KLA units (whom they had armed years ago). As the economic superpower of the EU, Germany—and its deutschemark—have become so invaluable to these countries that the war in Kosovo threatened the equilibrium of Europe itself. Kosovo represents the first time since 1945 that Germany has taken up offensive military operations. Some authors have been pandering to anti-German prejudice. Germany may have had a reckless past in Yugoslavia, especially under the Nazi dictatorship. The Serb regime's notion that Germany still has some diabolical agenda in place is absurd.

The French see themselves as leaders in world culture, and not only in the culinary arts. Ever since the fall of Napoleon, however, the French have been in decline (although they refuse to admit this). However, their jet fighter pilots performed admirably in the coalition war against Iraq. France has historic links to Serbia, like Germany's links to Croatia and Slovenia. And the French do not wish to leave Eastern Europe to their traditional rival, Germany; they prefer, instead, to piggyback on the Germans rather than on the English. Democracy has been the political form in France for as long as it has been in America. The French see themselves as a democratic alternative to the United States. Yet the country feels uncomfortable with the overbearing American cultural, military, and political swagger. The French are fearful of reaching a saturation point (which they almost did on the day they were saddled with the Paris version of Disneyland), and every Frenchman and Frenchwoman dreads the end of France's cultural preeminence. Typically, the Germans allow their high-strung Gallic neighbours to pitch the combined allied counterweight to American proposals.

Italy, under Prime Minister Massimo D'Alema, has been praised for its logistical support with its Adriatic air bases. Although American, British, German, and Spanish air forces led the air war, the facilities and manpower at the Italian bases were essential to that effort. At first Prime Minister Massimo D'Alema insisted it was time to halt the strikes and return to diplomacy. He soon changed his mind, however. The government's left-leaning allies threatened to remove support from his government if Italy allowed the use of its soldiers in any attacks.[15] The arrival of refugees in Italy raised memories of the Albanian refugee crisis that plagued Italy a few years earlier in the 1990s.

Spain was wary of getting involved in a war, given its own military history and the civil war that nearly tore the country apart. However, public opinion gave strong support to taking some part in the war effort in Kosovo. The Spanish military sent a number of planes to fight the air war. The Spanish public was strongly in favour of succouring the refugees.

Bulgaria was careful in its support in view of the fact that 30,000 Bulgarians live in Serbia. With its claims on Macedonia (which they claim as a cradle of Bulgarian culture, and the Macedonian people as western Bulgarians), Bulgaria, desperate to join both NATO and the EU, has kept down the rhetoric. Rumania is also eager to join NATO and the EU and is also worried about the Romanian population of Serbia. Both countries banned Yugoslav ships from their waters on the Danube after Serbia demanded that Romanian, Bulgarian, and Ukrainian ships apply for special permits to go through its part of the Danube waterway.

Greece also has claims on Macedonia, which it calls the Republic of Skopje. With strong religious ties to the Serbian Orthodox Church, most Greeks are fiercely pro-Serb. There were many violent anti-NATO demonstrations with the Athenian police force turning a blind eye to violence against Western consulates. Most of the demonstrators believed that the NATO action was the first step in adjusting borders all over the Balkans and didn't believe that the Albanians were really suffering. Given the history of the area, this is a surprising trend. As Dr. Basil Gouranis, a scholar on the "ethnic politics" of Greece, said: "Yesterday, the Serbs were the people who supported the communist takeover of Greece, eradicated Greek culture and communities north of the border and foisted the problem of Macedonian Slavs on us. Today, they are our ancient

Orthodox brethren who can do no wrong."[16] Although the government has cooperated with NATO, it has stated publicly that it won't cooperate. For Greece has its own problems with the Muslim Turks. Ankara supports Greek Turks and Athens supports the Kurds in Greece. And Macedonia is another sticky issue. The first and second Balkan Wars were fought over Macedonia, and that could happen again. Greece has publicly stated that it wants an end to sanctions against Serbia.

Slovakia let the Atlantic Alliance use its roads and railways. The three new members of NATO—Poland, the Czech Republic, and Hungary, which joined in March 1999—made their own contributions. Hungary feared for the Hungarian minority in Vojvodina but nonetheless declared that the NATO undertaking was just. The Czechs were less enthusiastic, although President Vaclav Havel is a strong proponent of NATO. President Alexander Kwasniewski and the government of Poland applauded NATO's actions in Kosovo. Although all three nations were not active in the military aspect of the operation, they provided humanitarian aid.

RUSSIA

Russians were and are still not happy with the entire Kosovo affair. They were angry at the American-led coalition for attacking their Slavic brothers. Russians are understandably annoyed at being marginalised; they resent being dismissed as a secondary power, and they resent no longer being in ascendancy. The Russians are treated at times as outcasts and feel they are ostracized in Europe. They believe the Serbs were targeted to humiliate them. Russian radio, television, and major newspapers constantly rebuke the United States for its "Protestant, puritan views of world order and peace."[17] At first they supported Serbia; they then suspended cooperation with NATO and withdrew their diplomatic missions from NATO countries.

Believing Albanian separatists had caused the war, many Russians took part in anti-NATO rallies. Soon after the war began, crowds pelted the American embassy in Moscow with ink, beer, and eggs, and volunteers in droves signed up for service in Serbia at the headquarters of the ultranationalist Liberal Democratic Party. Nearly three-quarters of Russian citizens had an unfavourable opinion of the Americans. The average Russian hoped NATO would be defeated so that it would not one day try to intervene in Chechnya.

Although the war has no doubt affected American-Russian relations, the Russians proved to be most expedient in the diplomatic phase in that they were directly involved in the final peace agreement with Milosevic. The Russian guarantees that its troops would be there to see that NATO didn't overstep its bounds constituted a very important incentive to get

Milosevic to agree.[18] The Russians' importance in the peacekeeping venture is also not to be underestimated. They even got in a little dig by arriving in Pristina before the Americans.

However, the practice of marginalising the Russians will eventually take its toll. Now that Boris Yeltsin has disappeared from the scene, the next leader may not be so pliant. How would Vladimir Putin react if the Russians were to take to the streets in large numbers? A nationalist Russia, an insular and militaristic Russia, could prove to be as great a danger as the Soviet Union once was.

CHECHNYA: KOSOVO'S PRECURSOR AND SUCCESSOR

Comparisons between (1) the current and past war between Russia and Chechnya, and (2) the war in Kosovo show eerie similarities. Perhaps if the West had paid attention to these similarities it might have found a way to divert the war in Kosovo. Both areas are Muslim and both lie on the crossroads of major empires (in the Chechen case, the Russian, Persian, and Ottoman). The Chechens were ruled by varied ethnic and religious factions and rarely enjoyed long periods of independence. They too practiced the tradition of blood revenge. The Russian Orthodox monarchy tried to assimilate the Chechens in much the same way as the Serbs did with the Kosovar Albanians. In 1785, the Caucasus was united under a Chechen Muslim, Shaykh Mansur Ushurma, to resist tsarist invasions and to unite Dagestan and Chechnya. A short-lived state was created in 1859.

After the Communists came to power in Russia, they promised equality and sovereignty for all peoples, including the right to separate. But soon after they gained power, they abdicated that imperative. After the revolution the Chechens and other nations of the Caucasus wanted to create a North Caucasian Emirate. Moscow refused. With 128 ethnic groups in Russia, the most expedient move was to create a "Soviet man," a *sovietskii chelovek*, who would belong to the whole country, not just one nationality (in Yugoslavia, Tito had tried to create a similar "Yugoslav man"). He/she was supposed to be an ideal, righteous, flawless individual of the future. Yet no one ever took the idea seriously. Many of the nationalities found this propaganda revolting and refused to cooperate. So disturbances broke out in 1940 and 1943, much like the Basmachi revolts in Turkic Central Asia of the 1930s. Enter Stalin, who decided to punish the nationalities. Under his leadership the Cossacks, Balts, Koreans, Chinese, Circassians, Kurds, Turks, Volga Germans, Karachai, Ingush, Balkars, Kalmyks, Crimean Tatars, Meskhetian Turks, Khemshens, Greeks, and Chechens were all brutally repressed. The Chechens were accused of collaborating with the Germans (which most Muslims did anyway) and in 1944 were moved out of their traditional homeland and sent to remote regions, where their rights were less than marginal. They were forced to do back-breaking physical labor and forbidden to promote their respective cultures. Millions were deported; tens of thousands perished in prison camps. Only in 1957 were they rehabilitated and allowed to return to their republics. Upon returning, they discovered that hundreds of thousands of Russians had already settled in their homelands.

During the Gorbachev era, liberalization and economic reform led to the creation of national movements. Cultural, social, and religious expression grew. The breakup of Russia produced a power vacuum on Russia's periphery. Today Moscow is anxious to control the oil deposits and the pipelines that run through this area. The Chechens have responded by refusing to ratify the 1992 Russian Federation Treaty. Doka Zabgaev, formerly first secretary of the Chechen-Ingush Autonomous Soviet Socialist Republic, launched the Chechen independence movement. A majority of Russians in prominent positions were removed from power. The Islamic faith was encouraged. Zabgaev was replaced by General Dzhokhar Dudaev, who also sought independence. Anti-Chechen sentiment spread across Russia as the independence movement grew. The Chechens, like the Albanians, were blamed for all the organized crime in Russia; indeed, Kremlin spin doctors call the Chechens "drug dealers," "arms merchants," "kidnappers," "rapists," "counterfeiters," and "terrorists." A lot of this rings true to anyone who has lived among Chechens; I myself have seen them operate in the murky underworld of Russian organized crime. But such labels also apply to Jews and Georgians and Armenians and Azeris and Russians themselves. To levy all these charges on the entire Chechen nation as some collective pathology is pure fabrication by Russia's public relations detachments.

On December 11, 1994, Russian armies, fresh from the ignominy of defeat in Afghanistan and Eastern Europe and eager to show their mettle, invaded Chechnya with the object of overthrowing the Chechen government, which had been in power since 1991. The Chechens had declared independence once again. Dudaev was killed in the fighting, but that paved the way for an even more obsessive nationalist, Zelimkhan Yandarbiev, to assert Chechen claims. The brutal war lasted until August 1996. Roughly 80,000 to 100,000 Chechens may have been killed, along with 3,700 Russian troops. Both sides committed human rights violations and atrocities. The Chechens kidnapped and used civilians as human shields. The Russians bombed civilian targets, used torture, massacred civilians, executed adult men, and indiscriminately used landmines. The International Court of Justice subsequently condemned the Russian military for its actions. International observers saw it as genocide against the Chechens. But the war was deemed an internal affair, so as not to upset the Russians. By 1995, the United States issued only mild criticism. Poland, the Baltic states, and the Muslim world sharply condemned the brutalities. The EU also reproached the Russian action. Yet Russia reappeared unscathed and unblemished on the world stage. If the international community had paid more attention to the circumstances that led to the war in Chechnya, it might have intervened in some form before the Kosovo situation got out of control.

In 1999, the tide turned against Chechnya again. In early August, Chechen militants began agitating in Dagestan, its neighbour, trying to whip the people into a frenzy of revolt. A 1,200-man force invaded Dagestan soon thereafter. Shamil Basayev, an Islamic fundamentalist, spearheaded the uprising along with a Jordanian militant known as Khattab. Both wanted to create an Islamic republic in Dagestan. Russian troops then began bombing villages and chasing rebels back into Chechnya. Chechen leader Aslan Maskhadov denied having anything to do with the rebels, but that didn't stop the Russian troops. When several shopping malls and apartment buildings were bombed, leading to a massive loss of life, most Russians decided the Chechens were to blame even though there was no direct evidence linking the group to the bombs. Xenophobia and hatred followed. On September 28, the Russian authorities launched Operation Whirlwind—virtually cracking down on all dark-skinned minorities whether they were Chechen or not. Chechen president Maskhadov faulted Russia for the terrorist bombs. Russia demanded that Chechnya extradite the "terrorists" and, until it does, refuses to meet with Maskhadov about ending the war.

The Russian army soon began an offensive against the Chechen republic. On September 17, 1999, Chechnya asked the international community to halt Russian aggression in this undeclared war. The air bombing of Chechen villages was causing extensive civilian casualties. Tens of thousands of refugees had fled the fighting. Up to 180,000 have fled since, most moving to Ingushetia (President Rusian Aushev has appealed for international help to handle the overload to his republic) and some to Georgia. On October 1, Russia asked the UN to help with the refugee problem. Later in the month Russian authorities closed all the Chechen borders, leaving the refugees trapped. The move was to stop Chechen guerrillas from launching terrorist attacks in Russia, said the Russian Internal Ministry, but it is patently obvious the "terrorists" could easily find another way across the border.

On September 30, the Russians launched a ground attack. They recognized an obscure group of pro-Moscow Chechen exiles as the only legitimate government of the region. The troops created a security buffer zone and took over large swaths of Chechnya. Maskhadov, meanwhile, frantically asked Georgian president Eduard Shevarnadze to mediate.

The Russian government still denies that it is bombing civilians, despite evidence to the contrary. Indeed, many civilian villages have been destroyed on the pretext that they are strongholds for rebel forces. On October 21, an attack on a Grozny market caused the death of 143 people and the wounding of over 250 more. At first the government declined to take responsibility, then blamed it on two Chechen gangs even though Russian missile fragments were found at the site. The newspaper *Izvestia* reported that the Russians had been shooting at a building where the guerrillas were meeting and that a bomb had gone off course. Then came the claim that the victims were terrorists, even though women and children were among them. A few days later, Russian jets began bombing Grozny, the Chechen capital.

The Moscow government will not allow journalists, Russian or foreign, into the war zone. Moscow's official broadcasts seem to be the only source of information. Does this sound like Serbia's propaganda war . . . revisited?

Why, indeed, have the Russians acted so harshly in Chechnya? As always, truth appears to be stranger than fiction. The Russian economy is in a shambles; the parliament, the ministries, the entire administration of justice under Boris Yeltsin was in complete disarray. It is small wonder Yeltsin finally quit his job and handed it over to Vladimir Putin. Elections for the Duma (the Russian Parliament) had already been set for mid-December. Then Putin won the presidential election, since, by law, Yeltsin could not run again. Putin had always been Yeltsin's chosen successor—why not? He had served Russia as security chief and as prime minister. Putin is Yeltsin's clone, as it were. Consider this: Yeltsin has let Putin take the credit for the bombing so that Putin can get himself elected. Sound familiar? Yeltsin has been taking lessons from Milosevic—how to keep the people from blaming him for Russia's woes.

What's the reaction? Russians are convinced that Chechens are savage riff-raff, a lawless breed, uncouth and uncivilized, cutthroats and misfits who are getting what they deserve. The West, on the other hand, has been harshly critical of the Russians in that their actions threaten the stability of the Caucasus. The Russian government dismisses this criticism by pointing to Kosovo, saying over and over that Russia is simply doing in Chechnya what the West did in Kosovo. Western calls for an end to the fighting only make it more popular with the Russians, who accuse the West of double standards. The Western press calls these rebels "freedom fighters." The West, argue the Russians, lost its moral superiority when NATO bombed Serbia. The Russian press believes that the West is siding with Chechnya to keep Russia weak. Foreign Minister Igor Ivanov stated that the West should actually be helping Moscow. Colonel-General Leonid Ivashov declared that Russia is only fulfilling its international duty (a phrase reminiscent of Soviet jargon when the official Communist press used the terms *ispolnyaet svoi mezhdunarodnyi dolg*) by fighting bandits and terrorists. For the time being, the West can do essentially nothing—cut off some aid, perhaps, but that's about all.[19]

Regardless of the outcome of the war in Chechnya, it means that other separatist elements in Russia will take a second look at their calls for independence.[20] Over 25 million Russians live in other republics. In Moldova, 60,000 Russians and Ukrainians created the Trans-Dneister Republic in 1992 because they feared Moldova would join Romania. Russians make up 40 percent of the population of Kazakhstan and 20 percent of the population in Kyrgyzstan. The Muslims of Russia have now been warned.

The West will never intervene in Russia, not as long as Russia keeps its nuclear arsenal. However, because Russia's coffers are empty, its private capital is in flight, and it is desperate for a handout (i.e., foreign currency), the West holds a few trump cards. The lessons of Chechnya and of Kosovo mean that Russia must rethink its strategies. If the Russians follow the ways of Milosevic, they must have the wealth and the economy to back up such actions. Then again, who will dare to call the Russians' bluff on their own turf? Geopolitics does make a difference.

ALBANIA

In Albania, unlike Kosovo, the Muslims, Roman Catholics, and Orthodox get along rather well. Albanians tend to see Kosovar Albanians as badly mannered, poorly educated, aggressive, and prone to criminal acts. The Kosovar Albanians tend to see Albanians as naive, backward, elitist, and incapable of operating successfully in the modern world.[21] The leaders, however, generally hail from the Orthodox, Greek-oriented south and have little affinity with the Kosovars. In the past, Sali Berisha's Democratic Party wanted to unite with Kosovo, especially after he lost power and sought a way back into the government. He abandoned his position after the Western promptings during the war in Bosnia. Before the war, the Albanian foreign minister saw the KLA as a band of terrorists. After the war, he wanted Kosovo to become a third republic in Yugoslavia. Parts of northern Albania on the Kosovo border are beyond the city of Tirana's control and may be the hideout of Kosovar guerrillas. The arrival of thousands of aid workers, journalists, and NATO troops (the Albania Force helped with the refugee problem and ended its mandate on September 1) provided the impoverished country with much-needed Western currency and led to vast improvements in infrastructure. The people here have no confidence in the police or their ability to keep order. The people are more concerned with their own economic problems than with the Kosovars' plight.

ARABS AND MUSLIMS IN GENERAL

The Arab world was angry with NATO for sidestepping the United Nations. Still, the Arab states donated money to the refugees and the Red Crescent organization set up refugee camps. Only the United Arab Emirates offered peacekeepers. Street protests broke out against the Serbs in Lebanon and by Palestinians. Paradoxically, Libya and Iraq (the international pariahs) supported Serbia. Turkey, a member of NATO, sent a 988-man contingent of peacekeepers, sheltered 20,000 refugees, and opened offices in Pristina to provide humanitarian assistance. With a small population of Turks in Kosovo, Turkey was concerned and has stated that if the crisis in Kosovo is allowed to get out of control, it could become a major source of instability in Europe.

ISRAEL AND WORLD JEWRY

Israel organized a large refugee aid mission to Macedonia when the war started. I would not belabour the point if I were to say that Israel has done more for Kosovar relief than any other non-NATO country. The Israelis sent doctors and nurses and sundry medical personnel and supplies for mothers, children, and orphans. The Preface to this book relates my own experience of this relief undertaking. In fact, more than 100 Muslim refugees were brought to Israel. This did not stop the Israelis, if not their government, from remaining ambivalent. Israelis are always reminded by their media how the Kosovars persecuted Jews and served with Hitler years ago. When war raged, Benjamin Netanyahu's supporters openly backed the Serbs (and they still do), contending that Kosovo was a base for Islamic extremism in Europe. Right-wing Israeli politician and war hero Ariel Sharon was a proponent of such unsubstantiated ideas. Israeli media has been reporting that the KLA was funded by Iran, Afghanistan, and Hezbollah; calls to Israel's "far-right talk radio station" have demanded that Israel send its Muslim Kosovar refugees to Iran or Saudi Arabia. At one point the United States was furious with Israel for allowing Belgrade to use the Israeli Amos-1 satellite for television broadcasts.[22]

American Jews, on the other hand, were quick to offer massive amounts of aid for the refugees. All manner of American-Jewish relief agencies were at work helping both Kosovars and Kosovar Jews under the general auspices of the American Jewish Joint Distribution Committee.[23] The vast majority of American Jews, whom I call mainstream American Jews, sided with the coalition against Milosevic. However, a small group of Jewish intellectuals—with Noam Chomsky leading the way—were appalled by the bombing of Yugoslavia and wrote a letter to the German Green Party to put pressure on NATO to stop the carnage. One will no doubt appreciate that any form of genocide or persecution, anywhere in the world, is reprehensible to all Jews. Moreover, the ranks of American Jews in the U.S. civil bureaucracy have swelled under President Clinton.[24] Jews have been in the limelight of the decision-making process. This fact has not been lost on Serbian public opinion, which castigated American Jews for directing the NATO campaign against Yugoslavia. Certain articles appearing in the Serbian press during the summer months of 1999, especially in the Belgrade dailies *Politika* and *Duga*, were blatantly anti-Semitic. Serbs were essentially saying that the powerful Jews of America orchestrated this entire war against the Yugoslav peoples. To this very day the Serbian media is trumpeting unflattering aspects of the Jews, sometimes without the slightest effort to differentiate between Israelis, whom the media always admired, and American and European Jews. If a split were discernible between diaspora Jews and Israelis, there would be nothing new in this. Dichotomies between these distinct cultures exist; Jewish opinion and behavior, in any event, are seldom celebrated for their uniformity. As for the outbursts of anti-Semitism among Serbs, that is an unfortunate situation born of Serbian frustrations.

CHINA

China came out promptly against the NATO bombing. It blamed everything on the Albanians and maintained that Serbia was only trying to keep its national unity. Beijing took the view that the United States was spreading its imperialist tentacles into Eastern Europe. The Chinese leadership called for an immediate end to the air strikes and criticized NATO for breaking international laws and for bypassing the United Nations. The bombing of the Chinese embassy in Belgrade set back relations between the Americans and the Chinese. Since then, the Americans have paid $4.5 million in compensation to the victims. On October 17, the London *Observer* quoted an unnamed intelligence officer as saying that NATO forces deliberately bombed the embassy because the Chinese were helping the Yugoslav army with military communications in order to gain access to radar-evading technology from a downed U.S. F-117 Stealth bomber. The United States and Britain denied the story. However, if the Chinese choose to believe it, relations between this fledgling superpower and the United States could reach a serious crisis one day. Former national security advisor Zbigniew Brzezinski has given an assessment of China's role if it turns against the United States. He lists some negative scenarios: intensification of nuclear cooperation with Pakistan or North Korea, mischief-making in Indonesia, strategic cooperation with Russia, and an anti-U.S. rapprochement with India. The Chinese, argues Brzezinski, always plan for the long term.

THE REST OF THE WORLD

Throughout the rest of the world, the actions of NATO were viewed with suspicion. From Japan and China to Latin America and Africa, most countries believe that the circumvention of the United Nations by NATO sets a bad precedent. Most countries believed when war began that NATO was being used as an instrument of American foreign policy. Latin American commentators, however, accepted the fact that the United States could and will intervene where and when it wants. Their own experience with the United States has taught them that harsh lesson. The fact that national sovereignty was essentially ignored is also a sticking point. China with problems in Tibet and India with problems in Kashmir are major critics of this policy.

RECOGNITION

Will Kosovo be recognized as an independent country by the international community? The Montevideo Convention of 1933 provided guidelines for the recognition of new states: clearly defined boundaries, a government in control, and a stable population. If these conditions are met, then the country deserves to have sovereignty. Do any of these conditions apply to Kosovo? Because of Serb claims on parts of Kosovo, the borders aren't set. There is no government in full control or accepted by all sides. The population is far from stable, with returning Albanian refugees and fleeing Serbs.

Although the 1975 Helsinki Accords guaranteed the prevailing borders of Europe, the Accords have been violated by the breakups of Yugoslavia and Czechoslovakia and the reunification of Germany. The West has already rejected the demands of the Kurds, Tibetans, Tamils, and other ethnic groups for independence. Will Kosovo be any different?

The fighting factions here may never find peace. As Istvan Deak wrote in 1997, "Not until the peoples of the region agree on an ethnically disinterested superior authority—perhaps in the form of the European Union—is there any hope for genuine reconciliation."[25] Once reconciliation takes place, independence ought to follow. But that is in a distant future.

The events in Kosovo have produced a major upheaval in the international system. But the future of Europe has not been altered irrevocably. Its destiny will now shift to the east, to the Balkans, to Russia, to the Caucasus, to Central Asia—where there is much wealth to be had.

Essentially, the success of the "intervention" in Kosovo has led to a new way of thinking. A new morality may have found its place in the world system, but it must be acted upon in every case. Lest we forget, there are areas in the world just as volatile as Kosovo.

NOTES

1. Thomas G. Weiss, "Rekindling Hope in U.N. Humanitarian Intervention" in *Learning from Somalia: The Lessons of Armed Humanitarian Intervention*, eds. Walter Clarke and Jeffrey Herbst (Boulder: Westview, 1997); p. 208.

2. Ibid.

3. Robert H. Jackson, "Armed Humanitarianism" in *International Journal*, vol. 8, Autumn 1993, p. 583.

4. Weiss, "Rekindling Hope," pp. 214–20.

5. Edward N. Luttwak, "Give War a Chance" in *Foreign Affairs*, vol. 78, no. 4, July/August 1999, p. 38.

6. Ibid. For example, UN troops in Srebenica in Bosnia could have saved thousands of lives if they had been more effective.

7. John Diamond, "General: Politicians Botched Kosovo" in *Chicago Tribune*, October 22, 1999.

8. "Outside Intervention New Norm in Civil Wars" in *Globe and Mail*, October 23, 1999, p. A12.

9. Many of the arguments in this paragraph are quoted from Charles Krauthammer, "Limits of Humanitarianism" in *Time*, September 27, 1999, p. 118.

10. Samantha Power, "Never Again: The World's Most Unfulfilled Promise," p. 8 (www.pbs.org/wgbh/pages/frontline/shows/karadzic/genocide/neveragain.html).

11. Ibid.

12. David Newsom, "Holbrooke's Daunting Task" in *Christian Science Monitor*, vol. 91, no. 179, August 11, 1999, p. 8.

13. Paul Knox, "UN Veto, a Divisive Reform Issue" in *Globe and Mail*, July 19, 1997.

14. "Kosovo, Drugs, the KLA and the West," *Australian Guardian* (http://members.tripod.com/kyeo/guardian.htm). The best account on the work of the Bundeswehr is contained in "Frieden im Kosovo, Europa Neu Begreifen," *Deutschland—Zeitschrift für Politik, Kultur, Wirtschaft und Wissenschaft*, no. 4, August/September 1999.

15. Gabriel Kahn, "The Unhappiest Allies: Italians Question NATO Moves in Kosovo as the Country Braces for More Refugees," March 26, 1999 (http://www.salonmagazine.com/news/1999/03/26newsa.html).

16. Thomas Goltz, "NATO's Achilles' Heel: History, Geography and Suspicion Underlie Popular Anti-NATO Sentiment in Greece," April

29, 1999 (http://www.salonmagazine.com/news/feature/1999/04/29/greece/index.html).

17. *Ogonek*, September 1999.

18. "It's the Russians, Stupid," p. 2 (www.stratfor.com/crisis/kosovo/specialreports/special87.htm).

19. Barry Renfrew, "Russia Rejects Chechnya Criticism," October 25, 1999 (http://dailynews.com/h/ap/19991025/wl/russia_rebuffing_the_west_1.html). See *Nezavisimaya Gazeta*, or any Russian English-language newspaper, for the last two weeks of October and early November 1999.

20. Currently, there are many major separatist movements in the Russian Federation: Altai-Khakassia, Bashkortostan, Buryatia, Chavashia, Chukotka, Circassia, Crimea, Don Cossacks, Hasava, Ingria, Ingushetia, Kalmykia, Karachai-Balkavia, Karelia, Koryakia, Kuban Cossacks, Mari-El, Mordvinia, Ossetia, Sakha Omuk, Siberia, Tannu Tuva, Tartarstan, Terek, Udmurtia, Uralia, Volga, and Zyria.

21. International Crisis Group, "South Balkans: The View from Tirana: The Albanian Dimension of the Kosovo Crisis," July 10, 1998 (www.crisisweb.org/projects/sbalkans/reports/kos03mai.htm).

22. *The Jerusalem Post*, November 4, 1999.

23. (http://www.jdc.org/news.kosovo.htm), November 6, 1999.

24. The following are but a few Jews close to President Clinton: Secretary of State Madeleine Albright, State Department spokesman James Rubin, Defense Secretary William Cohen, Congressman Mark Grossman, National Security Advisor Sandy Berger, Dmitri Simes of one reputable American think tank, and Henry Kissinger of another think tank.

25. Istvan Deak, "The Habsburg Empire" in *After Empire: Multiethnic Societies and Nation-Building: The Soviet Union and the Russian, Ottoman and Habsburg Empires*, eds. Karen Barkey and Mark Von Hagen (Boulder: Westview, 1997), pp. 138–39.

6

A SUMMING UP

It would be some time before I fully realized that the United States sees little need for diplomacy. Power is enough. Only the weak rely on diplomacy.... The Roman Empire had no need for diplomacy. Nor does the United States.

—Boutros Boutros-Ghali

We intentionally set the bar too high for the Serbs to comply. They need some bombing, and that's what they are going to get.
—a senior White House official talking to the media at Rambouillet

SHOPTALK

April, 2000. A year had elapsed since NATO first launched its bombing campaign of Yugoslavia. I needed to go over a series of legal matters with colleagues who could talk to me about what was going on at the War Crimes Tribunal at The Hague. The ICTY, as it is called, had been deliberating case after case of crimes committed against humanity. But, as in the rest of the world, opinion was divided; there were acquittals at The Hague, lack of evidence, briberies of witnesses. The sinister shadow of politics cast a pall over international law.

Percy McNair is a Harvard-educated professor who teaches the law of nations in a prominent New England college. Many years ago he and I had been graduate students in Switzerland on Guggenheim Fellowships. McNair is a pleasant, grey-haired man with a large face and intelligent blue eyes. He always leaned far to the left on the political spectrum—

something quite rare for American legal experts. After exams in late
April, he invited me over to Massachusetts for a few days. And we re-
sumed our endless discussions of war crimes in the Balkans. The talk,
as usual, turned to the rights and wrongs of the Kosovo war. His advice
was always welcome. I had told him about the book I was writing. He
immediately became engrossed in the subject of crime and listened in-
tently as I related a series of substantiated facts to him.

Our discussions had never lacked animation. "Good heavens, man!"
he exclaimed, after listening to my account. "I know their game," he
laughed mockingly. "I wouldn't fall for any of this NATO claptrap; it's
just the U.S. and the Monroe Doctrine all over again. You should always
doubt whatever you read." He stared at me for a moment, then
shrugged, a thin smile on his lips. "Have you read all the articles Noam
Chomsky wrote on the subject?" he inquired ruefully.

"Chomsky seems to love writing about our new world order," I said,
smirking and shaking my head. "And frankly," I said, drawing a long
breath, "I'm tired of Chomsky."

My host glared at me over his glasses.

"He's got much too much to say about the four corners of this globe.
The old linguistics professor just can't have the expertise on just about
everything, from Latin America to the Middle East, and the Balkans, and
Western Europe and Eastern Europe, the environment, the planet, he
says it all in one breath. They follow him around as if he were some
omniscient guru. Chomsky can dissect syntax all he likes," I explained,
"but hardly the correct and moral line on American foreign policy.
Chomsky is just as radical as the right-wing radicalism he denounces."

"Rezun," he interrupted, "Let's face it. Is it Chomsky you don't like,
or his following?"

"Both, but more of the latter," I told him. McNair sat tight-lipped and
silent.

I proceeded to relate to him how a significant number of people regard
all the leaders of NATO and Western heads-of-state as war criminals,
worthy of indictment for crimes committed against Serbia. I had been
thinking of the letter sent by a number of law professors from Canada's
Osgoode Hall Law School to Madam Justice Louise Arbour, who had
been chief prosecutor at the Hague.

"I know all about that," McNair said sarcastically. "Clinton and Blair
indeed, and the whole lot of them should be investigated for violations
of international humanitarian law under Articles 18.1 and 18.4 of the
Tribunal Statute. You know just as well as I do, Miron, that NATO
bombed bridges and civilians. Western leaders have openly admitted
targeting civilian infrastructure in addition to military targets."

"Military spokesmen said it was collateral damage." My voice may have sounded half serious. I was playing devil's advocate with him. "Most of the Serbs accused so far are indicted on crimes of genocide," I said.

His face became almost unreadable. "That's bunk," he suddenly spluttered. He shook his head and added, "There was never any genocide in Kosovo, and you know that. NATO lied. NATO faked the photographs and published pictures of mass graves for the press—it was all done to influence world opinion. Witnesses in Albania were talking about a massacre of 22,000 people by Serbian forces. When NATO troops went in there, the number of those murdered suddenly dwindled to about 11,000. Later it was 9,000. And it keeps getting smaller and smaller. Western media spoke of bodies down mine shafts, mass burials. But the death toll will be much, much lower. Once the bodies are all exhumed, the final body count may end up being hundreds, not thousands."

"There are about 2,000 villages in Kosovo," I answered. "If each village lost an average of five people, and that's a conservative estimate, that would mean at least 10,000 killed."

"The forensic experts sent there are not saying that," he said calmly. "Not a single mass grave has been found. For instance, there were no bodies in the Trepca mine shaft, nor was there any mass killing at Ljubenic," holding out a coloured map for me to see. "That so-called mass grave contained only five bodies; the forensics are saying the bodies that have been exhumed so far show no signs of mutilation; death, they say, was due to shrapnel or bullets. But just consider the case where a NATO plane strafed a highway and countless refugees were killed."

I wanted to ask him if he denied that Milosevic was a criminal in the eyes of the world. But I decided to drop that issue, and switched the discussion to the indictment of other Serbs. I showed him a UN document that described the horrid nightmare of dozens of women in a Serbian rape camp in the town of Foca during the Bosnian war. "Radomir Kovac, Dragoljub Kunarac, and Zoran Vukovic" I reeled off their names, "are the three Bosnian Serb commanders accused of forcing Muslim women into sexual slavery."

My friend asked me if this trial at the Hague marked the first time an international court was judging sexual assault as a crime against human dignity under international law. I answered that the first conviction for sexual assault as a crime of genocide was in 1998 by the International Tribunal for Rwanda. "But in Kosovo," I pointed out, "the women and girls, some of them only twelve, gang-raped every night by as many as eight soldiers; a number of the women fell pregnant and were forced to give birth; others suffered permanent gynecological damage and psychological trauma."

"Gynecological damage?" he asked, frowning.

"They were sadistically tortured," I said. "Beaten, brutalised, young daughters were forced to watch their mothers being probed and impaled with instruments, seeing them naked for hours on end."

McNair nodded and said, "The problem is that the media are still focussing on Serb atrocities. In the Bosnian war all sides resorted to rape—in dozens of camps across Bosnia. You will recall the earlier rape trial of Bosnian Croat Anto Furundzia."

How true, I thought to myself. "Most of the atrocities, though, were committed by Serbs," I replied evasively. It was then that I related my experiences at an Israeli field hospital in a Kosovar refugee camp.

My interlocutor's face became unreadable again.

I produced a written testimony of a rape survivor that was produced by the organization called Human Rights Watch. "This is what happened in Kosovo just two days before NATO troops arrived." And I started reading:

Then they took me. I was pregnant. I was holding my son. They took him away from me and gave him to my mother. They told me to get up and follow them. I was crying and screaming, "Take me back to my child!" They took me to another room. It was so bad I almost fainted. I can't say the words they said. They tortured me. Because I was pregnant, they asked me where my husband was. I was afraid to say that he was in the woods. So I said that he was in Italy. One of them said to another soldier, "Kick her and make the baby abort." They did this to me four times—they took me outside to the other place. All the girls were tortured the same way until they were taken for the last time.

While I was sitting apart from my mother in the yard, I could not see my mother or my sister, but I could hear my son crying. One man grabbed the child and brought him to me. He let the boy stay with me for a while and then they took him away. Then another man came at me. Three men took me one by one. Then they asked me, "Are you desperate for your husband?" and said, "Here we are instead of him." The paramilitaries released V.B. and put her inside with the other older women. A policeman sat outside, guarding the door. He wore a camouflage and blue uniform. After half an hour, however, other paramilitaries entered the room: They were coming in with knives and masks. And they would ask one another, "Are we going to cut them?" They did the same thing each time. They beat me, they bit me. The one who was finishing with me would take me to another one and say, "You take her now." One was very big with a shaved head and he tortured me very much. When he took me in his hands he tortured me so much that I fainted. I didn't know where I was.

When I woke up I was lying on the ground with no clothes and he was standing over me and laughing. I screamed but he put a machine gun in my face and said that he would shoot me if I screamed again. I didn't have any clothes on. I was afraid that since I was pregnant they would cut me. They were playing with their knives all the time. They said, "We will take the baby out." That man with the shaved head and a mask sharpened his knife in front of me. One gave himself an injection. The man with the shaved head did all these bad things. He cut his hand a little bit and drank blood in front of us. After I fainted they didn't take me anymore.

McNair answered, "Many refugees lied or magnified their stories. . . ." "Wait, let me just finish reading this other part by Human Rights Watch," I said. "It will corroborate some of the things I witnessed at the Macedonian refugee camp I visited." And I read to him as follows:

By July [1999], gynecologists in Kosovo and Albania interviewed by Human Rights Watch reported eight cases of rape in which they had provided abortions or other medical treatment. In Pec alone, a local gynecologist reported that three women had requested abortions because they had been raped. In Pristina, the chief gynecologist, Dr. S. Hoxha, performed two abortions on rape victims. In both cases the women, seventeen and twenty-one years of age, said they had been gang-raped by Serbian special police (MUP), one near Djakovica and the other near Klina.

"Elsewhere in the report," I continued, "it reads":

"Beyond the immediate fear of pregnancy, some women expressed shame that they had been raped," Dr. Hoxha, the chief gynecologist, told Human Rights Watch. "We think that this category of women will suffer consequences in the future—psychological consequences as well as family and social status consequences."
Women interviewed by Human Rights Watch appeared to be suffering from very high levels of trauma, exacerbated by cultural taboos associated with rape. Women returning to their families after hours of captivity often exhibited symptoms of trauma and extreme emotional distress. In one case, a twenty-two-year-old woman was taken away by Serbian soldiers in the village of Z. According to the testimony of eyewitnesses, in the morning on April 5, uniformed Serbs grabbed the woman and put a knife to her throat. A man who witnesses believed was an army captain told the woman's husband, "This woman is not yours anymore." An hour later when the woman returned, she fainted and wept.

She told her mother-in-law and the other women in her family that she had been raped. In shock, she tried to commit suicide by putting her fingers in a light socket.

At this point, seeing McNair's discomfort in speaking about women's issues, I brought the subject back to the atrocities committed in Bosnia a few years ago. I raised the issue of the Srebrenica slaughter, where, since 1995, at least 7,500 people are missing and are now presumed dead. "General Radislav Krstic was in charge then and had given the command. After the killings, Serb soldiers buried the bodies. When word of the massacre got out, the Serbs allegedly dug up many bodies and buried them elsewhere."

"Allegedly—still has to be proven in a court of law," the professor argued. "Even an international tribunal must comply with the notion of presumption of innocence," he said.

And so I continued by reading the report of further indictments. "You must know that Radovan Karadzic's top aide and successor, Krajisnik, is undergoing trial right now, as we speak—he faces charges of genocide, violations of the laws and customs of war, deportation and inhumane acts. The noose around Karadzic's neck is tightening, and also around General Ratko Mladic; both are still at large, although Mladic is more likely to be in Serbia right now."

McNair appeared to be quite unperturbed by all this. "Miron," he began, stroking his beard in that familiar way scholars do, "in your last book on Yugoslavia you wrote quite convincingly about this tribalism in the Balkans. Everyone's a part of the tribe! So why are you now suddenly finding fault with the Serbs?"

"I'm not," I said. "I'm certainly not leading to that in my book. But I'd like to know there is a sense of closure here. Tribalism, like cannibalism, is a minimalist way of looking at things."

"Minimalist?" McNair was plainly amused. "Well, then, you're a maximalist, and a romantic at that. Why even expect a happy ending?"

"I'm a transcendentalist, hoping there is justice for all," I insisted.

We had many conversations like this one. I now resign myself to the fact that closures readily come with some retribution; nor are happy endings an option in world politics.

BACK TO THE FUTURE

"Those who ignore the hard lessons of history are likely to relive them one day" is a saying that comes to mind again and again. The prophetic words are a fitting reminder to those faint of memory. As a general truth of inescapable fatalism, that saying could stand as a judgment of ethnic conflict—past, present, and future.

This turn-of-the-century's call to arms in the Balkans is what most conflicts will probably be like from now on: nasty, brutish, short; unfinished too. Yet the entire gamut has been run, replete with genocide, eviction, intervention, expulsions, revenge, and sanctions. The pattern in the Balkans seems predictable, like the cycle of life itself. One malefactor succeeds the next. One vengeful act begets another. Words like *retaliation* are already time-worn. Serbs who once persecuted ethnic Albanians are themselves being persecuted. Human beings become heroes today, victims tomorrow; sometimes, almost overnight, the heroes turn into antiheroes. Hunters become the hunted. A vortex of hateful passions drives communities to an irrational compulsion to persecute their neighbours, to evict their neighbours' children, violate their neighbours' women. One might remember that in the holy scriptures Christ pleaded with his tormentors and asked, "Why do you torment us so?" And Christ forgave them their trespasses, saying, "They know not what they do."

We are not all the children of Christ, however. To justify our self-righteousness we frequently need to identify the evil-doer. We want to hoist him up on Golgotha, self-righteously. There must be a villain. As the official broadcast world reminds us how to humanize one kind of victim and dehumanize another, we end up with half-truths about everyone and everything. We deal in myths. They are not total falsehoods, no more than saying, in one breath, that a cup may be half full and half empty. Disinformation, deception, and subterfuge dressed as journalism hardly does justice to the fifth estate. We must never suspect that the frontiers of villainy can be blurred. Slobodan Milosevic, the perpetrator of a catalogue of horrors, is cast as villain. His victims are regarded as saints. Western soldiers are portrayed as the flawless champions of virtue. "Joe Public" will scoop it up as an interesting *coup de théâtre*. We couldn't get enough of the jingoist hysteria that NATO whipped up to demonize the Serbs. Cynical journalists love writing about the knavish schemes that villains are up to, for an entertaining villain is a far more suitable character to hiss at than a dull hero.

Hence, the bad guy in our story, Milosevic, is no dullard. He holds on to power with might and main. One would have thought him incapable of resisting again. Indeed, foreigners and media mongers like to point to the swelling number of demonstrators in the streets of Belgrade. Western observers repeatedly relate how those streets resound with stormy cries of "Slobo to The Hague!" and "Down with Slobo!" And there is talk of "the opposition that controls the cities outside of Belgrade!" "Montenegro will separate!" Surely the people won't let Milosevic stay?

True, there are demonstrators shouting him down, but there were demonstrators on the streets when he lost the war in Bosnia. Milosevic is nothing if not cagey. He is already exploiting NATO's slowness in reacting to Albanian attacks on Serbs to rally his people away from the current situation in Serbia, giving them an enemy to react against.[1] West-erners now understand that the army is fully behind him. If his former supporters have turned against him, it is not because he is an insufferable tyrant ("Balkan culture easily breeds tyrants"); rather, they are seeking his ouster because he has failed to live up to his promises to create a greater Serbia. So now there is an official Serbian Renewal Movement to oust Milosevic. The idea that a dubious personality like Vuk Draskovic acts as leader of this front flies in the face of common sense and logic, for this erratic politician may one day find himself murdered by the regime's (read: Slobo's) gangsters. As if several attempts on his life have not been made already!

But who are Milosevic's gangsters? People who prop up the regime, no doubt. His own henchmen, some 300 persons. A rogue's gallery will eventually devour itself, as is said of any revolution that "devours its children." Factions begin to quarrel. After the Bosnian war of the early 1990s, Yugoslavia entered a period of high unemployment and economic decline. The underworld of illicit traders, money launderers, and rack-eteers thrived. Milosevic's supporters benefited from the illicit money, the drug trafficking, and the prostitution. Belgrade bristled with bars and bordellos. Living in the Serbian capital before the Kosovo war was like living in Caligula's Rome. Here was a microcosm of Slavic Eastern Europe, outperformed only by Russia and Ukraine. Milosevic's own son, Marko, was himself both player and patron of the crime syndi-cates. In this type of environment there will always be intrigue and jealousy and lust for more booty as the rogues are left to their own devices. In Yugoslavia some, if not all, were not only mobsters but sur-reptitious members of the political elite. The approximate number of "Slobo's elite" can today be gauged by the number of prominent men and women from Serbia and Montenegro who are banned from receiving EU visas. Most important are the four men whom the War Crimes Tri-bunal at the Hague has indicted, along with their patron—Milosevic himself (see Appendix E).

SLEIGHT-OF-HAND

The most notorious among the elite was Zeljko Raznatovic, better known as Arkan. His name was conspicuously absent from the public list of 75 war crimes indictments issued by The Hague in 1996. Barely a week into the twenty-first century he was gunned down in a hail of bullets in the lobby of Belgrade's Intercontinental Hotel. Who masterminded the slay-ing? Let us take a closer look at Arkan and what he represented. It will af-ford a deeper insight into Serbia's politics of pathology.

During the war in Bosnia in 1992, Arkan organized a private army, the Serb Volunteer Guard, or "Tigers." His men were incorporated in the Ministry of Internal Affairs. In 1991 he had orchestrated a series of massacres in Bosnia and Croatia, primarily against Muslims. In April 1992 some 1,400 Bosnians were murdered in various gruesome ways at Foca, the same place the Serbs set up a sexual enslavement camp, by his paramilitary groups. At Vukovar he had hospital patients taken out and shot. According to estimates of the Serbian Helsinki Committee, about 20,000 refugees from Krajina went through Arkan's extermination camp in Erdut in the fall of 1995 after being arrested and taken there by representatives of the Serbian Ministry of Internal Affairs. Arkan was personally involved in the mutilation and gasoline burnings of women and old men.

Arkan was a wheeler and dealer. He was a wanted man. He robbed like a petty crook from the rich and the poor. All the European police forces were after his hide. Even Interpol had been closing in on him, yet he made dashing escapes. A marked man, he was nonetheless re-elected chairman of the Party of Serbian Unity for four years; in 1998 it was by a unanimous vote. In elections the Kosovo Serbs chose him as their MP. He became rich from all of this; his holdings included a casino at Hotel Jugoslavija, a transport company, and a radio station, and he made a vast fortune through tobacco and petrol smuggling and protection of rackets. He did not seem to be very active in the Kosovo affair, although there were unconfirmed reports that his paramilitary forces were operating in the Srbica county of Kosovo. Night after night during the NATO bombing he would strut through the Hyatt Hotel lobby on the arm of his mini-skirted wife, Ceca, with bodyguards alongside him and bodyguards in front, a battery of thugs bringing up the rear. He lived in fear, aware that the process of liquidating those close to him had already begun. The Serbian State Security Service had been taking action against Arkan's lieutenants who had recruited volunteers for the Tigers—mainly from among criminals, prisoners, and residents of poor parts of the country. Arkan knew far too much and probably tried to distance himself from Milosevic. His bodyguards grew fewer and fewer. One wonders too whether Ceca was entirely reliable. She was his third wife, and he was known as a profligate. His lawyer in Italy had been in contact with the War Crimes Tribunal at The Hague on several occasions, and it is likely that a deal was afoot that would have bared the seamy side of the Milosevic empire. I myself do not believe that Arkan's assassination was a gangland plot, much less a foreign effort to scare the regime. It was certainly not the work of a French commando unit like the one that allegedly attempted to remove Milosevic by force, as Serbian propaganda would have us believe. The French simply would not have what it takes to carry out a hit such as this in a public hotel lobby.

By July 2000, the Serbian public prosecutor's office had charged at least ten people for the killing of Serbia's most prominent warlord and underworld don. But Arkan's murder was just one in a series of attacks against public figures in Yugoslavia. One month after he was gunned down, Defense Minister Pavle Bulatovic was shot dead in a Belgrade restaurant. At the end of May 2000, Goran Zugic, the national security adviser to Montenegro's president, was gunned down in front of his home in Podgorica. And an attempt was made again on Vuk Draskovic, who was injured in the head by a lone gunman.

So, I conclude that none other than Milosevic was behind all the murders.

The Serbian Renewal Movement is another name for the old, fractious opposition that constantly squabbles. It consists of 150 political parties and possibly 800 nongovernmental organizations (NGOs). Meanwhile, Milosevic's politically active wife vows that the Serbs will one day take Kosovo back. No one seems to heed these threats. The truth is that Westerners are more preoccupied with Montenegro's rock star, the bombshell Ceca (now that husband, Arkan, has passed from the scene), than they are with Montenegro's secession. And it is inconceivable that Serbia would one day let Montenegro go and lose the only coastal area it has.

How far out on the limb will NATO and the West go to help Montenegro?

Madeleine Albright and Montenegrin president Milo Djukanovic met in Washington on November 4, 1999, after the peacekeepers were deployed throughout Kosovo. Albright and Djukanovic had both been in contact with the leaders of the Yugoslav opposition. She said: "We understand the desire of all Yugoslavs in Serbia and Montenegro for monetary stability and full participation in the global economy."[2] Washington has already committed $55 million to this mountainous region and has exempted it from sanctions imposed on Serbia. Djukanovic, who could be ousted at any time by troops loyal to Belgrade, somehow persuaded the U.S. secretary of state that he was successfully insulating Montenegro economically from Milosevic's disastrous policies by legalizing the use of foreign currency. But not all foreign currency can be easily used as legal tender in Southeastern Europe; for example, the deutschmark cannot. The United States, moreover, can pledge many things to many countries as Washington sees fit; democratic reform, however, is not America's legacy to pass on to the Balkan people. Montenegro may or may not get the material support that Kosovo received if and when it decides to secede from the Yugoslav union. Djukanovic cries for an international community to be supportive of a democratically elected regime in Montenegro and, ultimately, its independence. So far Albright has given lip service to these aspirations, nothing more. And it does not seem to matter for the time being what Albright or Clinton or Sandy Berger say about the future of Montenegro. A Republican administration in the White House might abandon Montenegro altogether. In fact, just before the new millennium, in a show of force, the Yugoslav army cut off all air transport to and from Podgorica and temporarily closed down the airport.[3]

Too busy patting itself on the back for bringing Milosevic to heel, the West did not realize that its accomplishments were meagre. It failed to realize that the tragedy and horror could have been avoided years earlier if it had been more far-sighted during the breakup of Yugoslavia, if it had been willing to negotiate for minority rights for Serbs in Croatia and Bosnia during 1991 and 1992 rather than fully accepting Croatian independence. Perhaps the NATO powers might have pressured Milosevic for minority rights for the Albanians at the same time.[4]

Yet the failure of the West to see beyond the "now" is not new. It has happened to various empires, kingdoms, and governments since the dawn of civilization. The problem is that the West no longer has a credible villain to rail against. The Soviet Union is gone; the Russia that exists now is a mewing cat, not the raging bear of old. If one needed a villain, an ideology, a geopolitical advantage, an "us" versus "them," Russia no longer fits into that mould. Russia's rapid decline has shifted the balance of power in the Balkans and the Middle East toward the United States. Where there is a void now, the United States, Europe, and NATO are ready to fill it.

Many observers and analysts, moreover, have called the Kosovo war "Madeleine's war" (after the name of the U.S. secretary of state). That has not deterred many a British newscaster from calling it a British engagement from the very start, with responsibility for strategy firmly anchored in Downing Street. The British sense of primacy in this war should be regarded felicitously; Britain's burden was, if anything, a travesty—for in the Kosovo theater there were fewer than fifty British aircraft deployed. Not since World War I has Britain sounded so gung-ho in its media. Lest we forget, the lion's share of the financial assets and troops were deployed by the United States. Europe as a whole proved to be crucial to the equation, but we must be mindful that the EU has consistently maintained commercial, not strategic, interests in this corner of Europe. And Kosovo, in many ways, is unlike the rest of Europe.

This last point cannot be overstated. In terms of any semblance of democracy, Kosovo is light years behind all Europeans, even the Russians and Ukrainians. There is very little civic mindedness among the Kosovars; political culture is rough and crude. There is no tradition of legal norms, only tribal ones. Consequently the rule of law is absent, except that which the peacekeepers bring. Nationalistic male patriarchy gets the better of Kosovar men; women have little say outside the home, and civil society falters and degenerates into lawlessness.

The Kosovar crime syndicates are presently operating a flourishing underground market in drugs, oil, illegal arms, and prostitution. The economic collapse of Kosovo created an atmosphere that enabled the criminal element to thrive. Drug barons and arms dealers from both Kosovo and Albania now represent the new economic elite. Money from the illicit narcotics trade is currently being used to purchase black market weapons, weapons looted chiefly from Albania's military arsenal. These gangsters have extensive connections with Italian mafiosi in Sicily as well as with Western businesses. The money is laundered through Tirana where a graft-loving government routinely channels it through banks that are currently participating in market reform programs imposed by the IMF.

Seventy-five percent of all heroin entering Europe comes through Turkey, with the Kosovar-Albanian-Macedonian crime network controlling most of it. In fact, at this moment Kosovar crime operations—mainly racketeering and prostitution—in southern Italy have surpassed the Neapolitan and Calabria mafia clans in the amount of wealth that is generated.

Certainly all the Balkans suffer from this lawlessness; the Albanian Kosovars are the most notorious, though. The reader will recall that I began this book with a description of how Kosovar women, after being raped by Serbian predators, still had to hide their loss of face. The Albanians of Albania are no different in these social attitudes, which makes every Western statesman wince every time he or she hears of the imminent union of Kosovo and Albania.

It is strange how foreigners like to promote the democratization of Kosovo. Madeleine Albright, Sandy Berger, Bernard Kouchner (formerly with the Nobel Prize–winning Doctors Without Borders), President Bill Clinton himself—they have all made useless speeches about it. It reminds me of a passage in Machiavelli where it says that a statesman "who is ill advised, is himself not very wise." The Rambouillet agreement sought to bring an end to hostilities in Kosovo, to endow it with a communal police force and a criminal justice commission, all geared toward a civil public security system. But it was naive to even suggest in this interim accord that self-government was within the grasp of its citizens when they could hardly respect each other's basic human rights. What is required in Kosovo is policing and peacemaking, not premature "confidence-building measures."[5] Those who drafted the Rambouillet agreement must have known it was bound to fail. Albright never took it seriously. The terms that the Serbs accepted in June 1999 were virtually the same as those they themselves offered before the bombings began. Journalists who reported on the agreement used to laugh about it and say they had never even read it. Ian Black, the *Guardian*'s man at the British Foreign Office who reported the inebriated buffoonery at Rambouillet, admitted he never read the document in full.[6] The revelation that American reporters knew about a U.S. strategy to create a pretext for NATO's war on Yugoslavia—but did not report on it—raises serious questions about the independence of mainstream news organizations.

I am firmly convinced that the British and the Americans were keen on bringing about an armed conflict to push further ahead with Yugoslavia's dismemberment—the better to "divide and rule"! As for the problem of genocide, I am not sure that it is an apt description of what went on prior to NATO's bombing. Terrible events occurred, but nothing was what it seemed. The public was grossly misled. Yes, there was ethnic cleansing; yes, Milosevic would have evicted all the Albanians if he could; yes, there was outrage and brutality. But there was also deception on the part of NATO, "spin-doctoring on an unprecedented scale," some have called it. Journalists did lie, as McNair said. Photographs were faked. Mass graves turned out to be nothing more than plowed fields. Nevertheless, atrocities were definitely committed, men and women disappeared. The death toll will probably never be known—at the end, a reverse ethnic cleansing had begun.

We must use the term *genocide* with circumspection, lest it be corrupted to suggest the extent of the genocide of the Holocaust. Using a word like that is very emotive language. Consider the inaction of Western governments when faced with the "genocide" in Rwanda, where at least 500,000 people were butchered in thirteen weeks in 1994. Imagine for a moment that the American government actually forbade its officials to use the word *genocide* because of its moral and legal connotations.

But so much for the social and moral imperatives of how people acted in the Balkan crisis.

There is an economic side to all of this. The entire region should also be regarded as a potential market, under the economic influence of powerful global companies. A good example is the economic clout Germany wields in all of Eastern Europe. More important, Russia's weakness has opened potentially strategic oil deposits in Russia's Caspian Sea to American and German companies. German firms such as Siemens are part of the act in an area where the deutschmark rules. These Western companies in turn have inaugurated a lucrative pipeline-building network that in the long run might weaken Russia's influence over other members of the former Soviet Union. Recent turmoil in Muslim Dagestan and in Chechnya is only a case in point. When Russia accepted NATO's absorption of Poland, Hungary, and the Czech Republic in early 1999, it was on the understanding that the alliance was a defensive one, that Russia would have a voice, if not a veto, in NATO's policies in Eastern Europe. Then NATO intervened in what Russia saw as a civil war in Yugoslavia. The Clinton administration actually never wanted to enlist Russia as a strategic partner. Washington expected Moscow to acquiesce in whatever policies it undertook toward Milosevic's regime. Milosevic's Yugoslavia had thus become an identifiable enemy, with only token support from an insolvent Russia and moral backing from Greece, NATO's weakest (and, next to France, most eccentric) ally. The Serbs in Europe have always been the target; they have seldom, though, been an easy prey.

The Russians did not want intervention in Kosovo because it might have lead to intervention in their own backyard (i.e., Chechnya). The same could be said of China, a power waiting in the wings of the new century. Indeed, Beijing fears that American intervention on behalf of Kosovo might one day lead to a challenge on its claims to Taiwan and its hold on Tibet. Conversely, neither China nor the United States really want a strong War Crimes Tribunal because their own respective armed forces might be arraigned on charges (e.g., American actions in Vietnam; Chinese crackdown on dissidents, intellectuals, and secessionists in Tibet). A new way will have to be found to deal with international crises that won't involve infighting and delay.

China will likely continue to blow its horn over Kosovo, just as it did in international crises under Mao. Its embassy was shamefully bombed in Belgrade. However, China does not enter the equation of the Balkans so readily. Nor should one take China's siding with Russia over their mutual opposition to NATO's policies in Kosovo to be of major consequence, not in Europe at least. Europe's entire economy is in a slump. Unemployment and inflation have never been higher, and the new currency, the Euro, has fallen by at least 15 percent. Who needs Russia under such conditions? The Russian rubber-ruble economy is overrun by organized crime (something like $100 billion has been siphoned off overseas) while America posted a 6 percent annual growth rate in 1999, growing further in the year 2000. The turn of the century promises to be no less bullish—despite a few fits and starts—for North America. With America's benediction, the International Monetary Fund is now micromanaging Russia's economy, having committed more than $4.5 billion in loans to stave off a total collapse. At this rate, no nation will be threatening America's sole-superpower status for decades to come, certainly not the Russians or the Chinese—not just yet.[7]

What it all comes down to is that any American administration is well aware that the United States alone is capable of fuelling a world economic recovery. NATO is but a battering ram in that recovery. A Yugoslavia without Milosevic is bound to fall within that recovery umbrella, ultimately acceding to a huge European market.

How else, if not in economic terms and under these conditions, can one explain the European Union's support of NATO? With heavy investments in Slovenia, Croatia, and the emerging opportunities in Bosnia-Herzegovina, the EU felt the threat of the increasing chance that one of the major tactics used by Serbia would be to prolong the war by expanding it into the surrounding areas. With the Republic of Srpska ready to support its ethnic brother Serbia, the EU felt that the Balkan region could once more return to the state it was in during the early 1990s. Also, increasing pressure from newly established markets in Hungary and Bulgaria was beginning to have effects on sympathetic and eager trading partners. Finally, the fear that a new Iron Curtain would rise (had the war turned for the worse) sat heavily on the brows of expansionists hoping to break further into areas traditionally dominated by Middle Eastern markets. The idea of the threat of war expanding into the surrounding countries brought back haunting memories of the years 1991–1995.

As the history of European politics has proven, the EU believes in open and unrestricted markets among member states. If Serbia had been allowed to continue its actions in Kosovo and increase its trade with China and Russia, Serbia would have become a new front and offset the expansion of the European economy by creating an unequal political and economic power in what were already regarded as "European" Third World countries. Germany was concerned that a situation like this would spill over into the surrounding countries in which it has opened businesses and introduced private banking.

Several of the EU's economic formations have since developed strategies and agreements to be implemented in Kosovo and Eastern Europe. The British Trade International (BTI), for example, has offered assistance to the Balkans. BTI views the European Commission, the World Bank, the UN, and the British Department for International Development (DFID) as key players involved in rebuilding Kosovo through loans and foreign aid. This is but one example of the opportunists' market that is developing within Kosovo. Since the breakdown of the existing government agencies in Kosovo, which restricted the Kosovars from any benefits of privatization and international trade, the new economic situation has become extremely promising for the resurgence of new business and trade opportunities. Although there has been large-scale social, economic, and environmental damage, funds for restructuring Kosovo have begun flowing at a rapid rate, creating markets as well as strengthening and reinforcing existing infrastructures to a position not even reached under the previous administration. In view of the fact that these economies previous to the agreements were of nonsanctioned origin, the legitimization of such infrastructures will boost the economy greatly. Also, remittance money previously earned outside of Kosovo by the guest workers (Gastarbeiter) in Germany will continue to flow to the population.

Joint operations and economic reform plans by such groups as the IMF and World Bank will stabilize the country's economy and improve domestic business, unemployment, social conditions, and overall poverty. Also, the EU and other foreign investors will have the chance to establish footholds in a market that was previously dominated and controlled by

Belgrade, which many investors and businesses considered risky and constrictive.

On June 10, 1999, the foreign ministers of the EU met in Cologne to formulate a Stability Pact for South Eastern Europe. The result was a joint pact signed by over twenty organizations outlining the international civil aspects of economic restructuring and reform in the Balkans that would provide a stable environment for the conduct of local and international business.

Despite the embargo imposed on Yugoslavia, the major countries of Europe are pitching in to alleviate navigation problems on the Danube. This venerable waterway has so far remained closed to transit navigation. Winter flooding is acute. For some time now the barges and river boats that once plied between Germany and Austria and the Black Sea ports have sat idle at their moorings. In addition to the toxic poisons in the river from chemicals, the waterway is impassable at the city of Novi Sad in Serbia, where NATO warplanes destroyed three bridges. Billions of dollars have been lost owing to closure of the river. German shippers are losing most of the money. Thus, officials from the United States and the EU are, at the time of this writing, discussing the problem of clearing the debris and getting the Danube economies moving again.

If one day Kosovo were to become completely independent, who would the Serbs turn on next? Before the fall of Yugoslavia, their main antagonism was with the Croats. When the Croats were gone, it was the Bosnian Muslims. If the Kosovars go, will the Serbs turn to Vojvodina? There are large populations of Romanians, Ukrainians, and Hungarians there. Yet the Serbs might well run the risk of war with Romania. Ukrainians and Hungarians (the latter belong to NATO now) will surely not stand by and see these people get slaughtered. That could draw the wrath of NATO down on Serbia again. Romania is so desperate to join NATO and the EU that it might go to war just to show how Romanians wholeheartedly support NATO's policies.

One issue that I believe is worthwhile to raise is the legacy the Kosovo crisis has now left in Europe as a whole. As the European Union continues with its policies of enlargement, perhaps it will be necessary in the future to de-Balkanize the Balkans. The EU will always be the beacon to which the Balkan nations are drawn. However, my pessimism is copiously on record when I affirm with every conviction that the EU's absorptive capacity for further members is limited. It is even more limited than the immediate application of the EU's own "Euro." It will take many years more before a single currency can realistically take effect in so powerful an economic community. The Balkan nations can hardly make do with their national currencies, let alone an all-purpose Euro. But the problem of the Balkans is not the currency, really. It is—let me say this without inhibition—their culture. Before the Balkans are considered in any process of integration, they would have to undergo what I would like to call "Europeanization." Of course Europeanization means democratization.

I find it somewhat narrow-minded and stultifying that there are so many analysts in Europe and North America who are ready to forgive and accept these excesses of Balkan turmoil. As a university professor, I am quite dismayed that they are primarily found in academe more than in journalism and in government. They either do this or they are likely to put the entire blame squarely on the shoulders of Serbian nationalism. That is what McNair was driving at in his talk with me. Then you have the post-structuralists who find it annoying to have to use mega-narratives such as "the Serbs think..." and "the Albanians think..." They hate making sweeping characterizations of public opinion; they would have us look at the dynamics of Kosovo's internal politics. My question to them is how can we give so much attention to internal politics if their societies lack the kind of pluralism and rule of law needed for democratic discourse? We cannot help dealing in group stereotypes. The more "politically correct" among such people feel it is wrong to criticize a Balkan country, indeed the entire Balkan culture, no matter what it did.

Although I have argued that Western attitudes have been self-righteous, that Westerners were guilty of atrocities in the past, why should it be wrong for us to denounce a cabal of regressive nationalist bigots who insist on their race, their language, their religion, their villainy?

This brings me to the question of Jewish sympathies in this conflict. I touched upon this subject earlier. Serbs have called the war against Serbia "the Jewish war"—a subject of much diatribe in the Serbian media. The question is much debated on the pages of the *New York Times*. Serbian nationalists love to point to the Jewish decisionmakers sitting in Washington advising Congress and Clinton. This is an incontrovertible fact. So, too, is the fact that various sides have made efforts to manipulate Jewish opinion, which is so eclectic to begin with, not just pluralistic. What ultimately matters, perhaps, is what American Jews believe is a politically correct policy from an American point of view, regardless of what Israelis might think. American Jews will thus at least show that they support Albanian Kosovars on the same moral grounds that they are willing to support Israel. I do not wish to belabor this point—American Jews simply feel Muslims deserve support as well. How else will American Jewry continue justifying its lobby for Israel?

As for the United Nations, it is a tired policeman showing the signs of avuncular old age. The Universal Declaration of Human Rights was signed by the UN General Assembly in 1948 and guarantees liberty, security, fair trials, nationality, freedom of thought and religion, social security, work, and education, among other things. Yet many of the countries that signed this document do not allow these rights on their own soil. The UN can only be touted these days for its peacekeeping operations. Stepped over and forgotten in the mad dash to war, the UN was seemingly only useful for passing resolutions condemning the fighting. The fact that the UN needs restructuring is quite evident. It needs revitalization, a new purpose. The fifteen-member Security Council (of which China, Russia, the United States, England, and France are permanent members) is itself a cause of many problems. Most of what the Americans want, the Russians and Chinese veto for ideological purposes, and vice versa. This stalemate process led the Americans to overstep the UN entirely, resorting to NATO to legitimize the war in Kosovo because the Clinton administration knew the Chinese and Russians would never agree to it at the UN. However, the veto process was never intended to work in this way. The best way to reform the process is to give a two-thirds veto vote to all members of an expanded Security Council (incorporating Japan and Germany as permanent members). Only then will it become more effective and appear less as a tool of the Americans, Russians, and Chinese. Perhaps further reform could lead to the creation of a permanent international peacekeeping force.

The United Nations, moreover, has had a poor record of resolving ethnic conflict. An enhanced role for Germany in the UN might be welcomed for purely ethical and practical reasons. Germany plays a pre-eminent role in the European Union (EU) and the Conference on Security and Cooperation in Europe (CSCE), not to mention in NATO and in bilateral military arrangements with France. The problem, however, is the German military establishment and the vision of Germans as "peace-keepers." The Serbs take a dim view of this latter possibility, owing to the firm conviction that Germany has maintained historic interests in Croatia and Slovenia (Germany clings to them to this very day) and therefore cannot be expected to negotiate in an impartial manner. The Serbian perception (and this is not Milosevic speaking alone) is that Germany seeks hegemony in Europe and would make a bad third-party mediator. Of course, the same can be said of the Kosovars in regard to the Russians as peacekeepers. The Russians are feared by everyone except the Serbs. In Yugoslavia the Kosovars were averse to giving the Russians a separate peacekeeping sector. It was the Germans who insisted that the Russian force, initially 10,000 strong, be divided among the five sectors—the U.S., French, Italian, German, and British. The consequences of this potpourri are obvious. Fights among the peacekeepers and between the Russians and the local population have broken out with increased ferocity. Many Russian units have already started pulling out of Kosovo.[8]

The reason I am inclined to believe in a world body like the UN is clear and simple. Americans and their leaders cannot be the judges of right and wrong. What is truly needed is an international guarantor of human rights. A never-ending job, for sure; human rights abuses are legion in this world. This task is better left to a UN with an independent peace force that will work in a world where civilization has more and more respect for the rule of law.

The lessons of Kosovo speak volumes about how far the world has yet to come. The conflict shows that world governments cannot stand back and do nothing. Isolationist policies don't work in today's world. Economic reality has made that impossible. No nation can afford to disregard events in the rest of the world for economic ruin might result. Instead, the world needs a strengthened and revitalized organization like the United Nations, a body with the power and the ability to enforce its resolutions. NATO, weakened at the end of the Cold War, was vastly revitalized after the Kosovo conflict. It found a purpose. (Granted, it couldn't have done anything without the United States, but it's a promising first step.) What the UN needs now is a way to bypass the partisan politics of the Security Council and pass resolutions approving its own security force that can be deployed despite objections by the United States, Russia, and China. Perhaps only then can the first steps to true globalization be truly completed.

The world will not tolerate ethnic cleansing anymore, as recent events in East Timor indicate. Morality has indeed entered international politics. Interdependent economics plays a part, too. Even if the lies and the subterfuge continue, so will human accountability. Perhaps it is too late for some countries (e.g., Rwanda), but it is enough for future dictators and despots to think twice before they act. American policymakers, whether artful conspirators or benevolent world leaders, should be mindful at all times that those who wage wars also wear blinders. For man's reach, history has taught us so often, almost always exceeds his grasp.

NOTES

1. Almost every day one hears of Kosovars attacking and murdering innocent Serbs on the streets of Pristina and elsewhere in Kosovo. Muslim Kosovars even kill Muslim Bosnians who live in Kosovo. The NATO commanders are outraged by the behaviour and Bernard Kouchner has denounced it, but there is little they can do to stop the random attacks.

2. Washington File, International Information Programs, November 4, 1999 (www.usia.gov/cgi-bin/washfile/di . . .).

3. *New York Times*, December 9, 1999.

4. William W. Hagan, "The Balkans' Lethal Nationalisms" in *Foreign Affairs*, vol. 78, no. 4, July/August 1999, p. 60.

5. For the entire text of Rambouillet agreement, see *Le Monde Diplomatique*, April 17, 1999.

6. See Z Magazine, February 18, 2000.

7. Even the Europeans are not serious contenders. One European told me recently that what is important to Europe is how many shirts, tractors, and power stations it can sell in what, by the mid twenty-first century, will be the world's largest economy.

8. The media are saying that the Russian pullout is a result of troops needed for the war in Chechnya. See *New York Times*, December 7, 1999.

EPILOGUE

The fall of Milosevic is now a *fait accompli*. Most observers in the West expect nothing more than for "Slobo to be brought to The Hague." The European Union already began lifting sanctions on Serbia. Article after article in the press echoes the refrain that this is the last in a series of Eastern European revolutions. Since Vojislav Kostunica came to power, the scholars and journalists are saying there will at last be a period of peace in the Balkans. The Yugoslav canon has been silenced. Serbia will now hand over Milosevic to stand trial for war crimes. The other four Serbian leaders indicted (see Appendix E) will also join him. Radovan Karadzic and General Ratko Mladic of the Bosnian war will join them as well. Secretary of State Madeleine Albright, her term almost over after the U.S. presidential elections, repeatedly demanded that Milosevic be extradicted forthwith. NATO Secretary-general, Lord Robertson, welcomed Kostunica's new government in Yugoslavia; and he, too, raised the issue of "war criminals."

Be that as it may, Vojislav Kostunica is not about to give Milosevic a one-way ticket to The Hague. It may even prove difficult to try Milosevic in Yugoslavia. The Hague tribunal has indicted him for "crimes" commited in Kosovo in 1999 only—why not the crimes since 1991 in Bosnia, Croatia, and Slovenia? As it stands, his indictment is far too limited, based on dubious, circumstantial facts. So why all this talk about The Hague tribunal? Madeleine Albright and the others know this only too well. In my mind, they are just going through the motions. And why is that?

Many western European Union (EU) governments, including organizations such as the OSCE and NATO, would surely be raked over the coals if the world were to discover Milosevic's dealings these last few years, with both friend and foe. His dealings with the CIA, for instance, are an issue of concern. Western diplomats had repeatedly made deals and signed agreements and treaties with him. It was Milosevic, after all, who had signed the Dayton-Paris Agreement in 1995. Afterwards, his country received full recognition by the EU. When the German armed forces helped Tudjman's Croatia with logistics and expelled some 250,000 Serbs from land claimed by Croatia in 1995, Milosevic never retaliated. He could have. He certainly had the wherewithal. He must have accepted certain policies which the West would not compromise on. Besides, why had the West failed to indict Milosevic for atrocities committed by Serbs at Srebrenica?

If the West were to indict him for crimes committed through the 1990s, then why not indict Croatia's Franjo Tudjman (who died of cancer a few years ago) and Bosnian president Alija Izetbegovic? They were just as repsonsible for atrocities against the Serbs. Why not indict a high-level, Kosovo-Albanian military leader like the head of the KLA?

Furthermore, the number of reported Kosovars killed or missing, now that we know the true facts, was intentionally falsified and exaggerated all along. In Algeria's civil war alone, 100,000 perished—while the West turned a blind eye. The Ethiopian/Eritrean war claimed a greater number than that. The number of innocent Iraqi civilians and defenceless soldiers killed (or still dying) by UN-sponsored sanctions and a U.S.-led coalition is frighteningly higher, a thousand fold higher—just to punish a single Iraqi madman.

For sure, we need to examine things in scale, not just to take a worm's eye view of the situation. During the American elections, George W. Bush and his advisers believed they were thinking in scale. Condoleeza Rice, Dick Cheney, and other Republicans suggested the withdrawal of American ground forces from peacekeeping in the Balkans altogether. Will America go non-interventionist? Again, another instance of a worm's eye view. The Democrats are screaming that such a withdrawal would lead to general instability in Europe and the eventual dissolution of NATO as we know it. And what of China waiting in the wings as the next superpower?

Europe is decidedly in disarray. With EU enlargement eastward and a weakening Euro, it is caught between a rock and a hard place. It knows it must carry an increasing share of the burden anyway. For this reason, the EU is developing a European Security and Defense Policy (ESDP) while maintaining close ties with NATO. The ESDP will aim at EU-led operations in Europe that would undertake military crisis management. All Europe will become involved in this security system: the six European non-EU allies as well as the nine non-NATO EU accession candidates. To make it work, Europeans realize that Russia and Ukraine must not be excluded from the dialogue. This is the best possible option towards crisis prevention in Europe. With the end of the war in Kosovo, Yugoslavia and the Balkans may yet settle into the European fold. It might take a generation, maybe two. But Europe's nightmare would then be over for good.

APPENDIX A

RAMBOUILLET ACCORD

The Rambouillet text of February 23, 1999, a month before NATO began bombing, contains provisions that seem to have provided for NATO to occupy the entire Federal Republic of Yugoslavia, not just Kosovo. The Serbs rejected NATO troops in Kosovo. Here are some of the excerpts from that agreement that were unacceptable to the Serbs. The objectionable clauses are usually referred to as "Appendix B" of the accord.

Implementation II

Article I: General Obligations

1. The Parties undertake to recreate, as quickly as possible, normal conditions of life in Kosovo and to co-operate fully with each other and with all international organizations, agencies, and non-governmental organizations involved in the implementation of this Agreement. They welcome the willingness of the international community to send to the region a force to assist in the implementation of this Agreement.

   a. The United Nations Security Council is invited to pass a resolution under Chapter VII of the Charter endorsing and adopting the arrangements set forth in this Chapter, including the establishment of a multinational military implementation force in Kosovo. The Parties invite NATO to constitute and lead a military force to help ensure compliance with the provisions of this Chapter. They also reaffirm the sovereignty and territorial integrity of the Federal Republic of Yugoslavia (FRY).

   b. The Parties agree that NATO will establish and deploy a force (hereinafter IIKFORII) which may be composed of ground, air, and maritime units from NATO and non-NATO nations, operating under the authority and subject to the direction and the political control of the North Atlantic Council (NAC) through the NATO chain of command. The Parties agree to facilitate the deployment and operations of this force and agree also to comply fully with all the obligations of this Chapter.

Appendix B: Status of Multi-National Military Implementation Force

6. b. NATO personnel, under all circumstances and at all times, shall be immune from the Parties, jurisdiction in respect of any civil, administrative, criminal, or disciplinary offenses which may be committed by them in the FRY. The Parties shall assist States participating in the operation in the exercise of their jurisdiction over their own nationals.

c. Notwithstanding the above, and with the NATO Commander's express agreement in each case, the authorities in the FRY may exceptionally exercise jurisdiction in such matters, but only in respect of Contractor personnel who are not subject to the jurisdiction of their nation of citizenship.

7. NATO personnel shall be immune from any form of arrest, investigation, or detention by the authorities in the FRY. NATO personnel erroneously arrested or detained shall immediately be turned over to NATO authorities.

8. NATO personnel shall enjoy, together with their vehicles, vessels, aircraft, and equipment, free and unrestricted passage and unimpeded access throughout the FRY including associated airspace and territorial waters. This shall include, but not be limited to, the right of bivouac, maneuver, billet, and utilization of any areas or facilities as required for support, training, and operations.

9. NATO shall be exempt from duties, taxes, and other charges and inspections and custom regulations including providing inventories or other routine customs documentation, for personnel, vehicles, vessels, aircraft, equipment, supplies, and provisions entering, exiting, or transiting the territory of the FRY in support of the Operation.

10. The authorities in the FRY shall facilitate, on a priority basis and with all appropriate means, all movement of personnel, vehicles, vessels, aircraft, equipment, or supplies, through or in the airspace, ports, airports, or roads used. No charges may be assessed against NATO for air navigation, landing, or takeoff of aircraft, whether government-owned or chartered. Similarly, no duties, dues, tolls or charges may be assessed against NATO ships, whether government-

owned or chartered, for the mere entry and exit of ports. Vehicles, vessels, and aircraft used in support of the operation shall not be subject to licensing or registration requirements, nor commercial insurance.

11. NATO is granted the use of airports, roads, rails, and ports without payment of fees, duties, dues, tolls, or charges occasioned by mere use. NATO shall not, however, claim exemption from reasonable charges for specific services requested and received, but operations/movement and access shall not be allowed to be impeded pending payment for such services.

12. NATO personnel shall be exempt from taxation by the Parties on the salaries and emoluments received from NATO and on any income received from outside the FRY.

13. NATO personnel and their tangible moveable property imported into, acquired in, or exported from the FRY shall be exempt from all duties, taxes, and other charges and inspections and custom regulations.

14. NATO shall be allowed to import and to export, free of duty, taxes and other charges, such equipment, provisions, and supplies as NATO shall require for the operation, provided such goods are for the official use of NATO or for sale to NATO personnel. Goods sold shall be solely for the use of NATO personnel and not transferable to unauthorized persons.

15. The Parties recognize that the use of communications channels is necessary for the Operation. NATO shall be allowed to operate its own internal mail services. The Parties shall, upon simple request, grant all telecommunications services, including broadcast services, needed for the Operation, as determined by NATO. This shall include the right to utilize such means and services as required to assure full ability to communicate, and the right to use all of the electromagnetic spectrum for this purpose, free of cost. In implementing this right, NATO shall make every reasonable effort to coordinate with and take into account the needs and requirements of appropriate authorities in the FRY.

16. The Parties shall provide, free of cost, such public facilities as NATO shall require to prepare for and execute the Operation. The Parties shall assist NATO in obtaining, at the lowest rate, the necessary utilities, such as electricity, water, gas and other resources, as NATO shall require for the Operation.

17. NATO and NATO personnel shall be immune from claims of any sort which arise out of activities in pursuance of the operation; however, NATO will entertain claims on an ex gratia basis.

18. NATO shall be allowed to contract directly for the acquisition of goods, services, and construction from any source within and outside the FRY. Such contracts, goods, services, and construction shall not be subject to the payment of duties, taxes, or other charges. NATO may also carry out construction works with their own personnel.

19. Commercial undertakings operating in the FRY only in the service of NATO shall be exempt from local laws and regulations with respect to the terms and conditions of their employment and licensing and registration of employees, businesses, and corporations.

Source: Le Monde Diplomatique, April 17, 1999.

APPENDIX B

AGREEMENT BETWEEN AHTISAARI, CHERNOMYRDIN, AND MILOSEVIC

This is the actual agreement that has held. It was negotiated with Milosevic officially on behalf of the G8 and the European Union, not NATO. Readers will note that under its provisions, Milosevic is still indicted for war crimes by a UN tribunal. Also, KFOR is under UN, not NATO, auspices. International Force is deployed only in Kosovo, not throughout Yugoslavia.

- June 2, 1999. The Serb Parliament ratified this agreement on June 3. It was later incorporated into UN Security Council Resolution No. 1244, as Annex II.
- Deployment in Kosovo, under UN auspices, of efficient international civilian and security presences which would act as can be decided according to Chapter 7 of the UN Charter and be capable of guaranteeing fulfillment of joint goals.
- International security presence, with an essential NATO participation, must be deployed under a unified control and command and authorized to secure safe environment for all the residents in Kosovo and enable the safe return of the displaced persons and refugees to their homes.

KOSOVO MILITARY-TECHNICAL AGREEMENT
(Signed by representatives of NATO and Yugoslavia
on June 9, 1999)

General Obligations: The parties to this agreement reaffirm the document presented by President Ahtisaari to President Milosevic and approved by the Serb Parliament and the federal government on June 3, 1999, to include deployment in Kosovo under UN auspices of effective international civil and security presences. The parties further note that the UN Security Council is prepared to adopt a resolution, which has been introduced, regarding these presences.

UN Security Council Res. 1244 (June 10). Determined to ensure the safety and security of international personnel and the implementation by all concerned of their responsibilities under the present resolution, and acting for these purposes under Chapter VII of the Charter of the United Nations. . . . Decides on the deployment in Kosovo, under United Nations auspices, of international civil and security presences, with appropriate equipment and personnel as required, and welcomes the agreement of the Federal Republic of Yugoslavia to such presences . . .

Annex I (the G8 or Bonn Principles of May 6, 1999)

Deployment in Kosovo of effective international civil and security presences, endorsed and adopted by the United Nations, capable of guaranteeing the achievement of the common objectives . . .

Annex II (essentially the same text as the June 2–3 agreement)

Deployment in Kosovo under United Nations auspices of effective international civil and security presences, acting as may be decided under Chapter VII of the Charter, capable of guaranteeing the achievement of common objectives.

The international security presence with substantial North Atlantic Treaty Organization participation must be deployed under unified command and control and authorized to establish a safe environment for all people in Kosovo and to facilitate the safe return to their homes of all displaced persons and refugees.

APPENDIX C

RECOMMENDATIONS OF THE ORGANIZATION "HUMAN RIGHTS WATCH" RELATING TO THE SEXUAL VIOLATION OF WOMEN

Women victims of rape and other forms of sexual violence in Kosovo demonstrated courage in speaking of the abuses they suffered. The international community should respond to their willingness to speak with an effort to assist the women in pursuing justice, recovering from trauma, and rebuilding their lives. Particularly, Human Rights Watch makes the following recommendations:

To the International Criminal Tribunal for the Former Yugoslavia (ICTY):

- Conduct a diligent and independent investigation into the incidence and use of rape and other forms of sexual violence against women in Kosovo.

- Take steps to ensure that those alleged to have committed rape or other forms of sexual violence during the conflict in Kosovo, and those in positions of political or command authority who are alleged to have acquiesced in such abuse, are indicted, taken into custody, prosecuted, and brought to justice by the ICTY.

- Ensure that gender-integrated teams investigating rape and other forms of sexual violence have competence in investigating rape and conducting interviews with rape victims. As the Office of the Prosecutor (OTP) moves to make the investigation and prosecution of rape and other forms of sexual violence a normal part of OTP procedure, efforts to enhance and develop staff expertise necessary for rape investigations and prosecutions should increase. Whenever possible, interviews of rape victims should be conducted by female investigators with training in rape investigations.

- Include examinations for evidence of rape in autopsies of female bodies conducted by ICTY forensic teams.

- Ensure that all witnesses are protected now and subsequently from possible reprisals.

To the United Nations:

- Establish a specialist unit within the Office of the UN High Commissioner for Human Rights with a mission to develop expertise on the investigation of rape and other forms of sexual violence in conflict and the treatment of such victims. The unit would develop protocols for responding to rape in conflict, maintain a database of experts in the fields of investigation and trauma counseling, and monitor inclusion of rape and other forms of sexual violence in cases brought before tribunals and truth commissions internationally.

- Develop programs through the United Nations Interim Administration Mission in Kosovo (UNMIK) to assist women victims of rape and other forms of sexual violence and trauma in accessing job training programs, micro-credit programs, and psychological counseling programs in Kosovo.

To the Yugoslav Government:

- Cooperate with the ICTY by locating and arresting any person under indictment by the ICTY.

- Recognize the right of the ICTY to investigate all war crimes committed in the territory of the former Yugoslavia, including the area of Kosovo, as stated in UN Security Council Resolution 827 (1993) and repeatedly reaffirmed with particular reference to the Kosovo crisis in UN Security Council Resolutions 1160, 1199, and 1207.

- Hand over individuals already indicted for war crimes who are residing on the territory of Serbia and/or Montenegro.

To the NATO-led Kosovo Force (KFOR):

- Arrest without delay all persons present in Kosovo who have been or will be indicted by the ICTY for war crimes committed in Kosovo.

Source: UN Archives.

APPENDIX D

ACCORD BETWEEN KFOR AND THE KLA

This is the full text of the accord on the demilitarization of the Kosovo Liberation Army (KLA, known in Kosovo by its initials UCK) signed by KLA chief Hashim Thaci and KFOR commander Lieutenant-General Mike Jackson in Pristina on June 21, 1999:

UNDERTAKING THE DEMILITARIZATION AND TRANSFORMATION OF THE KLA

1. This Undertaking provides for a cease-fire by the KLA, their disengagement from the zones of conflict, subsequent demilitarization and reintegration into civil society, in accordance with the terms of UNSCR 1244 and taking account of the obligations agreed to at Rambouillet and the public commitments made by the Kosovar Albanian Rambouillet delegation.

2. The KLA undertake to renounce the use of force, to comply with the directions of the Commander of the international security force in Kosovo (COMKFOR), and where applicable the head of the interim civil administration for Kosovo, and to resolve peacefully any questions relating to the implementation of this undertaking.

3. The KLA agree that the International Security Presence (KFOR) and the international civil presence will continue to deploy and operate without hindrance within Kosovo and that KFOR has the authority to take all necessary action to establish and maintain a secure environment for all citizens of Kosovo and otherwise carry out its mission.

4. The KLA agrees to comply with all of the obligations of this Undertaking and to ensure that with immediate effect all KLA forces in Kosovo and in neighboring countries will observe the provisions of this Undertaking, will refrain from all hostile or provocative acts, hostile intent and freeze military movement in either direction across international borders or the boundary between Kosovo and other parts of the FRY, or any other actions inconsistent with the spirit of UNSCR 1244. The KLA in Kosovo agree to commit themselves publicly to demilitarize in accordance with paragraphs 22 and 23, refrain from activities which jeopardize the safety of international governmental and non-governmental personnel including KFOR, and to facilitate the deployment and operation of KFOR.

5. For purposes of this Undertaking, the following expressions shall have the meanings as described below:

a) The KLA includes all personnel and organizations within Kosovo, currently under KLA control, with a military or paramilitary capability and any other groups or individuals so designated by Commander KFOR (COMKFOR).

b) "FRY Forces" includes all of the FRY and Republic of Serbia personnel and organisations with a military capability. This includes regular army and naval forces, armed civilian groups, associated paramilitary groups, air forces, national guards, border police, army reserves, military police, intelligence services, Ministry of Internal Affairs, local, special, riot and anti-terrorist police, and any other groups or individuals so designated by Commander KFOR (COMKFOR).

c) The Ground Safety Zone (GSZ) is defined as a 5-kilometre zone that extends beyond the Kosovo province border into the rest of FRY territory. It includes the terrain within that 5-kilometre zone.

d) Prohibited weapons are any weapon 12.7mm or larger, any anti-tank or anti-aircraft weapons, grenades, mines or explosives, automatic and long barrelled weapons.

6. The purposes of this Undertaking are as follows:

a) To establish a durable cessation of hostilities.

b) To provide for the support and authorisation of the KFOR and in particular to authorise the KFOR to take such actions as are required, including the use of necessary force in accordance with KFOR's rules of engagement, to ensure compliance with this Undertaking and protection of the KFOR, and to contribute to a secure environment for the international civil implementation presence, and other international organisations, agencies, and non-governmental organisations and the civil populace.

7. The actions of the KLA shall be in accordance with this Undertaking. "The KFOR" commander in consultation, where appropriate, with the interim civil administrator will be the final authority regarding the interpretation of this Undertaking and the security aspects of the peace settlement it supports. His determinations will be binding on all parties and persons.

Cessation of Hostilities

8. With immediate effect on signature the KLA agrees to comply with this Undertaking and with the directions of COMKFOR. Any forces which fail to comply with this Undertaking or with the directions of COMKFOR will be liable to military action as deemed appropriate by COMKFOR.

9. With immediate effect on signature of this Undertaking all hostile acts by the KLA will cease. The KLA Chief of General Staff undertakes to issue clear and precise instructions to all units and personnel under his command, to ensure contact with the FRY forces is avoided and to comply fully with the arrangements for bringing this Undertaking into effect. He will make announcements immediately following final signature of this Undertaking, which will be broadcast regularly through all appropriate channels to assist in ensuring that instructions to maintain this Undertaking reach all the forces under his command and are understood by the public in general.

10. The KLA undertakes and agrees in particular:

    a) To cease the firing of all weapons and use of explosive devices.

    b) Not to place any mines, barriers or checkpoints, nor maintain any observation posts or protective obstacles.

    c) The destruction of buildings, facilities or structures is not permitted. It shall not engage in any military, security, or training related activities, including ground or air defence operations, in or over Kosovo or GSZ, without the prior express approval of COMKFOR.

    d) Not to attack, detain or intimidate any civilians in Kosovo, nor shall they attack, confiscate or violate the property of civilians in Kosovo.

11. The KLA agrees not to conduct any reprisals, counter-attacks, or any unilateral actions in response to violations of the UNSCR 1244 and other extant agreements relating to Kosovo. This in no way denies the right of self-defence.

12. The KLA agrees not to interfere with those FRY personnel that return to Kosovo to conduct specific tasks as authorised and directed by COMKFOR.

13. Except as approved by COMKFOR, the KLA agrees that its personnel in Kosovo will not carry weapons of any type:

a) Within 2 kilometres of VJ and MUP assembly areas;

b) Within 2 kilometres of the main roads and the towns upon them listed at Appendix A;

c) Within 2 kilometres of external borders of Kosovo;

d) In any other areas designated by COMKFOR.

14. Within 4 days of signature of this Undertaking:

a) The KLA will close all fighting positions, entrenchments, and checkpoints on roads, and mark their minefields and booby traps.

b) The KLA Chief of General Staff shall report in writing completion of the above requirement to COMKFOR and continue to provide weekly detailed written status reports until demilitarisation, as detailed in the following paragraphs, is complete.

Cross-Border Activity

15. With immediate effect the KLA will cease the movement of armed bodies into neighboring countries. All movement of armed bodies into Kosovo will be subject to the prior approval of COMKFOR.

Monitoring the Cessation of Hostilities

16. The authority for dealing with breaches of this Undertaking rests with COMKFOR. He will monitor and maintain and if necessary enforce the cessation of hostilities.

17. The KLA agrees to co-operate fully with KFOR and the interim civil administration for Kosovo. The Chief of the General Staff of the KLA will ensure that prompt and appropriate action is taken to deal with any breaches of this Undertaking by his forces as directed by COMKFOR.

18. Elements of KFOR will be assigned to maintain contact with the KLA and will be deployed to its command structure and bases.

19. KFOR will establish appropriate control at designated crossing points into Albania and the FYROM.

Joint Implementation Commission (JIC)

20. A JIC will be established in Pristina within 4 days of the signature of this Undertaking. The JIC will be chaired by COMKFOR, and will

comprise the senior commanders of KFOR and the KLA, and a representative from the interim civil administration for Kosovo.

21. The JIC will meet as often as required by COMKFOR throughout the implementation of this Undertaking. It may be called without prior notice and representation by the KLA is expected at a level appropriate with the rank of the KFOR chairman. Its functions will include:

a) Ensuring compliance with agreed arrangements for the security and activities of all forces;

b) The investigation of actual or threatened breaches of this Undertaking;

c) Such other tasks as may be assigned to it by COMKFOR in the interests of maintaining the cessation of hostilities.

Demilitarization and Transformation

22. The KLA will follow the procedures established by COMKFOR for the phased demilitarization, transformation and monitoring of KLA forces in Kosovo and for the further regulation of their activities. They will not train or organise parades without the authority of COMKFOR.

23. The KLA agrees to the following timetable which will commence from the signature of this Undertaking:

a) Within 7 days, the KLA shall establish secure weapons storage sites, which shall be registered with and verified by the KFOR;

b) Within 7 days the KLA will clear their minefields and booby traps, vacate their fighting positions and transfer to assembly areas as agreed with COMKFOR at the JIC. Thereafter only personnel authorised by COMKFOR and senior Officers of the KLA with their close protection personnel not exceeding 3, carrying side arms only, will be allowed outside these assembly areas.

c) After 7 days automatic small arms weapons not stored in the registered weapons storage sites can only be held inside the authorized assembly areas.

d) After 29 days, the retention of any non automatic long barrelled weapons shall be subject to authorization by COMKFOR.

e) Within 30 days, subject to arrangements by COMKFOR if necessary, all KLA personnel who are not of local origin, whether or not they are legally within Kosovo, including individual advisors, freedom fighters, trainers, volunteers, and personnel from neighbouring and other States, shall be withdrawn from Kosovo.

f) Arrangements for control of weapons are as follows:

(1) Within 30 days the KLA shall store in the registered weapons storage sites all prohibited weapons with the exception of automatic small arms. 30 per cent of their total holdings of automatic small arms weapons will also be stored in these sites at this stage. Ammunition for the remaining weapons should be withdrawn and stored at an approved site authorised by COMKFOR separate from the assembly areas at the same time.

(2) At 30 days it shall be illegal for KLA personnel to possess prohibited weapons, with the exception of automatic small arms within assembly areas, and unauthorized long barrelled weapons. Such weapons shall be subject to confiscation by the KFOR.

(3) Within 60 days a further 30 per cent of automatic small arms, giving a total of 60 per cent of the KLA holdings, will be stored in the registered weapons storage sites.

(4) Within 90 days all automatic small arms weapons will be stored in the registered weapons storage sites. Thereafter their possession by KLA personnel will be prohibited and such weapons will be subject to confiscation by KFOR.

g) From 30 days until 90 days the weapons storage sites will be under joint control of the KLA and KFOR under procedures approved by COMKFOR at the JIC. After 90 days KFOR will assume full control of these sites.

h) Within 90 days all KLA forces will have completed the processes for their demilitarization and are to cease wearing either military uniforms or insignia of the KLA.

i) Within 90 days the Chief of General Staff KLA shall confirm compliance with the above restrictions in writing to COMKFOR.

24. The provisions of this Undertaking enter into force with immediate effect of its signature by the Kosovar Albanian representative(s).

25. The KLA intends to comply with the terms of the United Nations Security Council Resolution 1244, and in this context that the international community should take due and full account of the contribution of the KLA during the Kosovo crisis and accordingly give due consideration to:

a) Recognition that, while the KLA and its structures are in the process of transformation, it is committed to propose individual current members to participate in the administration and police forces of Kosovo, enjoying special consideration in view of the expertise they have developed.

b) The formation of an Army in Kosovo on the lines of the US National Guard in due course as part of a political process designed to

determine Kosovo's future status, taking into account the Rambouillet Accord.

26. This Undertaking is provided in English and Albanian and if there
is any doubt as to the meaning of the text the English version has
precedence.

Source: UN Archives.

APPENDIX E

THE INTERNATIONAL CRIMINAL TRIBUNAL FOR THE FORMER YUGOSLAVIA

The indictment alleges that, between January 1st and late May 1999, forces under the control of the five accused persecuted the Kosovo Albanian civilian population on political, racial, or religious grounds. By the date of the indictment, approximately 740,000 Kosovo Albanians, about one-third of the entire Kosovo Albanian population, had been expelled from Kosovo. Thousands more are believed to be internally displaced. An unknown number of Kosovo Albanians have been killed in the operations by forces of the FRY and Serbia. Specifically, the five indictees are charged with the murder of over 340 persons identified by name in an annex to the indictment, which I did not include. Of course, it is believed that there were far more than that number killed.

**THE PROSECUTOR OF THE TRIBUNAL
AGAINST
SLOBODAN MILOSEVIC
MILAN MILUTINOVIC
NIKOLA SAINOVIC
DRAGOLJUB OJDANIC
VLAJKO STOJILJKOVIC**

INDICTMENT

The Prosecutor of the International Criminal Tribunal for the former Yugoslavia, pursuant to her authority under Article 18 of the Statute of the Tribunal, charges:

Slobodan Milosevic
Milan Milutinovic
Nikola Sainovic
Dragoljub Ojdanic
Vlajko Stojiljkovic

with CRIMES AGAINST HUMANITY and VIOLATIONS OF THE
LAWS OR CUSTOMS OF WAR as set forth below:

Background

1. The Autonomous Province of Kosovo and Metohija is located in the
   southern part of the Republic of Serbia, a constituent republic of the
   Federal Republic of Yugoslavia (hereinafter FRY). The territory now
   comprising the FRY was part of the former Socialist Federal Republic
   of Yugoslavia (hereinafter SFRY). The Autonomous Province of Kosovo and Metohija is bordered on the north and north-west by the
   Republic of Montenegro, another constituent republic of the FRY. On
   the south-west, the Autonomous Province of Kosovo and Metohija
   is bordered by the Republic of Albania, and to the south, by the
   Former Yugoslav Republic of Macedonia. The capital of the Autonomous Province of Kosovo and Metohija is Pristina.

2. In 1990 the Socialist Republic of Serbia promulgated a new Constitution which, among other things, changed the names of the republic
   and the autonomous provinces. The name of the Socialist Republic
   of Serbia was changed to the Republic of Serbia (both hereinafter
   Serbia); the name of the Socialist Autonomous Province of Kosovo
   was changed to the Autonomous Province of Kosovo and Metohija
   (both hereinafter Kosovo); and the name of the Socialist Autonomous
   Province of Vojvodina was changed to the Autonomous Province of
   Vojvodina (hereinafter Vojvodina). During this same period, the Socialist Republic of Montenegro changed its name to the Republic of
   Montenegro (hereinafter Montenegro).

3. In 1974, a new SFRY Constitution had provided for a devolution of
   power from the central government to the six constituent republics
   of the country. Within Serbia, Kosovo and Vojvodina were given
   considerable autonomy including control of their educational systems, judiciary, and police. They were also given their own provincial assemblies, and were represented in the Assembly, the
   Constitutional Court, and the Presidency of the SFRY.

4. In 1981, the last census with near universal participation, the total
   population of Kosovo was approximately 1,585,000 of which
   1,227,000 (77%) were Albanians, and 210,000 (13%) were Serbs. Only
   estimates for the population of Kosovo in 1991 are available because

Kosovo Albanians boycotted the census administered that year. General estimates are that the current population of Kosovo is between 1,800,000 and 2,100,000 of which approximately 85–90% are Kosovo Albanians and 5–10% are Serbs.

5. During the 1980s, Serbs voiced concern about discrimination against them by the Kosovo Albanian–led provincial government while Kosovo Albanians voiced concern about economic underdevelopment and called for greater political liberalisation and republican status for Kosovo. From 1981 onwards, Kosovo Albanians staged demonstrations which were suppressed by SFRY military and police forces of Serbia.

6. In April 1987, Slobodan MILOSEVIC, who had been elected Chairman of the Presidium of the Central Committee of the League of Communists of Serbia in 1986, travelled to Kosovo. In meetings with local Serb leaders and in a speech before a crowd of Serbs, Slobodan MILOSEVIC endorsed a Serbian nationalist agenda. In so doing, he broke with the party and government policy which had restricted nationalist expression in the SFRY since the time of its founding by Josip Broz Tito after the Second World War. Thereafter, Slobodan MILOSEVIC exploited a growing wave of Serbian nationalism in order to strengthen centralised rule in the SFRY.

7. In September 1987 Slobodan MILOSEVIC and his supporters gained control of the Central Committee of the League of Communists of Serbia. In 1988, Slobodan MILOSEVIC was re-elected as Chairman of the Presidium of the Central Committee of the League of Communists of Serbia. From that influential position, Slobodan MILOSEVIC was able to further develop his political power.

8. From July 1988 to March 1989, a series of demonstrations and rallies supportive of Slobodan MILOSEVIC's policies—the so-called "Anti-Bureaucratic Revolution"—took place in Vojvodina and Montenegro. These protests led to the ouster of the respective provincial and republican governments; the new governments were then supportive of, and indebted to, Slobodan MILOSEVIC.

9. Simultaneously, within Serbia, calls for bringing Kosovo under stronger Serbian rule intensified and numerous demonstrations addressing this issue were held. On 17 November 1988, high-ranking Kosovo Albanian political figures were dismissed from their positions within the provincial leadership and were replaced by appointees loyal to Slobodan MILOSEVIC. In early 1989, the Serbian Assembly proposed amendments to the Constitution of Serbia which would strip Kosovo of most of its autonomous powers, including control of the police, educational and economic policy, and choice of

official language, as well as its veto powers over further changes to the Constitution of Serbia. Kosovo Albanians demonstrated in large numbers against the proposed changes. Beginning in February 1989, a strike by Kosovo Albanian miners further increased tensions.

10. Due to the political unrest, on 3 March 1989, the SFRY Presidency declared that the situation in the province had deteriorated and had become a threat to the constitution, integrity, and sovereignty of the country. The government then imposed "special measures" which assigned responsibility for public security to the federal government instead of the government of Serbia.

11. On 23 March 1989, the Assembly of Kosovo met in Pristina and, with the majority of Kosovo Albanian delegates abstaining, voted to accept the proposed amendments to the constitution. Although lacking the required two-thirds majority in the Assembly, the President of the Assembly nonetheless declared that the amendments had passed. On 28 March 1989, the Assembly of Serbia voted to approve the constitutional changes effectively revoking the autonomy granted in the 1974 constitution.

12. At the same time these changes were occurring in Kosovo, Slobodan MILOSEVIC further increased his political power when he became the President of Serbia. Slobodan MILOSEVIC was elected President of the Presidency of Serbia on 8 May 1989 and his post was formally confirmed on 6 December 1989.

13. In early 1990, Kosovo Albanians held mass demonstrations calling for an end to the "special measures." In April 1990, the SFRY Presidency lifted the "special measures" and removed most of the federal police forces as Serbia took over responsibility for police enforcement in Kosovo.

14. In July 1990, the Assembly of Serbia passed a decision to suspend the Assembly of Kosovo shortly after 114 of the 123 Kosovo Albanian delegates from that Assembly had passed an unofficial resolution declaring Kosovo an equal and independent entity within the SFRY. In September 1990, many of these same Kosovo Albanian delegates proclaimed a constitution for a "Republic of Kosovo." One year later, in September 1991, Kosovo Albanians held an unofficial referendum in which they voted overwhelmingly for independence. On 24 May 1992, Kosovo Albanians held unofficial elections for an assembly and president for the "Republic of Kosovo."

15. On 16 July 1990, the League of Communists of Serbia and the Socialist Alliance of Working People of Serbia joined to form the Socialist Party of Serbia (SPS), and Slobodan MILOSEVIC was elected its President. As the successor to the League of Communists, the SPS

became the dominant political party in Serbia and Slobodan MILO-SEVIC, as President of the SPS, was able to wield considerable power and influence over many branches of the government as well as the private sector. Milan MILUTINOVIC and Nikola SAINOVIC have both held prominent positions within the SPS. Nikola SAINOVIC was a member of the Main Committee and the Executive Council as well as a vice-chairman; and Milan MILUTINOVIC successfully ran for President of Serbia in 1997 as the SPS candidate.

16. After the adoption of the new Constitution of Serbia on 28 September 1990, Slobodan MILOSEVIC was elected President of Serbia in multi-party elections held on 9 and 26 December 1990; he was re-elected on 20 December 1992. In December 1991, Nikola SAINOVIC was appointed a Deputy Prime Minister of Serbia.

17. After Kosovo's autonomy was effectively revoked in 1989, the political situation in Kosovo became more and more divisive. Throughout late 1990 and 1991 thousands of Kosovo Albanian doctors, teachers, professors, workers, police and civil servants were dismissed from their positions. The local court in Kosovo was abolished and many judges removed. Police violence against Kosovo Albanians increased.

18. During this period, the unofficial Kosovo Albanian leadership pursued a policy of non-violent civil resistance and began establishing a system of unofficial, parallel institutions in the health care and education sectors.

19. In late June 1991 the SFRY began to disintegrate in a succession of wars fought in the Republic of Slovenia (hereinafter Slovenia), the Republic of Croatia (hereinafter Croatia), and the Republic of Bosnia and Herzegovina (hereinafter Bosnia and Herzegovina). On 25 June 1991, Slovenia declared independence from the SFRY, which led to the outbreak of war; a peace agreement was reached on 8 July 1991. Croatia declared its independence on 25 June 1991, leading to fighting between Croatian military forces on the one side and the Yugoslav People's Army (JNA), paramilitary units and the "Army of the Republic of Srpska Krajina" on the other.

20. On 6 March 1992, Bosnia and Herzegovina declared its independence, resulting in wide scale war after 6 April 1992. On 27 April 1992, the SFRY was reconstituted as the FRY. At this time, the JNA was re-formed as the Armed Forces of the FRY (hereinafter VJ). In the war in Bosnia and Herzegovina, the JNA, and later the VJ, fought along with the "Army of Republika Srpska" against military forces of the Government of Bosnia and Herzegovina and the "Croat Defence Council." Active hostilities ceased with the signing of the Dayton peace agreement in December 1995.

21. Although Slobodan MILOSEVIC was the President of Serbia during the wars in Slovenia, Croatia and Bosnia and Herzegovina, he was nonetheless the dominant Serbian political figure exercising de facto control of the federal government as well as the republican government and was the person with whom the international community negotiated a variety of peace plans and agreements related to these wars.

22. Between 1991 and 1997 Milan MILUTINOVIC and Nikola SAIN-OVIC both held a number of high ranking positions within the federal and republican governments and continued to work closely with Slobodan MILOSEVIC. During this period, Milan MILUTINOVIC worked in the Foreign Ministry of the FRY, and at one time was Ambassador to Greece; in 1995, he was appointed Minister of Foreign Affairs of the FRY, a position he held until 1997. Nikola SAINOVIC was Prime Minister of Serbia in 1993 and Deputy Prime Minister of the FRY in 1994.

23. While the wars were being conducted in Slovenia, Croatia and Bosnia and Herzegovina, the situation in Kosovo, while tense, did not erupt into the violence and intense fighting seen in the other countries. In the mid-1990s, however, a faction of the Kosovo Albanians organised a group known as Ushtria Çlirimtare e Kosovës (UÇK) or, known in English as the Kosovo Liberation Army (KLA). This group advocated a campaign of armed insurgency and violent resistance to the Serbian authorities. In mid-1996, the KLA began launching attacks primarily targeting FRY and Serbian police forces. Thereafter, and throughout 1997, FRY and Serbian police forces responded with forceful operations against suspected KLA bases and supporters in Kosovo.

24. After concluding his term as President of Serbia, Slobodan MILO-SEVIC was elected President of the FRY on 15 July 1997, and assumed office on 23 July 1997. Thereafter, elections for the office of the President of Serbia were held; Milan MILUTINOVIC ran as the SPS candidate and was elected President of Serbia on 21 December 1997. In 1996, 1997 and 1998, Nikola SAINOVIC was re-appointed Deputy Prime Minister of the FRY. In part through his close alliance with Milan MILUTINOVIC, Slobodan MILOSEVIC was able to retain his influence over the Government of Serbia.

25. Beginning in late February 1998, the conflict intensified between the KLA on the one hand and the VJ, the police forces of the FRY, police forces of Serbia, and paramilitary units (all hereinafter forces of the FRY and Serbia), on the other hand. A number of Kosovo Albanians and Kosovo Serbs were killed and wounded during this time. Forces of the FRY and Serbia engaged in a campaign of shelling predomi-

nantly Kosovo Albanian towns and villages, widespread destruction of property, and expulsions of the civilian population from areas in which the KLA was active. Many residents fled the territory as a result of the fighting and destruction or were forced to move to other areas within Kosovo. The United Nations estimates that by mid-October 1998, over 298,000 persons, roughly fifteen percent of the population, had been internally displaced within Kosovo or had left the province.

26. In response to the intensifying conflict, the United Nations Security Council (UNSC) passed Resolution 1160 in March 1998 "condemning the use of excessive force by Serbian police forces against civilians and peaceful demonstrators in Kosovo," and imposed an arms embargo on the FRY. Six months later the UNSC passed Resolution 1199 (1998) which stated that "the deterioration of the situation in Kosovo, Federal Republic of Yugoslavia, constitutes a threat to peace and security in the region." The Security Council demanded that all parties cease hostilities and that "the security forces used for civilian repression" be withdrawn.

27. In an attempt to diffuse tensions in Kosovo, negotiations between Slobodan MILOSEVIC, and representatives of the North Atlantic Treaty Organisation (NATO), and the Organisation for Security and Co-operation in Europe (OSCE) were conducted in October 1998. An "Agreement on the OSCE Kosovo Verification Mission" was signed on 16 October 1998. This agreement and the "Clark-Naumann agreement," which was signed by Nikola SAINOVIC, provided for the partial withdrawal of forces of the FRY and Serbia from Kosovo, a limitation on the introduction of additional forces and equipment into the area, and the deployment of unarmed OSCE verifiers.

28. Although scores of OSCE verifiers were deployed throughout Kosovo, hostilities continued. During this period, a number of killings of Kosovo Albanians were documented by the international verifiers and human rights organisations. In one such incident, on 15 January 1999, 45 unarmed Kosovo Albanians were murdered in the village of Racak in the municipality of Stimlje/Shtime.

29. In a further response to the continuing conflict in Kosovo, an international peace conference was organised in Rambouillet, France, beginning on 7 February 1999. Nikola SAINOVIC, the Deputy Prime Minister of the FRY, was a member of the Serbian delegation at the peace talks and Milan MILUTINOVIC, President of Serbia, was also present during the negotiations. The Kosovo Albanians were represented by the KLA and a delegation of Kosovo Albanian political and civic leaders. Despite intensive negotiations over several weeks, the peace talks collapsed in mid-March 1999.

30. During the peace negotiations in France, the violence in Kosovo continued. In late February and early March, forces of the FRY and Serbia launched a series of offensives against dozens of predominantly Kosovo Albanian villages and towns. The FRY military forces were comprised of elements of the 3rd Army, specifically the 52nd Corps, also known as the Pristina Corps, and several brigades and regiments under the command of the Pristina Corps. The Chief of the General Staff of the VJ, with command responsibilities over the 3rd Army and ultimately over the Pristina Corps, is Colonel General Dragoljub OJDANIC. The Supreme Commander of the VJ is Slobodan MILOSEVIC.

31. The police forces taking part in the actions in Kosovo are members of the Ministry of Internal Affairs of Serbia in addition to some units from the Ministry of Internal Affairs of the FRY. All police forces employed by or working under the authority of the Ministry of Internal Affairs of Serbia are commanded by Vlajko STOJILJKOVIC, Minister of Internal Affairs of Serbia. Under the FRY Act on the Armed Forces, those police forces engaged in military operations during a state of war or imminent threat of war are subordinated to the command of the VJ whose commanders are Colonel General Dragoljub OJDANIC and Slobodan MILOSEVIC.

32. Prior to December 1998, Slobodan MILOSEVIC designated Nikola SAINOVIC as his representative for the Kosovo situation. A number of diplomats and other international officials who needed to speak with a government official regarding events in Kosovo were directed to Nikola SAINOVIC. He took an active role in the negotiations establishing the OSCE verification mission for Kosovo and he participated in numerous other meetings regarding the Kosovo crisis. From January 1999 to the date of this indictment, Nikola SAINOVIC has acted as the liaison between Slobodan MILOSEVIC and various Kosovo Albanian leaders.

33. Nikola SAINOVIC was most recently re-appointed Deputy Prime Minister of the FRY on 20 May 1998. As such, he is a member of the Government of the FRY, which, among other duties and responsibilities, formulates domestic and foreign policy, enforces federal law, directs and co-ordinates the work of federal ministries, and organises defence preparations.

34. During their offensives, forces of the FRY and Serbia acting in concert have engaged in a well-planned and co-ordinated campaign of destruction of property owned by Kosovo Albanian civilians. Towns and villages have been shelled, homes, farms, and business burned, and personal property destroyed. As a result of these orchestrated actions, towns, villages, and entire regions have been made unin-

habitable for Kosovo Albanians. Additionally, forces of the FRY and Serbia have harassed, humiliated, and degraded Kosovo Albanian civilians through physical and verbal abuse. The Kosovo Albanians have also been persistently subjected to insults, racial slurs, degrading acts based on ethnicity and religion, beatings, and other forms of physical mistreatment.

35. The unlawful deportation and forcible transfer of thousands of Kosovo Albanians from their homes in Kosovo involved well-planned and co-ordinated efforts by the leaders of the FRY and Serbia, and forces of the FRY and Serbia, all acting in concert. Actions similar in nature took place during the wars in Croatia and Bosnia and Herzegovina between 1991 and 1995. During those wars, Serbian military, paramilitary and police forces forcibly expelled and deported non-Serbs in Croatia and Bosnia and Herzegovina from areas under Serbian control utilising the same method of operations as have been used in Kosovo in 1999: heavy shelling and armed attacks on villages; widespread killings; destruction of non-Serbian residential areas and cultural and religious sites; and forced transfer and deportation of non-Serbian populations.

36. On 24 March 1999, NATO began launching air strikes against targets in the FRY. The FRY issued decrees of an imminent threat of war on 23 March 1999 and a state of war on 24 March 1999. Since the air strikes commenced, forces of the FRY and Serbia have intensified their systematic campaign and have forcibly expelled hundreds of thousands of Kosovo Albanians.

37. In addition to the forced expulsions of Kosovo Albanians, forces of the FRY and Serbia have also engaged in a number of killings of Kosovo Albanians since 24 March 1999. Such killings occurred at numerous locations, including but not limited to, Bela Crkva, Mali Krusa/Krushe e Vogel—Velika Krusa/Krushe e Mahde, Dakovica/Gjakovë, Crkovez/Padalishte, and Izbica.

38. The planning, preparation and execution of the campaign undertaken by forces of the FRY and Serbia in Kosovo, was planned, instigated, ordered, committed or otherwise aided and abetted by Slobodan MILOSEVIC, the President of the FRY; Milan MILUTINOVIC, the President of Serbia; Nikola SAINOVIC, the Deputy Prime Minister of the FRY; Colonel General Dragoljub OJDANIC, the Chief of the General Staff of the VJ; and Vlajko STOJILJKOVIC, the Minister of Internal Affairs of Serbia.

39. By 20 May 1999, over 740,000 Kosovo Albanians, approximately one-third of the entire Kosovo Albanian population, were expelled from Kosovo. Thousands more are believed to be internally displaced. An

unknown number of Kosovo Albanians have been killed in the operations by forces of the FRY and Serbia.

The Accused

40. Slobodan MILOSEVIC was born on 20 August 1941 in the town of
Pozarevac in present-day Serbia. In 1964 he received a law degree
from the University of Belgrade and began a career in management
and banking. Slobodan MILOSEVIC held the posts of deputy director and later general director at Tehnogas, a major gas company,
until 1978. Thereafter, he became president of Beogradska banka
(Beobanka), one of the largest banks in the SFRY, and held that post
until 1983.

41. In 1983 Slobodan MILOSEVIC began his political career. He became
Chairman of the City Committee of the League of Communists of
Belgrade in 1984. In 1986 he was elected Chairman of the Presidium
of the Central Committee of the League of Communists of Serbia
and was re-elected in 1988. On 16 July 1990, the League of Com-
munists of Serbia and the Socialist Alliance of Working People of
Serbia were united; the new party was named the Socialist Party of
Serbia (SPS), and Slobodan MILOSEVIC was elected its President.
He holds the post of President of the SPS as of the date of this indictment.

42. Slobodan MILOSEVIC was elected President of the Presidency of
Serbia on 8 May 1989 and re-elected on 5 December that same year.
After the adoption of the new Constitution of Serbia on 28 September
1990, Slobodan MILOSEVIC was elected to the newly established
office of President of Serbia in multi-party elections held on 9 and
26 December 1990; he was re-elected on 20 December 1992.

43. After serving two terms as President of Serbia, Slobodan MILO-
SEVIC was elected President of the FRY on 15 July 1997 and he began
his official duties on 23 July 1997. At all times relevant to this indictment, Slobodan MILOSEVIC has held the post of President of the
FRY.

44. Milan MILUTINOVIC was born on 19 December 1942 in Belgrade in
present-day Serbia. Milan MILUTINOVIC received a degree in law
from Belgrade University.

45. Throughout his political career, Milan MILUTINOVIC has held numerous high level governmental posts within Serbia and the FRY.
Milan MILUTINOVIC was a deputy in the Socio-Political Chamber
and a member of the foreign policy committee in the Federal Assembly; he was Serbia's Secretary for Education and Sciences, a member
of the Executive Council of the Serbian Assembly, and a director of

the Serbian National Library. Milan MILUTINOVIC also served as an ambassador in the Federal Ministry of Foreign Affairs and as the FRY Ambassador to Greece. He was appointed the Minister of Foreign Affairs of the FRY on 15 August 1995. Milan MILUTINOVIC is a member of the SPS.

46. On 21 December 1997, Milan MILUTINOVIC was elected President of Serbia. At all times relevant to this indictment, Milan MILUTINOVIC has held the post of President of Serbia.

47. Nikola SAINOVIC was born on 7 December 1948 in Bor, Serbia. He graduated from the University of Ljubljana in 1977 and holds a Master of Science degree in Chemical Engineering. He began his political career in the municipality of Bor where he held the position of President of the Municipal Assembly of Bor from 1978 to 1982.

48. Throughout his political career, Nikola SAINOVIC has been an active member of both the League of Communists and the Socialist Party of Serbia (SPS). He held the position of Chairman of the Municipal Committee of the League of Communists in Bor. On 28 November 1995, Nikola SAINOVIC was elected a member of the SPS's Main Committee and a member of its Executive Council. He was also named president of the Committee to prepare the SPS Third Regular Congress (held in Belgrade on 2–3 March 1996). On 2 March 1996 Nikola SAINOVIC was elected one of several vice chairmen of the SPS. He held this position until 24 April 1997.

49. Nikola SAINOVIC has held several positions within the governments of Serbia and the FRY. In 1989, he served as a member of the Executive Council of Serbia's Assembly and Secretary for Industry, Energetics and Engineering of Serbia in 1989. He was appointed Minister of Mining and Energy of Serbia on 11 February 1991, and again on 23 December 1991. On 23 December 1991, he was also named Deputy Prime Minister of Serbia. Nikola SAINOVIC was appointed Minister of the Economy of the FRY on 14 July 1992, and again on 11 September 1992. He resigned from this post on 29 November 1992. On 10 February 1993, Nikola SAINOVIC was elected Prime Minister of Serbia.

50. On 22 February 1994, Nikola SAINOVIC was appointed Deputy Prime Minister of the FRY. He was re-appointed to this position in three subsequent governments: on 12 June 1996, 20 March 1997 and 20 May 1998. Slobodan MILOSEVIC designated Nikola SAINOVIC as his representative for the Kosovo situation. Nikola SAINOVIC chaired the commission for co-operation with the OSCE Verification Mission in Kosovo, and was an official member of the Serbian delegation at the Rambouillet peace talks in February 1999. At all times

relevant to this indictment, Nikola SAINOVIC has held the post of Deputy Prime Minister of the FRY.

51. Colonel General Dragoljub OJDANIC was born on 1 June 1941 in the village of Ravni, near Uzice in what is now Serbia. In 1958, he completed the Infantry School for Non-Commissioned Officers and in 1964, he completed the Military Academy of the Ground Forces. In 1985, Dragoljub OJDANIC graduated from the Command Staff Academy and School of National Defence with a Masters Degree in Military Sciences. At one time he served as the Secretary for the League of Communists for the Yugoslav National Army (JNA) 52nd Corps, the precursor of the 52nd Corps of the VJ now operating in Kosovo.

52. In 1992, Colonel General Dragoljub OJDANIC was the Deputy Commander of the 37th Corps of the JNA, later the VJ, based in Uzice, Serbia. He was promoted to Major General on 20 April 1992 and became Commander of the Uzice Corps. Under his command, the Uzice Corps was involved in military actions in eastern Bosnia during the war in Bosnia and Herzegovina. In 1993 and 1994 Dragoljub OJDANIC served as Chief of the General Staff of the First Army of the FRY. He was Commander of the First Army between 1994 and 1996. In 1996, he became Deputy Chief of the General Staff of the VJ. On 26 November 1998, Slobodan MILOSEVIC appointed Dragoljub OJDANIC Chief of General Staff of the VJ, replacing General Momcilo Perisic. At all times relevant to this indictment, Colonel General Dragoljub OJDANIC has held the post of Chief of the General Staff of the VJ.

53. Vlajko STOJILJKOVIC was born in Mala Krsna, in Serbia. He graduated from the University of Belgrade with a law degree, and then was employed at the municipal court. Thereafter, he became head of the Inter-Municipal Secretariat of Internal Affairs in Pozarevac. Vlajko STOJILJKOVIC has served as director of the PIK firm in Pozarevac, vice-president and president of the Economic Council of Yugoslavia, and president of the Economic Council of Serbia.

54. By April 1997, Vlajko STOJILJKOVIC became Deputy Prime Minister of the Serbian Government and Minister of Internal Affairs of Serbia. On 24 March 1998, the Serbian Assembly elected a new Government, and Vlajko STOJILJKOVIC was named Minister of Internal Affairs of Serbia. He is also a member of the main board of the SPS. At all times relevant to this indictment, Vlajko STOJILJKOVIC, has held the post of Minister of Internal Affairs.

Superior Authority

55. Slobodan MILOSEVIC was elected President of the FRY on 15 July 1997, assumed office on 23 July 1997, and remains President as of the date of this indictment.

56. As President of the FRY, Slobodan MILOSEVIC functions as President of the Supreme Defence Council of the FRY. The Supreme Defence Council consists of the President of the FRY and the Presidents of the member republics, Serbia and Montenegro. The Supreme Defence Council decides on the National Defence Plan and issues decisions concerning the VJ. As President of the FRY, Slobodan MILOSEVIC has the power to "order implementation of the National Defence Plan" and commands the VJ in war and peace in compliance with decisions made by the Supreme Defence Council. Slobodan MILOSEVIC, as Supreme Commander of the VJ, performs these duties through "commands, orders and decisions."

57. Under the FRY Act on the Armed Forces of Yugoslavia, as Supreme Commander of the VJ, Slobodan MILOSEVIC also exercises command authority over republican and federal police units subordinated to the VJ during a state of imminent threat of war or a state of war. A declaration of imminent threat of war was proclaimed on 23 March 1999, and a state of war on 24 March 1999.

58. In addition to his de jure powers, Slobodan MILOSEVIC exercises extensive de facto control over numerous institutions essential to, or involved in, the conduct of the offences alleged herein. Slobodan MILOSEVIC exercises extensive de facto control over federal institutions nominally under the competence of the Assembly or the Government of the FRY. Slobodan MILOSEVIC also exercises de facto control over functions and institutions nominally under the competence of Serbia and its autonomous provinces, including the Serbian police force. Slobodan MILOSEVIC further exercises de facto control over numerous aspects of the FRY's political and economic life, particularly the media. Between 1986 and the early 1990s, Slobodan MILOSEVIC progressively acquired de facto control over these federal, republican, provincial and other institutions. He continues to exercise this de facto control to this day.

59. Slobodan MILOSEVIC's de facto control over Serbian, SFRY, FRY and other state organs has stemmed, in part, from his leadership of the two principal political parties that have ruled in Serbia since 1986, and in the FRY since 1992. From 1986 until 1990, he was Chairman of the Presidium of the Central Committee of the League of Communists in Serbia, then the ruling party in Serbia. In 1990, he was elected President of the Socialist Party of Serbia, the successor

party to the League of Communists of Serbia and the Socialist Alliance of the Working People of Serbia. The SPS has been the principal ruling party in Serbia and the FRY ever since. Throughout the period of his Presidency of Serbia, from 1990 to 1997, and as the President of the FRY, from 1997 to the present, Slobodan MILOSEVIC has also been the leader of the SPS.

60. Beginning no later than October 1988, Slobodan MILOSEVIC has exercised de facto control over the ruling and governing institutions of Serbia, including its police force. Beginning no later than October 1988, he has exercised de facto control over Serbia's two autonomous provinces—Kosovo and Vojvodina—and their representation in federal organs of the SFRY and the FRY. From no later than October 1988 until mid-1998, Slobodan MILOSEVIC also exercised de facto control over the ruling and governing institutions of Montenegro, including its representation in all federal organs of the SFRY and the FRY.

61. In significant international negotiations, meetings and conferences since 1989, Slobodan MILOSEVIC has been the primary interlocutor with whom the international community has negotiated. He has negotiated international agreements that have subsequently been implemented within Serbia, the SFRY, the FRY, and elsewhere on the territory of the former SFRY. Among the conferences and international negotiations at which Slobodan MILOSEVIC has been the primary representative of the SFRY and FRY are: The Hague Conference in 1991; the Paris negotiations of March 1993; the International Conference on the Former Yugoslavia in January 1993; the Vance-Owen peace plan negotiations between January and May 1993; the Geneva peace talks in the summer of 1993; the Contact Group meeting in June 1994; the negotiations for a cease fire in Bosnia and Herzegovina, 9–14 September 1995; the negotiations to end the NATO bombing in Bosnia and Herzegovina, 14–20 September 1995; and the Dayton peace negotiations in November 1995.

62. As the President of the FRY, the Supreme Commander of the VJ, and the President of the Supreme Defence Council, and pursuant to his de facto authority, Slobodan MILOSEVIC is responsible for the actions of his subordinates within the VJ and any police forces, both federal and republican, who have committed the crimes alleged in this indictment since January 1999 in the province of Kosovo.

63. Milan MILUTINOVIC was elected President of Serbia on 21 December 1997, and remains President as of the date of this indictment. As President of Serbia, Milan MILUTINOVIC is the head of State. He represents Serbia and conducts its relations with foreign states and

international organisations. He organises preparations for the defence of Serbia.

64. As President of Serbia, Milan MILUTINOVIC is a member of the Supreme Defence Council of the FRY and participates in decisions regarding the use of the VJ.

65. As President of Serbia, Milan MILUTINOVIC, in conjunction with the Assembly, has the authority to request reports both from the Government of Serbia, concerning matters under its jurisdiction, and from the Ministry of the Internal Affairs, concerning its activities and the security situation in Serbia. As President of Serbia, Milan MILUTINOVIC has the authority to dissolve the Assembly, and with it the Government, "subject to the proposal of the Government on justified grounds," although this power obtains only in peacetime.

66. During a declared state of war or state of imminent threat of war, Milan MILUTINOVIC, as President of Serbia, may enact measures normally under the competence of the Assembly, including the passage of laws; these measures may include the reorganization of the Government and its ministries, as well as the restriction of certain rights and freedoms.

Source: International Criminal Tribunal for the former Yugoslavia (ICTY), May 4, 1999.

BIBLIOGRAPHY

BOOKS

Allcock, John B., Marko Milivojevic, and John J. Horton, eds. *Conflict in the Former Yugoslavia: An Encyclopedia*. Denver: ABC-CLIO, 1998.

Allport, Gordon W. *The Nature of Prejudice*. Boston: Beacon Press, 1954.

August, Ray. *Public International Law*. Englewood Cliffs, NJ: Prentice-Hall, 1995.

Banac, Ivo. "The Origins and Development of the Concept of Yugoslavia (to 1945)." In *Yearbook of European Studies #5: The Disintegration of Yugoslavia*, eds. Martin van den Heuvel and Jan G. Siccama. Atlanta: Rodopi, 1992.

Barkey, Karen. "Thinking about Consequences of Empire." In *After Empire: Multiethnic Societies and Nation-Building: The Soviet Union and the Russian, Ottoman and Habsburg Empires*, eds. Karen Barkey and Mark Von Hagen. Boulder: Westview, 1997.

Beloff, Nora. *Tito's Flawed Legacy: Yugoslavia and the West, 1939–84*. London: Victor Gollancz, 1985.

Bennis, Phyllis. *Calling the Shots: How Washington Dominates Today's UN*. New York: Olive Branch Press, 1996.

Biberaj, Elez. *Albania: A Socialist Maverick*. Boulder: Westview, 1990.

Bugajski, Janusz. *Nations in Turmoil: Conflict and Cooperation in Eastern Europe*. Boulder: Westview, 1993.

Cortright, David, and George A. Lopez. "Carrots, Sticks, and Cooperation: Economic Tools of Statecraft." In *Cases and Strategies for Preventive Action*, ed. Barnett R. Rubin. New York: Century Foundation Press, 1998.

Crnobrnja, Mihailo. *The Yugoslav Drama*. Montreal: McGill–Queen's University Press, 1996.

Curtis, Glenn E., ed. *Yugoslavia: A Country Study*. Washington, DC: Federal Research Division, Library of Congress, 1992.

Deak, Istvan. "The Habsburg Empire." In *After Empire: Multiethnic Societies and Nation-Building: The Soviet Union and the Russian, Ottoman and Habsburg Empires*, eds. Karen Barkey and Mark Von Hagen. Boulder: Westview, 1997.

Djilas, Aleksa. *The Contested Country: Yugoslav Unity and Communist Revolution, 1919–1953*. Cambridge, MA: Harvard University Press, 1991.

Djordjevic, Dimitrije, and Stephen Fischer-Galati. *The Balkans' Revolutionary Tradition*. New York: Columbia University Press, 1981.

Howard, Harry. "Historical Evolution: A Chronology." In *Yugoslavia*, ed. Robert Kerner. Berkeley: University of California Press, 1949.

Hutchinson, John, and Anthony D. Smith, eds. *Nationalism*. New York: Oxford University Press, 1994.

Maliqi, Shkelzen. "The Albanians of Kosovo: Self-Determination through Nonviolence." In *Why Bosnia? Writings on the Balkan War*, eds. Rabia Ali and Lawrence Lifschultz. Stony Creek, CT: Pamphleteer's Press, 1993.

Marmullaku, Ramadan. *Albania and the Albanians*. London: C. Hurst and Company, 1975.

Nossal, Kim Richard. *The Patterns of World Politics*. Scarborough, Ontario: Prentice-Hall Allyn and Bacon Canada, 1998.

Poulton, Hugh. *Balkans: Minorities and States in Conflict*. London: Minority Rights Publications, 1991.

Pratkanis, Anthony R., and Elliot Aronson. *Age of Propaganda: The Everyday Use and Abuse of Persuasion*. New York: W. H. Freeman and Co., 1991.

Ramet, Pedro. *Nationalism and Federalism in Yugoslavia 1963–1983*. Bloomington: Indiana University Press, 1984.

Ramet, Sabrina. *Balkan Babel: The Disintegration of Yugoslavia from the Death of Tito to the War for Kosovo*, 3rd ed. Boulder: Westview Press, 1999.

————. *Nationalism and Federalism in Yugoslavia 1962–1991*. Bloomington: Indiana University Press, 1992.

Rechetar, John S., Jr. *The Soviet Polity: Government and Politics in the USSR*. New York: Harper and Row, 1978.

Rezun, Miron. *Europe and War in the Balkans: Toward a New Yugoslav Identity*. New York: Praeger, 1995.

Seton-Watson, R. W., and R. G. D. Laffam. "Yugoslavia Between the Wars." In *A Short History of Yugoslavia: From Early Times to 1966*, ed. Stephen Clissold. Cambridge: Cambridge University Press, 1966.

Shoup, Paul. *Communism and the Yugoslav National Question*. New York: Columbia University Press, 1968.

———. "Titoism and the National Question in Yugoslavia: A Reassessment." In *Yearbook of European Studies #5: The Disintegration of Yugoslavia*, eds. Martin van den Heuvel and Jan G. Siccama. Atlanta: Rodopi, 1992.

Singleton, F. B. "The First World War and the Birth of Yugoslavia." In *Yugoslavia*, eds. Muriel Heppell and F. B. Singleton. New York: Praeger, 1961.

Smith, Anthony D. *National Identity*. Reno: University of Reno Press, 1991.

Spillman, Kurt, and Joachim Krause, eds. *Kosovo: Lessons Learned for International Security*. Peter Lang: Born/Berlin, 2000.

Stiglmayer, Alexandra, ed. *Mass Rape: The War against Women in Bosnia-Herzegovina*. Lincoln: University of Nebraska Press, 1994.

Stoianovich, Traian. *Balkan Worlds: The First and Last Europe*. Armonk, NY: M. E. Sharpe, 1994.

Tishkov, Valery. *Ethnicity, Nationalism and Conflict in and after the Soviet Union: The Mind Aflame*. London: SAGE Publications, 1997.

Tomasevich, Jozo. *War and Revolution in Yugoslavia 1941–1945: The Chetniks*. Stanford, CA: Stanford University Press, 1975.

Udovicki, Jasminka, and James Ridgeway, eds. *Burn This House: The Making and Unmaking of Yugoslavia*. Durham: Duke University Press, 1997.

Vuckovic, Gojko. *Ethnic Cleavages and Conflict: The Sources of National Cohesion and Disintegration: The Case of Yugoslavia*. Brookfield: Ashgate, 1997.

Weiss, Thomas G. "Rekindling Hope in U.N. Humanitarian Intervention." In *Learning from Somalia: The Lessons of Armed Humanitarian Intervention*, eds. Walter Clarke and Jeffrey Herbst. Boulder: Westview, 1997.

Zickel, Raymond, and Walter R. Iwaskiw, eds. *Albania: A Country Study*. Washington, DC: Federal Research Division, Library of Congress, 1994.

INTERNET SOURCES

http://albanian.com/main/countries/kosova/documents/ducellier.html (Alain Ducellier, "Have the Albanians Occupied Kosova?")

http://anthro.spc.uchicago.edu/~mdzivkov/course/BB.html (Marko Zivkovic, "Ballads and Bullets in Bosnia: How Dangerous Are the Epics of Mountain Serbs?")

http://asia.yahoo.com/headlines/030699/world/928406340-
90603103928.newsworld.html ("71 Days of War in the Balkans: A Chronology")

http://call.army.mil/call/fmso/fmsopubs/issues/yugo-ram.htm (Jacob
W. Kipp and Timothy L. Thomas, "International Ramifications of Yu-
goslavia's Serial Wars: The Challenge of Ethno-National Conflicts for a
Post–Cold War, European Order," through Foreign Military Studies
Office)

http://cnn.com/WORLD/europe/9906/09/kosovo.plan.01 ("Timetable
for Kosovo Transition")

http://dailynews.yahoo.com/h/ap/19990922/wl/us_kosovo_serbs_2
.html (Barry Schweid, "Albright Defends New Kosovo Force," September
22, 1999)

http://dailynews.yahoo.com/h/ap/19990923/wl/nato_kosovo_1.html
(Robert Burns, "NATO Chief: No Kosovo Independence," September 23,
1999)

http://dailynews.yahoo.com/h/ap/19991009/wl/yugoslavia_last_
serbs_1.html (George Jahn, "Few Serbs Remain in Kosovo Capital," October 9, 1999)

http://dailynews.yahoo.com/h/ap/19991012/pl/army_of_the_future_
1.html (Robert Burns, "Army Reveals Changes in Land Forces," October
12, 1999)

http://dailynews.yahoo.com/h/ap/19991018/wl/italy_kosovo_1.html
("Milosevic's Wife Vows Serb Revenge," October 18, 1999)

http://dailynews.yahoo.com/h/ap/19991018/wl/yugoslavia_kosovo_
21.html (George Jahn, "NATO Trains Serbs, Ethnic Albanians," October
18, 1999)

http://dailynews.yahoo.com/h/ap/19991023/wl/yugoslavia_
montenegro_6.html (Danilo Burzan, "Montenegro Seeks Fiscal Independence," October 23, 1999)

http//dailynews.yahoo.com/h/ap/19991025/wl/russia_rebuffing_the_
west_1.html (Barry Renfrew, "Russia Rejects Chechnya Criticism," October 25, 1999)

http://dailynews.yahoo.com/h/ap/19991025/wl/yugoslavia_
montenegro_12.html (Dusan Stojanovic, "Serbs, Montenegrins Discuss
Future," October 25, 1999)

http://fourthfreedom.org/inforum/yugo.html ("The Case of Yugoslavia" on sanctions)

http://idt.net/~qosja/albquestion.html (Rexhep Qosja, "The Albanian
National Question in the Serb Political Programs during 1937–1944")

http://kennedy.soc.surrey.ac.uk/socresonline/2/1/8.html   (Paul Treanor, "Structures of Nationalism," in *Sociological Research Online*, 1997)

http://members.tripod.com/kyeo/guardian.htm ("Kosovo, Drugs, the KLA and the West," from Australian *Guardian*)

http://news.bbc.co.uk//

http://web.inter.nl.net/users/Paul.Treanor/genocide.html (Paul Treanor, "Genocide, World Order, and State Formation")

http://web.inter.nl.net/users/Paul. Treanor/post-kfor.html (Paul Treanor, "Europe after KFOR")

http://www.access.ch/tuerkei/GRUPF/racism1.html ("The Etiology of Racism in Europe," sections 1–9)

http://www.afsouth.nato.int/deteagle/eagle.htm ("Operation Eagle Eye")

http://www.afsouth.nato.int/detforce/force.htm ("Operation Allied Force")

http://www.afsouth.nato.int/kvcc/kvcc.htm ("The Kosovo Verification Coordination Centre")

http://www.amina.com/article/relig_root.html (David Damrel, "The Religious Roots of Conflict: Russia and Chechnya")

http://www.amina.com/article/warstart.html ("How the War Started," on war in Chechnya)

http://www.amnesty.org/ailib/aipub/1998/EUR/46300298.htm (Amnesty International, "Bosnia-Herzegovina: All the Way Home")

http://www.coffeeshoptimes.com/watk7.html (Mark Watkins, "Milosevic 2, Clinton 0")

http://www.cpss.org/casiabk/chap3.txt (on war in Chechnya)

http://www.crisisweb.org/projects/sbalkans/reports/ba02main.htm (International Crisis Group, "Balkans: The Balkan Refugee Crisis: Regional and Long-Term Perspectives," June 1, 1999)

http://www.crisisweb.org/projects/sbalkans/reports/kos03mai.htm (International Crisis Group, "South Balkans: The View from Tirana: The Albanian Dimension of the Kosovo Crisis," July 10, 1998)

http://www.crisisweb.org/projects/sbalkans/reports/kos12main.htm (International Crisis Group, "South Balkans: Unifying the Kosovar Factions: The Way Forward," March 12, 1999)

http://www.crisisweb.org/projects/sbalkans/reports/kos20main.htm (International Crisis Group, "South Balkans: War in the Balkans: Consequences of the Kosovo Conflict and Future Options for Kosovo and the Region," April 19, 1999)

http://www.crisisweb.org/projects/sbalkans/reports/kos23main.htm
(International Crisis Group, "South Balkans: The New Kosovo Protectorate")

http://www.crisisweb.org/projects/sbalkans/reports/kos25main.htm
(International Crisis Group, "South Balkans: Back to the Future: Milosevic Prepares for Life after Kosovo," June 28, 1999)

http://www.crisisweb.org/projects/sbalkans/reports/kos27main.htm
(International Crisis Group, "South Balkans: Who's Who in Kosovo,"
August 31, 1999)

http://www.crisisweb.org/projects/sbalkans/reports/kos28main.htm
(International Crisis Group, "South Balkans: Waiting for UNMIK: Local
Administration in Kosovo," October 18, 1999)

http://www.crisisweb.org/projects/sbalkans/reports/mac03main.htm
(International Crisis Group, "South Balkans: The Albanian Question in
Macedonia: Implications of the Kosovo Conflict for Inter-Ethnic Relations
in Macedonia," August 11, 1998)

http://www.crisisweb.org/projects/sbalkans/reports/mont01main.htm
(International Crisis Group, "South Balkans: Montenegro Briefing: Calm
before the Storm," August 18, 1999)

http://www.crisisweb.org/projects/sbalkans/reports/yu01main.htm
(International Crisis Group, "South Balkans: Serbia: The Milosevic Factor," February 24, 1998)

http://www.crisisweb.org/projects/sbalkans/reports/yu02main.htm
(International Crisis Group, "South Balkans: Slobodan Milosevic's Ma-
nipulation of the Kosovo Dispute," May 6, 1998)

http://www.crisisweb.org/projects/sbalkans/reports/yu04main.htm
(International Crisis Group, "South Balkans: Sandzak: Calm for Now,"
November 9, 1998)

http://www.crisisweb.org/projects/sbalkans/reports/yu05maina.htm
(International Crisis Group, "South Balkans: Sidelining Slobodan: Getting Rid of Europe's Last Dictator," March 15, 1999)

http://www.crisisweb.org/projects/sbalkans/reports/yu06brfmain.htm
(International Crisis Group, "South Balkans: Milosevic to Move on Montenegro," April 23, 1999)

http://www.crisisweb.org/projects/sbalkans/reports/yu07main.htm
(International Crisis Group, "South Balkans: Milosevic's Aims in War
and Diplomacy," May 12, 1999)

http://www.crisisweb.org/projects/sbalkans/reports/yu10main.htm
(International Crisis Group, "South Balkans: Transforming Serbia: The
Key to Long Term Stability," August 12, 1999)

http://www.crisisweb.org/projects/sbalkans/reports/yugobrf01main. htm (International Crisis Group, "South Balkans: Fear and Loathing in Belgrade: What the Serbian State Media Say about Kosovars," January 26, 1999)

http://www.csmonitor.com/durable/1999/05/25/pls3.htm   (Justin Brown, "An Heir to Milosevic: Is He Better?" in *Christian Science Monitor*, May 25, 1999)

http://www.dixienet.org/spatriot/vol2no2/member4.html   (Franklin Sanders, "The Global Rise of Ethnic Nationalism")

http://www.du.edu/~mmishima/intervention-index.htm (on multinational intervention)

http://www.european-digest.com/docs/digest08.htm ("Where History Boils Over . . . and Over," June 1999)

http://www.foreignaffairs.org/oxford/990811.html   ("Kosovo—New Dawn for an Ethical Foreign Policy?" weekly column from *Oxford Analytica*, August 11, 1999)

http://www.freerepublic.com/forum/a3700bb310e37.htm   (Thomas Friedman, "Bomb, Talk, Deal," in *New York Times*, March 30, 1999)

http://www.geocities.com/Athens/Delphi/6875/nexhat.html   (Nexhat Ibrahimi, "Islam's First Contacts with the Balkan Nations")

http://www.globalpolicy.org/security/reform/sc99-2.htm (Judith Miller, "U.N. Security Council Relegated to Sidelines," in *New York Times*, March 14, 1999)

http://www.globescope.com/karen/genocide.html (Karen V. Lawrence, "International Dimensions of Genocide")

http://www.hrw.org/reports/1999/kosov2/ ("Federal Republic of Yugoslavia: Abuses against Serbs and Roma in the New Kosovo," in *Human Rights Watch*, vol. 11, no. 10, August 1999)

http://www.igc.apc.org/globalpolicy/security/issues/djhnstne.htm (Diana Johnstone, "The War NATO Wanted")

http://www.iwpr.net/balkans/news/bcr030699_2_eng.htm   (Anthony Borden, "The Next Serbian Conflict")

http://www.lib.msu.edu/sowards/balkan/lecture1.html (Steven W. Sowards, "Geography and Ethnic Geography of the Balkans to 1500")

http://www.monde-diplomatique.fr/dossiers/kosovo/rambouillet. html ("Interim Agreement for Peace and Self-Government in Kosovo," the Rambouillet Agreement)

http://www.monde-diplomatique.fr/en/1999/05/?c=01leader (Ignacio Ramonet, "A Fine Mess," in *Le Monde Diplomatique*, May 1999) http://www.newsday.com/ap/rnmpin1m.htm (Tony Czuczka, "Russia, NATO Agree on Kosovo Plan")

http://www.nytimes.com/specials/bosnia/context/apchrono.html (*New York Times*, "Chronology, 1990–1995")

http://www.pathfinder.com/time/magazine/articles/0,3266,22232,00. html (Timothy Garton Ash, "The New Adolf Hitler?" in *Time*, April 6, 1999)

http://www.pbs.org/wgbh/pages/frontline/shows/karadzic/genocide/ neveragain.html (Samantha Power, "Never Again: The World's Most Un-fulfilled Promise")

http://www.rec.org/REC/Bulletin/Bull84/EnvEffects.html ("Environ-mental Effects in Yugoslavia," in *The Bulletin, Quarterly Magazine of Regional Environmental Center for Central and Eastern Europe*)

http://www.rferl.org/ (RFE/RL Newsline)

http://www.royalty-magazine.com/features/serbia.html (Jean St. Clair, "The Blood-Stained Throne of Serbia")

http://www.salon.com/news/feature/1999/06/21/reconstruction/index. html (Mark Boal, "Businesses Are Waiting to Cash In on the Rebuilding of Kosovo," June 21, 1999)

http://www.salonmagazine.com/news/1999/03/26newsa.html (Gabriel Kahn, "The Unhappiest Allies: Italians Question NATO Moves in Ko-sovo as Country Braces for More Refugees," March 26, 1999)

http://www.salonmagazine.com/news/feature/1999/04/29/greece/ index.html (Thomas Goltz, "NATO's Achilles Heel: History, Geography and Suspicion Underlie Popular Anti-NATO Sentiment in Greece," April 29, 1999)

http://www.serbia-info.com/news/1999-06/14/12573.html   ("NATO Crimes in Yugoslavia: Planned Annihilation of the Entire Nation")

http://www.smh.com.au/news/9910/04/world/world9.html   (Chris Bird, "Fear of Civil War Saps Serbs' Spirit," October 4, 1999)

http://www.srpska-mreza.com/bookstore/kosovo/kosovo1.htm   (Tho-mas Emmert, "The Kosovo Legacy")

http://www.state.gov/www/regions/eur/bosnia/dayton.html   (Sum-mary of the Dayton Peace Agreement released by the Bureau of Public Affairs, December 11, 1995)

http://www.state.gov/www/regions/eur/fs_980716_bosqanda.html (Summary of U.S. government policy on Bosnia released by the Bureau of European and Canadian Affairs, U.S. Department of State, July 16, 1998)

http://www.stratfor.com/crisis/kosovo/specialreports/special87.htm ("It's the Russians, Stupid") http://www.thenation.com/issue/990628/0628falk.shtml (Richard Falk, "Reflections on the War")

http://www.unac.org/unreform/gordon.html (Nancy Gordon and Gregory Wirick, "Humanitarian Intervention as an Instrument of Human Rights," March 1996)

http://www.usafa.af.mil/jscope/JSCOPE95/Whitman95.html (Jeffrey Whitman, "An End to Sovereignty?")

http://zagreb.hic.hr/books/greatserbia/garasanin.htm (Ilija Garasanin, *Nacertanije* [1844])

http://zagreb.hic.hr/books/greatserbia/sanu.htm (Serbian Academy of Arts and Sciences Memorandum, 1986)

ENGLISH LANGUAGE JOURNALS

Albright, Madeleine K. "The Testing of American Foreign Policy." *Foreign Affairs*, vol. 77, no. 6, November/December 1998.

Banac, Ivo. "The Fearful Asymmetry of War: The Causes and Consequences of Yugoslavia's Demise." *Daedalus*, vol. 121, no. 2, Spring 1992.

Bell-Fialkoff, Andrew. "A Brief History of Ethnic Cleansing." *Foreign Affairs*, vol. 72, no. 3, Summer 1993.

Bringa, Tone R. "Nationality Categories, National Identification and Identity Formation in 'Multinational' Bosnia." *Anthropology of East European Review*, vol. 11, nos. 1–2, Autumn 1993.

Chomsky, Noam. "Judge the U.S. by Deeds, Not Words." *New Statesman*, vol. 128, no. 4431, April 9, 1999.

Conry, Barbara. "The Futility of U.S. Intervention in Regional Conflicts." *Policy Analysis*, no. 209, May 19, 1994.

Cornell, Svante E. "International Reactions to Massive Human Rights Violations: The Case of Chechnya." *Europe-Asia Studies*, vol. 51, no. 1, January 1999.

Costa, Nicholas J. "Kosovo: A Tragedy in the Making." *East European Quarterly*, vol. 21, no. 1, March 1987.

Cranshaw, Steve. "A Whole Nation Goes Mad." *New Statesman*, vol. 128, no. 4438, May 31, 1999.

Denitch, Bogdan. "Kosovo: The Beginning of the End." *Dissent*, vol. 46, no. 2, Spring 1999.

Djilas, Aleksa. "A Profile of Slobodan Milosevic." *Foreign Affairs*, vol. 72, no. 3, Summer 1993.

Ferfila, Bogomil. "Yugoslavia: Confederation or Disintegration?" *Problems of Communism*, vol. 40, July/August 1991.

Gobarev, Viktor. "Feeling Threatened." *The World Today*, vol. 55, no. 6, June 1999.

Goldhagen, Daniel Jonah. "A New Serbia." *The New Republic*, vol. 220, May 17, 1999.

Granville, Brigitte. "Time for a Rescue." *The World Today*, vol. 55, no. 7, July 1999.

Hagan, William W. "The Balkans' Lethal Nationalisms." *Foreign Affairs*, vol. 78, no. 4, July/August 1999.

Hedges, Chris. "Kosovo's Next Masters?" *Foreign Affairs*, vol. 78, no. 3, May/June 1999.

Hroch, Miroslav. "Nationalism and National Movements: Comparing the Past and the Present of Central and Eastern Europe." *Nations and Nationalism*, vol. 2, no. 1, 1996.

Huntington, Samuel P. "The Clash of Civilizations?" *Foreign Affairs*, vol. 72, no. 3, Summer 1993.

———. "The Lonely Superpower." *Foreign Affairs*, vol. 78, no. 2, March/April 1999.

Jackson, Robert H. "Armed Humanitarianism." *International Journal*, vol. 48, August 1993.

Kearns, Ian. "Kosovo Will Be Worse Than Bosnia." *New Statesman*, vol. 127, no. 4389, June 12, 1998.

Klein, Jacques Paul. "Stopping the Whirlwind." *The World Today*, vol. 55, no. 6, June 1999.

Korb, Lawrence J. "U.S. Defense Policy and the Management of International Conflicts." In *America's Quest for a New Contract with the World*, eds. Charles-Phillippe David and Onnig Beylerian. Centre D'Etudes des Politiques Étrangères et de Sécurité, Université du Quebec à Montréal, October 1995.

Lind, Michael. "In Defense of Liberal Nationalism." *Foreign Affairs*, vol. 73, no. 3, May/June 1994.

Lloyd, John. "How the Doves Turned Hawkish." *New Statesman*, vol. 128, no. 4430, April 2, 1999.

———. "Kosovo: A Rich and Comfortable War." *New Statesman*, vol. 128, no. 4440, June 14, 1999.

Luttwak, Edward N. "Give War a Chance." *Foreign Affairs*, vol. 78, no. 4, July/August 1999.

Malcolm, Noel. "Kosovo: Only Independence Will Work." *National Interest*, no. 54, Winter 1998/1999.

Nicarchos, Catherine N. "Women, War, and Rape: Challenges Facing the International Tribunal for the Former Yugoslavia." *Human Rights Quarterly*, vol. 17, no. 4, 1995.

Pavkovic, Aleksandar. "From Yugoslavism to Serbism: The Serb National Idea, 1986–1996." *Nations and Nationalism*, vol. 4, no. 4, 1998.

Pipa, Arshi. "The Political Situation of the Albanians in Yugoslavia with Particular Attention to the Kosovo Problem: A Critical Approach." *East European Quarterly*, vol. 23, no. 2, June 1989.

Ramet, Sabrina. "Serbia's Slobodan Milosevic: A Profile." *Orbis*, vol. 35, no. 1, Winter 1991.

Roberts, Elizabeth. "Next Balkan Flashpoint?" *The World Today*, vol. 55, no. 4, April 1999.

Silber, Laura. "Milosevic Family Values." *The New Republic*, no. 4415, August 30, 1999.

Sullivan, Stacy. "Milosevic's Willing Executioners." *The New Republic*, vol. 220, no. 19, May 10, 1999.

Taylor, Philip M. "Propaganda and the Web War." *The World Today*, vol. 55, no. 6, June 1999.

Velebit, Vladimir. "Kosovo: A Case of Ethnic Change of Population." *East European Quarterly*, vol. 33, no. 2, Summer 1999.

Williams, Michael C. "Ties That Bind." *The World Today*, vol. 55, no. 5, May 1999.

Wills, Garry. "Bully of the Free World." *Foreign Affairs*, vol. 78, no. 2, March/April 1999.

Wright, Eske. "A Balkan Version of the IRA?" *New Statesman*, vol. 128, no. 4431, April 9, 1999.

Zakaria, Fareed. "Keeping Kosovo." *National Review*, vol. 51, no. 18, September 27, 1999.

Zimmermann, Warren. "The Demons of Kosovo." *National Interest*, no. 52, Summer 1998.

Zivkovic, Marko. "Stories Serbs Tell Themselves." *Problems of Post Communism*, vol. 44, no. 4, July 1, 1997.

MAGAZINES

Annan, Kofi. "Two Concepts of Sovereignty." *Economist*, September 18, 1999.

Calabresi, Massimo. "No to Reconciliation." *Time*, September 28, 1998.

Came, Barry. "The Albanian Dream." *Maclean's*, April 19, 1999.

Cirjakovic, Zoran. "A Summer of Discontent." *Newsweek*, July 12, 1999.

"Exporting Misery." *Economist*, April 17, 1999.

Gutman, Roy. "U.N.'s Deadly Deal: How Troop-Hostage Talks Led to Slaughter of Srebrenica." *Newsday*, May 29, 1996.

Isaacson, Walter. "Madeleine's War." *Time*, May 17, 1999.

Jordan, Michael J. "In Albania: A Return to 'Eye for Eye.' " *Christian Science Monitor*, August 7, 1997.

Junger, Sebastian. "The Forensics of War." *Vanity Fair*, October 1999.

Kennedy, William. "Masters of Deception." *George*, vol. 3, no. 2, February 1998.

Kissinger, Henry A. "Doing Injury to History." *Newsweek*, April 5, 1999.

Krauthammer, Charles. "Limits of Humanitarianism." *Time*, September 27, 1999.

McGeary, Johanna. "The Ethnic Cleanser." *Time*, vol. 153, no. 13, April 5, 1999.

Newsom, David. "Holbrooke's Daunting Task." *Christian Science Monitor*, vol. 91, no. 179, August 11, 1999.

"No Place for Them Both." *Economist*, April 3, 1999.

Nordland, Rod. "Daddy, They're Killing Us." *Newsweek*, June 28, 1999.

Peterson, Scott. "The Trail of a Bullet." *Christian Science Monitor*, vol. 91, no. 217.

Starr, Paul. "The Choice in Kosovo." *The American Prospect*, July–August 1999.

NEWSPAPERS

Bell, Stewart, and Juliette Terzieff. "The New Power Brokers." *National Post*, May 29, 1999, p. E8.

Cherney, Elena. "Kosovar Refugees Are the Lucky Ones." *National Post*, May 29, 1999, p. E16.

Chwialkowska, Luiza. "Draskovic Has Been Dumped, Discredited." *National Post*, May 29, 1999, p. E19.

Cienski, Jan. "One of the Oldest Ways Societies Deal with Their Minorities." *National Post*, May 29, 1999, p. E14.

Diamond, John. "General: Politicians Botched Kosovo." *Chicago Tribune*, October 22, 1999.

Dobbs, Michael. "Leaders Spar in the Other Yugoslav War." *Guardian Weekly*, April 25, 1999.

Drozdiak, William. "Cold Snap Could Cool Support for Milosevic." *Washington Post*, October 22, 1999, p. A25.

Edwards, Steven. "Family 'Moving Fortune Out of the Country.' " *National Post*, May 29, 1999, p. E3.

Erlanger, Steven. "The Dayton Accords: A Status Report." *New York Times*, June 10, 1996.

Finn, Peter. "Forces of Intolerance Threaten to Consume Kosovo." *Washington Post*, October 13, 1999, p. A1.

———. "Support Dwindles for Kosovo Rebels: Ethnic Albanians Dismayed by KLA's Violence, Arrogance." *Washington Post*, October 17, 1999, p. A1.

Finn, Peter, and R. Jeffrey Smith. "Kosovo's Homeless Shudder as Balkan Winter Threatens: U.N. Officials Race to Provide Temporary Shelter, Heat, Food." *Washington Post*, October 19, 1999, p. A12.

Graham, Patrick. "Balancing on a Razor's Edge." *National Post*, May 29, 1999, p. E18.

Honore, Carl. "The Most Wanted Men in Serbia." *National Post*, May 29, 1999, p. E11.

———. "Prosecuting the Criminals." *National Post*, May 29, 1999, p. E10.

————. "Serbia's Pretty-Boy Psychopath." *National Post*, May 29, 1999, p. E11.

Jagger, Bianca. "The Betrayal of Srebrenica." *The European*, September 25–October 1, 1995.

Jimenez, Marina. "Rugova's Pacifism Swept Away by War." *National Post*, May 29, 1999, p. E19.

————. "Will Thaci's Political Skills Match Up to the Task Ahead?" *National Post*, May 29, 1999, p. E19.

Judah, Tim. "Cycle of Revenge Haunts Kosovo." *Guardian Weekly*, April 11, 1999.

Knox, Paul. "UN Veto a Divisive Reform Issue." *Globe and Mail*, July 19, 1997.

Krauze, Jan. "NATO's Newcomers Get Rude Awakening." *Guardian Weekly*, April 25, 1999.

Krogh, Peter F. "Scold and Bomb: Clinton's Failed Foreign Policy." *Wall Street Journal*, April 28, 1999.

McMahon, Colin, and Charles M. Madigan. "Autopsy of a War: Bringing Charges." *Chicago Tribune*, September 7, 1999.

————. "Following the Trail to Milosevic." *Chicago Tribune*, September 6, 1999.

————. "Nightmare Strikes at Dawn." *Chicago Tribune*, September 5, 1999.

————. "The Vicious Tide Turns: Kosovo's Victims Become the Aggressors." *Chicago Tribune*, September 5, 1999.

Medvedev, Roy. "Why Muscovites Are Saying Nyet." *Guardian Weekly*, May 9, 1999.

Mertus, Julie. "Hope, Hunger and Serbia." *Washington Post*, October 21, 1999, p. A29.

"Outside Intervention New Norm in Civil Wars." *Globe and Mail*, October 23, 1999, p. A12.

Rose, Alexander. "1878 Invasion Was First Clash with Ethnic Albanians." *National Post*, May 29, 1999, p. E6.

————. "The Battle That Cast Long Shadows." *National Post*, May 29, 1999, p. E7.

————. "The KLA Accepts Rambouillet Accord." *National Post*, May 29, 1999, p. E16.

————. "NATO Goes to War for the First Time." *National Post*, May 29, 1999, p. E18.

————. "No Surrender Is a Central Theme in Serb Folklore." *National Post*, May 29, 1999, p. E4.

————. "We Have Become Another Bosnia." *National Post*, May 29, 1999, p. E4.

Smith, R. Jeffrey. "Specter of Independent Kosovo Divides U.S., European Allies." *Washington Post*, September 28, 1999, p. A19.

Tamayo, Juan O. "Old Europe Is Dying a Tempestuous Death." *The Kan-sas City Star*, July 12, 1992.

Traynor, Ian. "Expedient Band of Slav Brothers." *Guardian Weekly*, April 25, 1999.

Vick, Karl. "Africa Has Refugees, Kosovo Gets Money: Needs of War Exiles Deplete Donations." *Washington Post*, October 8, 1999, p. A24.

Weymouth, Lally. "I Can Only Be Proud of My Role." *Guardian Weekly*, January 3, 1999.

FOREIGN LANGUAGE SOURCES

Russian Documentation

Argumenty I Fakty

Ejenedel'nik

Literaturnaya Gazeta

Moskovskie Novosti

Nezavisimaya Gazeta

Ogonek

Pravda

Rossijskaya Gazeta

Russkaya Mysl'

Vecherniy Klub

German Documentation

Der Spiegel

Deutschland: Zeitschrift für Politik, Kultur, Wirtschaft und Wissenschaft, 4 & 5/99, August/September and October/November.

Die Zeit

Frankfurter Allgemeine

Neue Zürcher Zeitung

Yugoslav Newspapers

Duga

Politika

French Newspapers

Le Monde
Le Monde Diplomatique

Italian Newspaper

Corriere della sera

INDEX

About the Author

MIRON REZUN teaches political science and the economics of transition at the University of New Brunswick in Canada. He has published eleven works of non-fiction, including *Saddam Hussein's Gulf Wars* (Praeger, 1992), *Europe and the War in the Balkans: Toward a New Yugoslav Identity* (Praeger, 1995), and *Science, Technology, and Ecopolitics in the USSR* (Praeger, 1996). He has also published two novels.